WAR STORIES III

THE HEROES WHO DEFEATED HITLER

OLIVER L. NORTH

WITH JOE MUSSER

Since 1947
**REGNERY
PUBLISHING, INC.**
An Eagle Publishing Company • Washington, DC

Cataloging-in-Publication data on file with the Library of Congress

ISBN 0-89526-014-X

Published in the United States by
Regnery Publishing, Inc.
One Massachusetts Avenue, NW
Washington, DC 20001

www.regnery.com

Distributed to the trade by
National Book Network
Lanham, MD 20706

Printed on acid-free paper
Manufactured in the United States of America

10   9   8   7   6   5   4   3   2   1

Books are available in quantity for promotional or premium use. Write to Director of Special Sales, Regnery Publishing, Inc., One Massachusetts Avenue NW, Washington, DC 20001, for information on discounts and terms or call (202) 216-0600.

*To my parents and their peers, who gave so much that
we could prevail as the home of the brave and land of the free—
with hope that we remain worthy of their sacrifice.*

CONTENTS

INTRODUCTION

More than fifty-five million people were killed in World War II. Seven times that number were wounded, injured, or suffered serious deprivation. The global war affected people on every continent except Antarctica, and arguably caused greater political, cultural, and demographic change than any other armed conflict in the human record.

In this book and the accompanying DVD are the personal, eyewitness accounts of American and Allied men and women who lived through the epic battles of the European theater during this brutal conflict. Their stories are inspirational—yet most of these heroes are unknown except to their families and neighbors. Their first-person accounts serve as a reminder that the price of liberty in blood and treasure can be very high indeed.

For more than forty years, it has been my privilege to keep company with heroes—those who place themselves at risk for the benefit of others. All of us involved in these *War Stories* books—and the award-winning FOX News documentaries on which they are based—are dedicated to preserving for posterity the record of people like these in this volume who have served on the front lines of freedom.

These World War II participants are now in their twilight years. Most are in their eighties and nineties and they will not be with us much longer to share their stories—for they are dying at the rate of about 1,000 a day. I am grateful that we were able to capture these priceless narratives while there was yet time, as a legacy for future generations of our great nation.

This book was also written at a time when brave men and women, serving at home and abroad, are once again engaged in an armed struggle against a deadly foe. Like Hitler and the other Axis leaders, today's adversaries are brutal, murderous, and fanatically refuse to abide by civilized rules or laws. These stories from the past are replete with lessons to teach us about our country's future, and the principles that govern and guide us despite the passage of time.

In 1941, Winston Churchill spent Christmas in Washington, D.C. He came to the United States in secret, but at the lighting of the national tree on Christmas Eve, President Roosevelt asked him to say a few words. Churchill urged all Americans to "cast aside, for this night at least, the cares and dangers which beset us and make for the children an evening of happiness in a world of storm."

"Let the children have their night of fun and laughter," Churchill said. "Let us grown-ups share to the full in their unstinted pleasures—before we turn again to the stern tasks and the formidable years that lie before us, resolved that by our sacrifice and daring these same children shall not be robbed of their inheritance or denied their right to live in a free and decent world."

In the days after Churchill's remark, nearly all Americans would experience stern tasks and be called to daring deeds. Whether for those who saw these heroes firsthand, or those who know of them only through the shared stories of family and friends, this book can help bring insight, understanding, pride, and even closure. From 1941 to 1945, almost every American family had a loved one—brother, father, husband, son, sister, or daughter—who served in some capacity during World War II. Theirs are *War Stories* that deserve to be told.

Semper Fidelis,
Oliver North
21 October 2005

CHAPTER 1
WAR CLOUDS
1938–1941

World War II in Europe was both inevitable and preventable. It was a war started by a military dictator who came to power not by a coup, but by the ballot box. One man—Adolf Hitler—precipitated the carnage, and he was able to do so because the German people and the democracies of the world were unwilling to confront his growing evil until it was too late.

A World War I veteran, unsuccessful artist, and failed businessman, Hitler was a charismatic demagogue, xenophobe and racist. From 1919 to 1923, with Germany reeling in the chaotic political environment after World War I and crippled by reparations imposed by the Treaty of Versailles, he and a half-dozen other political unknowns organized the nucleus of what was to become the National Socialist—or Nazi—Party.

In the autumn of 1923, the French army occupied the Ruhr River valley, Germany's industrial heartland, in an effort to force Berlin to pay its World War I reparations. The value of the German currency plummeted and Hitler convinced himself—and several thousand followers—that the hyper-inflation and French "invasion" had created conditions conducive to a coup that would bring down the national government.

The "Beer Hall *Putsch,*" in Munich on 9 November 1923, failed miserably. Had Hitler and his co-conspirators been sentenced to lengthy jail terms, that might well have ended any threat that he and his *Sturmabteilung*—the "SA," brown-shirted "Storm-troopers"—posed to the Weimar Republic and the security of Europe. But as it turned out, he only served nine months, just enough time to dictate his political manifesto, *Mein Kampf* (My Struggle) to his leading accomplice Rudolf Hess, a fellow World War I veteran.

Once freed, Hitler spent the next eight years building a political machine—and a 400,000-man private army. In the elections of 1932, the Nazi party won more than 37 percent of the vote and a plurality of seats in the *Reichstag,* the German parliament. Beset by the catastrophic effects of the worldwide "Great Depression," six million unemployed workers, and the rising specter of Communist-inspired revolution, Paul von Hindenburg, a World War I hero and the figurehead president of the republic, installed Hitler as chancellor on 30 January 1933.

National Archives

Nazi brownshirts saluting Hitler (1935).

The following month the Reichstag was destroyed by fire. The Nazis claimed that the fire had been set by Communists and used the incident to pass the infamous "Enabling Bill," which suspended legislative authority and gave Hitler near absolute power to make new laws. In June of 1934 he had all of his rivals in the SA brutally murdered, and when Hindenburg died in August of that year, Hitler combined the offices of chancellor and president in a new post: *Führer*. From that moment on, war was practically inevitable.

Hitler immediately set about consolidating his hold on absolute power. By 1935 his public works projects: railroads, motorways (he called them *autobahnen*), airports, military conscription, and armaments industries, had cut German unemployment to a fraction of that in the rest of the world. Meanwhile, Europe's leaders did little but debate about what to do about the growing menace in the heart of the continent.

The French, alarmed at Hitler's withdrawal from the League of Nations and his unilateral abrogation of the Versailles Treaty, did little but double the term of service for their army conscripts and speed up work on their border fortifications—the Maginot Line. The British, in the first of many acts of appeasement, agreed that Germany was no longer bound by naval restrictions imposed by the Versailles Treaty. In Moscow, Josef Stalin was busy purging his military and establishing a totalitarian police state that oppressed, tortured, and killed millions. In Rome, Hitler's philosophical ally and fellow fascist, Benito Mussolini, was engaged in his own imperial ambitions in Africa. Militarism and expansionism also gained ground in Asia, as the Japanese expanded their territorial ambitions in the heart of China from Manchuria, which it had occupied in 1930.

Emboldened by the impotence of his neighbors, in March 1936, Hitler sent troops into the "demilitarized" Rhineland, in violation of the Treaty of Versailles. In October that same year, Hitler and Mussolini signed the Rome-Berlin Axis Agreement—expanded a year later to include a military agreement under the so-called Anti-Comintern Pact—pledging military support to one another in the event of war with the Soviet Union.

In late 1937 the Führer also reorganized the German military and established a new strategic command structure—the *Obercommando der*

Wermacht (OKW)—and put himself at its head. In November of that year, Hitler convened a secret conference in the Reich Chancellery, where he outlined for his cabinet and senior military commanders his plan to gain *Lebensraum*—"living space"—for the "Aryan" race, a term for the German people that he'd first articulated in *Mein Kampf.*

The broad strokes of Hitler's plan called for expanding German territory to the east, seizing resources, "purifying" German-held territory of "non-Aryan" peoples and "confronting Communism." In his grand plan for creating a "Third Reich," he envisioned massive propaganda campaigns, the use of disinformation to spread fear, the use of espionage operations in an enemy's heartland, and "lightning stroke" military maneuvers to overwhelm adversaries without the static attrition that had characterized combat in World War I. He correctly surmised that the French would have to be beaten militarily but wrongly assumed that both the Soviet Union and Great Britain could be cowed into submission.

The Führer's strategic premise—that the Western democracies would be powerless to stop the German juggernaut—was supported by assessments of

his military intelligence service, the *Abwehr*. By the time he finished laying out his plan for European domination, no one in the Nazi party had any doubt that Hitler was ready for war.

On 12 March 1938 Germany annexed Austria in what the Führer called an *Anschluss*—or "re-unifying annexation." The European democracies filed a diplomatic protest. When Hitler arrayed his army on the border of Czechoslovakia that September, Neville Chamberlain and Édouard Daladier—the British and French prime ministers—flew to

Molotov and Ribbentrop sign non-aggression treaty in Moscow.

Munich in an effort to appease the German dictator. On his return to London, Chamberlain, quoting an old hymn, promised that they had secured "peace for our time." Less than six months later, on 15 March 1939, the grey-clad, jack-booted *Wehrmacht* marched into Prague, Czechoslovakia, without resistance. Only then did the British and French start serious preparations for war.

While London and Paris scrambled to accelerate military production and conscription, Hitler engaged in a diplomatic offensive with his sworn enemy to the east—the Soviet Union. On 22 August 1939 foreign ministers Vyacheslav Molotov and Joachim von Ribbentrop signed a secret non-aggression pact in Moscow, effectively dividing Poland in two—giving Hitler free reign east to the Vistula—and a German promise not to intervene if the Soviets annexed the Baltic states of Estonia, Latvia, and Lithuania.

When the sixty-two divisions and 1,300 aircraft of the Nazi war machine invaded Poland on 1 September 1939, it took three full days for Britain, France, Australia, and New Zealand to declare war on Germany. Poland's ill-equipped army fought the *blitzkrieg*—"lightning war," a term coined by British newspapers—as best they were able, hoping for a rapid Allied response. But the unprepared Poles were no match for the modernized German army, and when Warsaw fell on 27 September, no allied forces were yet fully mobilized. Rather than surrender to Hitler's legions, several hundred thousand Polish troops fled east—only to be captured by the Soviets, who promptly murdered every officer who fell into their hands.

The Führer spent the remainder of the autumn and the winter of 1939–1940 preparing for an expected Franco-British intervention in the west that never came—and arguing with his generals as to how best to capture France. Stalin, believing himself secured from Hitler's voracious territorial appetite by the Molotov-Ribbentrop Pact, sent his own army into Finland on 30 November 1939, earning nothing more than expulsion from the League of Nations.

Hitler watched the "Winter War" in Finland with great interest. The poor performance of more than a million Soviet troops—fighting fewer than 200,000 Finns—convinced the Führer that Stalin's Red Army was no match for his Wehrmacht. By the time Moscow and Helsinki inked an armistice on 12 March 1940, members of the General Staff in Berlin—instigated by Grand Admiral Erich Raeder—had convinced Hitler that the

Third Reich had to have Norway in order to ensure access from the Baltic into the North Atlantic.

On 9 April 1940 German troops occupied a totally undefended and neutral Denmark—and simultaneously invaded Norway. Though the Wehrmacht quickly captured Oslo, secured their objectives in the south, and forced the royal family to flee, the British Navy fought back tenaciously and succeeded in doing serious damage to the German invasion fleet at Narvik. Only Hitler's long-planned invasion of Holland, Belgium, and France saved the German invaders from the 25,000 or so Norwegian, British, and French troops fighting their way south down the rough Scandinavian coastline.

Hitler called his plan for seizing France—and the rest of northwestern Europe—*Sichelschnitt*: "Sickle Stroke." It involved three German army groups—120 infantry divisions, ten Panzer divisions with 2,400 tanks, two paratroop divisions, thousands of tracked and wheeled vehicles, more than 2,500 aircraft—and the most important requirement of all, the element of surprise. At 0430 on the morning of 10 May 1940, the "Phony War" ended as the largest mechanized army yet assembled on earth began a slashing assault across the neutral Netherlands, Belgium, and Luxembourg—and into the heart of France. That evening the government of Neville Chamberlain collapsed and Winston Churchill was named prime minister.

Within fourteen days the outnumbered and outgunned British Expeditionary Force and the remnants of the once-proud French First Army Group had been pushed into a pocket along the French Coast—the English Channel to their backs. From 24 May to 6 June, a flotilla of nearly a thousand small boats in "Operation Dynamo" evacuated more than 338,000 Allied troops from the beaches of Dunkirk, carrying them across the cold, choppy waters of the channel to the eastern thumb of Kent, England. On 4 June 1940, as "Dynamo" was coming to a close, a defiant Churchill promised, "We shall fight on the beaches, we shall fight on the landing grounds, we shall fight in the fields and in the streets, we shall fight in the hills—we shall *never* surrender."

On 10 June, Italy declared war on France and Mussolini dispatched twenty-eight of his divisions across the Alps to invade France from the south—only to be held in check by four under-strength French divisions. But in the north it was a different story. By 14 June, most French units were simply out of ammunition and Paris, declared an "open city" to spare its destruction, was occupied by German troops. On 16 June, the aged Marshal Philippe Petain—a World War I hero—was appointed prime minister of France. Five days later the old man authorized an armistice—dividing France into an "Occupied Zone" and moving the "sovereign" French government first to Bordeaux and then to Vichy.

The terms of the cease-fire were onerous. Some 90,000 Frenchmen were dead, almost half a million wounded, and nearly two million others became prisoners of the Reich. Across the English Channel, a defiant Winston Churchill, leader of the only democracy left in Europe but Switzerland, told his countrymen to prepare for an invasion—while at the same time trying to persuade America into war.

✪ ✪ ✪

Americans had done their best to avoid getting drawn into another war in Europe. Following World War I many American politicians and ordinary citizens proudly described themselves as "isolationists." By the 1930s, most U.S. citizens were overwhelmed with their own concerns. The Great Depression had robbed a great many of them of their farms, homes, businesses, and way of life. Heartbreaking as Nazi and Japanese atrocities sounded, most Americans had to face their own anxieties. Their families and jobs were more important than what was happening on the other side of the Atlantic or Pacific oceans during one of the darkest and bleakest periods of American history.

As Hitler's rise to power threatened stability in Europe, prominent American business and political leaders counseled that whatever happened "over there"—it was not our fight. Robert Wood, the chairman of Sears Roebuck Company, emphasized the consequences and the terrible economic losses that war left in its wake. Most newspapers echoed those sentiments and urged that we remain neutral as war clouds enveloped Europe and Asia.

Curiously, the famous record-setting aviator Charles Lindbergh also promoted isolationism, but at the same time seemed to be courting

Germany and Hitler. Lindbergh's heritage was German, and he held views that some said were anti-Semitic and pro-Nazi. During 1935–39, in his visits to Germany, where he praised German aviation, Lindbergh was presented with a medal from the Nazis. A member of an isolationist movement calling itself "America First," Lindbergh was also a featured speaker during a neo-Nazi rally of the "German-American *Bund*" when they met at Madison Square Garden in 1941.

Though President Franklin Delano Roosevelt viewed developments in Europe and Asia with growing concern, he was unable to convince Congress not to pass a series of five "Neutrality Acts" between 1935 and 1939.

These laws effectively prohibited the United States government or its citizens from becoming a party to either side in the overseas conflicts by banning the shipment of war materiel and restricting travel abroad by U.S. citizens "except at their own risk." FDR—who favored opposing German, Japanese, and Italian aggression—walked a tight line. He wanted to soften the country's isolationist position, but at the same time didn't want to alienate Congress by vetoing any of the neutrality bills. He was unwilling to jeopardize legislation that he wanted passed which he believed would help ameliorate the effects of the Depression.

But just weeks after FDR signed the first Neutrality Act in 1935, Hitler's National Socialist Party passed the Nurenburg laws—revoking the citizenship of German Jews. The Nazis then forbade marriage between Jews and "pure-blooded" Germans. Seeing the handwriting on the wall, many Jews living in Germany decided to leave the country. But America, like most other countries, turned them away.

The U.S. had tightened immigration policies some ten years earlier, and lawmakers were unwilling to ease those restrictions—after all, America was still deep within the Depression and many unemployed Americans were afraid that a flood of refugees would make it even harder to find a job. Polls showed that three-fourths of the country opposed raising refugee quotas.

The international response to the Jewish refugee situation was no better. The matter was debated in European capitals, but none volunteered to open the doors to the Jewish refugees. That only encouraged further Nazi oppression of the Jews in Germany. In 1938 Hitler arrested 17,000 Jews of Polish citizenship—many of whom had been living in Germany—and relocated them in "work camps" on the Polish border after Poland refused to take them back.

In November 1938, violence organized by the Nazis erupted in what became known as *Kristallnacht*—the "night of broken glass"—and over 7,000 Jewish shops and a hundred synagogues and homes were ransacked, robbed, and burned. In the aftermath, more than 25,000 Jews were sent to concentration camps.

In 1939, several hundred Jewish refugees sailed on the liner *St. Louis* from Hamburg for Havana, Cuba. On board were 937 Jews fleeing Nazi persecution after the horror of *Kristallnacht* the previous November. Each passenger of the *St. Louis* carried a valid visa providing for temporary entry into Cuba.

However, as the ship neared Havana, the Cuban government announced that the visas were no longer valid and denied entry to the nearly one thousand passengers. The *St. Louis* then sailed for the United States but the American government—adhering to its strict immigration policy—also denied them entry and even refused to let the ship dock. After weeks of futility and pleas for asylum, the *St. Louis* returned to Europe, docking at Antwerp, where the king and prime minister permitted 200 passengers to enter Belgium. The British, French, and Dutch governments finally agreed to grant temporary asylum for the refugees, but by then the passengers had disembarked at Amsterdam. When the Nazis invaded the Netherlands on 10 May 1940, many of the Jews from the *St. Louis* were still there—and found themselves once again in Hitler's clutches. For most, their hapless and hopeless story finally ended in a Nazi death camp as part of Hitler's "Final Solution."

In 1939, President Roosevelt called Congress into special session to amend the earlier neutrality acts. FDR presented them with a plan he called "cash-and-carry," which permitted Americans to sell arms and munitions to "democratic countries" able to pay for them in cash and carry them away from American docks in their own ships. Some isolationists in Congress protested the plan, but the Neutrality Act of 1939 finally allowed Britain and France to buy American weapons and war materiel. It was not until March 1941 that Congress passed the Lend-Lease Act—permitting the president to "sell, transfer title to, exchange, lease, lend, or otherwise dispose of," war materiel to other governments deemed "vital to the defense of the United States." FDR was authorized to provide up to $1 billion to England in such aid.

But all of this military aid would come too late for the Dutch, Belgian, British, and French armies that had to face the German onslaught in May 1940. Within days of the Dunkirk evacuation, the president asked for Congress to authorize more funds for America's own national defense—and for the Selective Training and Service Act—the first U.S. peacetime military draft. This bill, considered by isolationist opponents to be "jingoistic," and too "provocative for a neutral nation," would eventually make it possible to recruit more than sixteen million Americans—but it had to be reauthorized the following year. Accordingly, the number of infantrymen who were assigned to specific organized U.S. Army units actually *decreased* between mid-1939 and the start of 1940 to a total of just under 50,000 men. It wasn't until 12 August 1941 that the law was amended, authorizing U.S. military conscripts to be sent overseas. It passed the U.S. House of Representatives by a single vote.

By then, it was becoming apparent to most Americans that it wouldn't be long before the country would be called upon to do more than simply provide arms and munitions in what was fast becoming a global conflagration. One of those who saw it coming was a young U.S. Army aviator from Florida named John Alison.

SECOND LIEUTENANT JOHN ALISON, USAAF
Moscow, Russia
2 July 1940

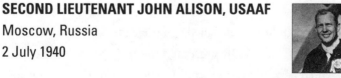

I was commissioned as a second lieutenant in the field artillery of the United States Army in 1935. When I graduated in June of '36, I went almost directly to the Army Flying School in Randolph Field. I had to resign my commission in order to enroll as a flying cadet, and attend the Army Flying School at San Antonio, Texas. I completed my training and was assigned in 1937 to Langley Field, Virginia, flying a PB-2A.

At this time America was antiwar. I don't think we had really one ready division in the United States Army at the beginning of World War I. And now, just before World War II, we were only a little better off. The country just didn't want to prepare for war. If we'd had the level of preparedness for the beginning of World War II that we had two years later, the war would've much shorter. And cost far less. And we would've saved the lives of a lot of really good kids.

I'd been flying for two years when General Claire Chennault asked me to demonstrate a new P-40 fighter aircraft for some Chinese who were buying the planes for China to use against the Japanese, and right after that, I was sent to England with the P-40s to help the RAF assimilate this new American aircraft under the Lend-Lease Plan.

I think our greatest help was as a morale booster, giving them hope that the Americans were going to come in and help them fight this war. But we only flew over Britain. When we left General "Hap" Arnold pointed his finger at us and said, "Look . . . you know, the antiwar sentiment that's going on in the United States today. Your RAF friends are going to say, come on, fly over France with us. If you do, I'm not going to court martial you—I'm going to have you shot! If an American officer is shot down over France and we're not at war, the antiwar sentiment and the active press that we'll be getting, if you're shot down, it'll do us tremendous damage. So don't you dare cross the channel!" So, of course we took that seriously.

Then Hitler invaded Russia. The president was interested in keeping Russia in the war because he anticipated that later on, we were going to be involved too. When the Germans attacked the Russians, the president sent his assistant Mr. Harry Hopkins and me to Moscow.

We tried to find out from the Russians what they really needed most but they were very secretive. As matter of fact I never saw one act of genuine cooperation between the Russians and our side. I met with the Russian generals and Hopkins met with Stalin; we tried to find out about their tanks—whether we could improve on them; The flat answer was, "We have a good tank." Artillery pieces—"We have good artillery." Airplanes? "We have good airplanes." But finally it was agreed that we would send the P-40s to Russia. They didn't need much training but we put together a system to supervise the assembly of the airplanes. And my partner and I test-flew every airplane before we delivered it to the Russians.

I was in Moscow when the Germans got to the city in October. We had to evacuate. The provisional capital had been moved from Moscow to the Caucuses. I requested that I be relieved of my assignment in Moscow and sent back to my unit in the United States—because I knew by now that America was getting ready for war. It hadn't happened yet, but I knew it was coming.

When the war in Europe began, the American army was the seventeenth largest in the world—just behind that of Romania. What troops we had were issued the old "bell style" helmets left over from World War I, and the men drilled with wooden guns. That didn't dismay many of those who were suddenly "called up." In the midst of the Great Depression, joining the Army paid a dollar a day, and provided a bunk and three square meals a day. That sounded pretty good to a lot of people.

Seventeen-year-old Joe Boitnott, a fresh-faced high school dropout, needed work, and by his own account, "a little discipline in my life," so he decided to join the Iowa National Guard for that dollar a day that they paid for every drill. Joe told his friend, a farm boy named Duane Stone, "Why don't you join? It's a dollar a drill. And we're gonna go to Minnesota for twenty-one days. And that's $21." And $21 was big money for a teenager in Depression-era Iowa.

Angelo Montemaro grew up in Brooklyn during the Great Depression and after graduating from high school was one of the lucky ones to find a job. He became a bellhop for the Hotel Commodore on Lexington and 42nd Street in New York City. One of the perks of being a bellhop was that he occasionally got to hear the Big Band sounds of an orchestra playing in the hotel ballroom. For this young teenager, life—despite the Depression—seemed good, and war was something he scarcely thought of.

JOSEPH BOITNOTT
Des Moines, Iowa
2 July 1940

I joined the National Guard December 21, 1939. At that time, my father and mother had been divorced and I was living with my sister, in Des Moines, Iowa. So, I joined the National Guard, to gain both discipline and money. In the summer of 1940, we went to Camp Ripley, Minnesota, on maneuvers. We had come back from that twenty-one-day encampment, and we settled in to do more training, in our armory there in Des Moines.

And later, we were mobilized from the National Guard of Iowa, Minnesota, and South Dakota into the Army of the United States, and were sent to Camp Claiborne, Louisiana, for a year's training. We trained on forced marches, ten-mile marches, with full field pack. And we had to dig foxholes and let a tank go over, to make sure we got that training. We had no amphibious training or desert training.

We trained with very old World War I equipment. Our rifles were 1903 Springfield rifles. We had some Colt .45s, but revolvers—not the automatic pistols. The Army Air Corps would "bomb" us during the maneuvers—they'd drop flour bags as bombs. And some of our units had wooden guns. And our bayonet training, and hand-to-hand combat, was very limited.

But in the meantime, they started the Selective Service. We received these Selective Service draftees into our unit. We then trained at Camp Claiborne throughout the summer on basic maneuvers. Later in the year the Japs bombed Pearl Harbor, in December. We were alerted, and sent to guard different structures in Louisiana and along the Texas border.

And then, we come back, and were ordered to get on a troop train. Our destination was unknown. We later found out we were going to Fort Dix, New Jersey. There we waited to be shipped out. Every day we marched around the field, or ran around the perimeter of Fort Dix doing calisthenics. And it was cold, living and sleeping in those tattered tents. We were scheduled to leave on the USS *Normandy*. But the *Normandy* caught fire and burned. So we were delayed two or three weeks, until another ship could be refitted for troops. They used these luxury liners, and refitted them for us. Everything was done in a hurry. And before long we sailed on the *Mariposa*.

When we boarded the ship and sailed, our convoy rendezvoused at Nova Scotia. We picked up other ships for the crossing. And we still, at that point, didn't know where our destination was. But we landed in Ireland, and after six or eight months, we were transferred to Scotland where we trained some more without the proper weapons and equipment.

✪ ✪ ✪

DUANE STONE
Des Moines, Iowa
2 July 1940

My friend had joined the National Guard and asked me to join too. He said, "It's a dollar a drill. And we're gonna go to Minnesota for twenty-one days of maneuvers." Well, that seemed like big money in the middle of the Depression.

My family and I lived on a farm. My dad worked as a laborer, for the farm. My older brother and I got work shocking wheat and oats. But, for fifty cents a day, it wasn't much money. So, the opportunity came along to enlist. And we were paid—every three months we got twelve bucks. It paid for a lot of little things here and there. In fact, it paid for my graduation suit when I graduated in May of 1940.

My cousin always believed that we were going to have trouble with Japan—not Germany. I mean, he wasn't a college graduate, but he was well-educated enough from reading the papers and books that Japan was going to be our enemy. And we weren't at war with either Japan or Germany then. But France and England were. And the U.S. was trying to supply them with ammunition, weapons, and war equipment. That was what we were supposed to do—help France and England. But not get into the fighting.

Well, most Americans realized what the situation was. I think our parents back then—a lot of them had sons in the service—they had to know what was going on. They had to realize that their sons would soon be involved with the war.

✪ ✪ ✪

ANGELO MONTEMARO
Brooklyn, New York
2 July 1940

I was working then at the Hotel Commodore as a bellhop. I had been doing that for three years. The Depression was terrible—that's when Franklin Delano Roosevelt started the WPA. I had three brothers on the WPA. When Hitler went into Poland, the U.S. started mandatory conscription, and you had to go into the service. That's why my brother Joe was in the service already.

I graduated high school in 1937. I wanted to go to college but I couldn't go because my family was pretty poor. So I got my higher education at the Hotel Commodore. When the war finally started, I got my draft notice about six months later. Now we were five brothers in the service, and our folks were pretty proud. My brother Mike was in the Marine Corps. He went to Iwo Jima. My brother Vincent was a doctor, and a colonel in the Army Medical Corps. My brother Joe was with an artillery unit and my youngest brother, Peter, was in the Army Air Force. I was in the infantry.

I had ninety days in Camp Cross. Then they took us to Fort Mead, Maryland. From there we went to Fort Kilmer, and then to Camp Miles Standish in Boston. From there we went across the North Atlantic in a convoy that took us twenty-three days to get to Plymouth, England. They were really happy to see us.

✪ ✪ ✪

Following his 1940 reelection, President Roosevelt declared that the United States should become "the great arsenal of democracy." In August 1941 FDR and British prime minister Winston Churchill announced new Allied goals for dealing with Hitler's aggression, presented in what they called the Atlantic Charter. Britain and America each pledged to respect "the right of all peoples to choose the form of government under which they will live." Both also promised a free world without war "after the final destruction of Nazi tyranny."

By then, the Royal Air Force had all but won perhaps one of the most lopsided and revolutionary series of engagements in the history of warfare—the "Battle of Britain." As America slowly mobilized to confront the great peril of Hitler's aggression, the Royal Air Force and the German Luftwaffe were dueling in the skies over the British Isles. The 10 July–30 October 1940 aerial battle made it possible for Britain to survive. Winston Churchill characterized it as "their finest hour."

CHAPTER 2
THE BATTLE OF BRITAIN AND THE LONDON BLITZ
JULY–OCTOBER 1940

The fall of France on 22 June 1940 presented Hitler with a new strategic dilemma: what to do about the British Isles. Still hoping that Churchill would come to some kind of accommodation with Germany, the Nazi leader decided to pressure the pesky Brits by ordering highly visible preparations for Operation Sea Lion—the invasion of England.

Brushing aside the anxieties of his General Staff, Hitler directed that a fleet of barges, tugs, and landing craft assemble at captured Dutch, Belgian, and French ports. And then, to ratchet up the pressure, on 10 July, he ordered the first significant cross-channel air raids against British shore defenses, merchant ports, and naval installations on the south coast of England.

The Battle of Britain had begun. Its outcome would determine Great Britain's survival as an independent nation.

For six days, groups of twenty to thirty German Dornier 17s, Heinkel 111s, Junkers 87 (Stukas) and Ju-88s, escorted by Messerschmitt 109s and twin-engine Me-110s, flew from hastily repaired French and Belgian airfields. This amazing aircraft armada flew into the teeth of well-prepared British defenses. When these limited attacks produced no softening in

National Archives

"Never in the field of human conflict was so much owed by so many to so few."

Churchill's resolve, the Reich chancellor issued Führer Directive No. 16, ordering accelerated preparations for Operation Sea Lion. Hitler correctly surmised that without total control of the air over the Channel and the invasion beaches, any attack on England would be doomed to failure.

The Luftwaffe was ordered to both prepare the way for Wehrmacht assault forces and "prevent all air attacks" by the Royal Air Force. But now, for the first time since German aggression began in 1938, Hitler learned that just because he ordered something didn't necessarily make it so.

RAF Fighter Command's Supermarine Spitfires and Hawker Hurricanes, vectored by fifty "Chain Home" radar stations, swarmed up to meet the attacking Luftwaffe formations. Hermann Goering, Hitler's air minister, responded by ordering an increase in the number of Me-109 and Me-110 fighter escorts for their bombers.

On 19 July, Hitler summoned the Reichstag—Germany's now impotent legislature—all of the puppet governors from the conquered territories, the diplomatic corps, and the world press to Berlin's Kroll Opera House for a "victory celebration." At the conclusion of his lengthy speech, the German dictator made a blatant call for British capitulation: "I feel it is my duty, before my own conscience to appeal once more to reason and common sense in Great Britain and elsewhere. I consider myself in a position to make this appeal since I am not the vanquished begging for favors, but the victor speaking in the name of reason. I see no reason why this war must go on."

While waiting for Churchill to accept the futility of further resistance, the Luftwaffe continued its daily raids—with inevitable dogfights over the Channel and the fields of southern England. By the end of the month the Luftwaffe had lost more than 100 bombers and eighty fighters while the RAF had lost just seventy Spitfires and Hurricanes. While almost half the British pilots had parachuted to safety over friendly territory, nearly all the downed German airmen were killed or captured.

On 30 July Hitler summoned his commanders to Berghof, his Bavarian retreat. There he reiterated his decision to double the number of Panzer divisions from ten to twenty and increase the Wehrmacht from 120 to 180 divisions. Two days later he issued Führer Directive No. 17, launching Operation Eagle and ordering the Luftwaffe to "overpower the English air force."

Goering commanded his pilots to effectively double the number of strikes against British "flying units," bases, aircraft plants, and anti-aircraft installations and predicted that his pilots would "crush Britain." Fortunately for the British, the Luftwaffe never developed a coherent plan for doing so—nor did

German Dornier planes over Britain.

Associated Press

Goering, a World War I ace, ever seem to grasp the importance that radar played in defeating the German air offensive.

For another two weeks Luftwaffe bombers pounded RAF fighter bases and bomber fields, the piers at Portsmouth, munitions plants, and shipping along the Thames and in the English Channel. Only once were any of the radar stations hit—and none of the German raids succeeded in disrupting the carefully integrated RAF early warning and control centers.

When he met with his senior military commanders at the Reich Chancellery on 14 August, Hitler once again expressed his hopes that the air campaign would bring the stubborn British to some accommodation, to protect their "Asian colonies and trade from Japanese aggression." But the next day, losses of Stukas and pilots were so high that Kesselring and Sperrle, commanders of the Luftwaffe 2nd and 3rd Air Fleets, stopped sending the dive-bombers across the channel.

For the German Me-109 pilots escorting the bombers, each trip over England became increasingly dangerous as the RAF fighter pilots gained proficiency and experience. Gunther Raal, a young pilot from Stuttgart, Germany, saw this transition firsthand from the cockpit of his Me-109.

GUNTHER RAAL, LUFTWAFFE PILOT
Qoquel Airfield, Near Calais, France
15 August 1940

I joined the army as a cadet at the age of eighteen. Then I changed to become an officer to the air force when I was twenty years old because I wanted to fly. I was not politically orientated—and besides, active duty officers weren't allowed to join political parties. I just wanted to serve my country.

I went to a famous fighter pilot school northeast of Berlin. Just when I finished the course, the war started. In those days we didn't count flying hours, not even takeoffs or sorties. Once you got your wings you decided whether to go into bombers or fighters. My temperament is for a fighter pilot. I wanted to sit alone in my airplane and fight, not as part of a crew in a plane. That's not my temperament.

I was just twenty-two years old when I saw combat for the first time. When the war started, my squadron of Messerschmitt Me-109 fighters was on the frontier with France and there was hesitation on both sides about flying across the border. The French flew down the Rhine on the western side, and we on the eastern side. Then in May '40, the Wehrmacht moved into France and we had our first air-to-air contact. Mine was against a Curtis P-36 and it was my first victory.

After the French surrendered, we were told to prepare for the invasion of England. I was a lieutenant in one of the fighter units with the mission of escorting the bombers to their targets in England. At first our assignment was to escort Stuka Ju-87 dive-bombers. These were very slow flying airplanes, and our fighter escorts had to stay close by. We would meet them at a rendezvous point over France and then lead them over to England. Our Messerschmidt 109s—the escorts—were good aircraft, but as we approached the coast, the British Spitfires would be waiting for us upstairs. And we lost a lot of pilots.

At first they just had us go after military targets—not the cities. But even after we switched to using just the Dornier and Heinkel bombers—they were faster than the Stukas—but the Luftwaffe wasn't a strategic air force. Precision bombing was not that far developed, and our fighters didn't have the range to escort the bombers all the way to targets on the west side of the island. The whole concept was wrong. The weather was terrible—and just got worse as the summer wore on.

The British pilots had the advantage of defending their own territory—and many of them were very good. As we lost pilots and planes, the British just kept getting more of both. Their Spitfires and Hurricanes were no better than our Me-109s—but they could stay up longer because they were fighting right over their own airfields. We could only engage for a few minutes before we had to turn and go back across the channel before we ran out of fuel.

I was credited with shooting down 275 planes because I flew fighters in combat for five and a half years, except when I was in hospital. The best pilots are those who fly many missions. The best British pilots were the ones who flew hundreds of missions—that's what makes a good pilot. All of us had the greatest respect for the Royal Air Force. Their tactics and skills were excellent.

By mid-August, Goering and his high command decided that the only way to bomb England more effectively would be to eliminate the British fighter threat to the Dornier and Heinkel bombers. Accordingly, the Luftwaffe was ordered to shift the focus of their attacks and concentrate on "obliterating" the RAF Fighter Command bases. For the next three weeks, nearly every Spitfire and Hurricane station in southeast England was hit as the Germans launched thousands of sorties against the British defensive network.

By the end of the month, losses of RAF fighters and pilots were almost double that of the Luftwaffe. In the last week of August and the first week of September, RAF Fighter Command lost nearly 300 Spitfires and Hurricanes. And although the RAF managed to down more than 375 German aircraft, fewer than half were fighters.

Bigham Hill—a key sector station for Eleven Group of RAF Fighter Command, twelve miles south of London—was hit multiple times a day for nearly a week. And though it never went completely out of service, scores of ground support personnel were killed and numerous fighters damaged in the German raids. One of the young pilots flying from Bigham Hill throughout the onslaught was twenty-two-year-old Hurricane pilot Pete Brothers.

PETER BROTHERS, RAF PILOT
Bigham Hill, South of London, England
29 August 1940

I joined the Air Force after we were given the talk by a First World War fighter ace, who said, "There's going to be another war and you chaps are going to be in it. I'll give you one piece of advice. When you get into your first combat you'll be frightened. Always remember the chap in the other cockpit is twice as frightened as you are."

He was right. When I got into my first combat, I was practically hysterical but I thought of those words, and then said, "Well then, the poor chap in the German cockpit must be going insane, so I'd better put him out of his misery." Which I did.

I applied to join the Royal Air Force as soon as I was seventeen and then in January 1936, they sent me a letter saying to report. I was lucky because I had already done 100 to 150 hours flying at a training school. The RAF gave me a couple of checks, put me through some drills, a little ground school, and then my instructor said, "Fine, you know how to fly, you've done it." So I was selected to fly fighters and assigned to a Hurricane squadron.

Nobody had imagined that the Germans would roll up to the coast of France so fast. We reckoned the only aircraft we were going to see were bombers. But my first fight was against Messerschmidt 109s. And as they were coming toward us I thought they were specks on the windscreen— when suddenly they grew larger, coming right at us. I vividly remember the first one I shot down. He came out of a cloud about thirty feet above me—so close that I could see oil streaks from underneath his engine cowlings and missing chips of paint. He swept over the top of me and he was turning around, coming in to attack. As he did, he overshot, so I got on his tail and shot him down.

Within a couple of weeks the British Expeditionary Force in France was surrounded at Dunkirk and they pulled my squadron back to Bigham Hill. From there, I flew cover over Dunkirk, trying to protect the troops being evacuated and providing cover for them from attacks by German bombers and fighter aircraft. We were amazed that so many troops were able to get out and across the Channel. France capitulated shortly after that. We said, "It's up to us now . . . and nobody is going to muck us about anymore."

After Dunkirk there was a lull while the Germans got ready to launch their heavy strikes on England. And then the raids started in what the newspaper people called the Battle of Britain, and it began to get very hectic.

At first they went after the ports and beach defenses and the like. Then, after a few weeks, the Germans started to mount heavy raids on our airfields with 200 to 250 bombers—escorted by a similar number of fighters flying above them. We'd take a look and say, "Well...where do we start?" Our tactics had us going this way and that, and it wasn't very successful. After we had lost a number of our mates, someone said, "I tell you what—let's take the Germans head on. They probably won't like that— the gunner in a bomber is sitting in a Plexiglas nose—and we've got eight guns and he's only got two. So let's take them head on. That should split them up." And it did.

The Germans' instinct was to pull up, over the top of someone that they thought was about to collide with them. And that's a bad instinct. We learned to always push forward and fly underneath for two reasons: one, you expect the other chap to pull up, and two, you gain more speed shoving the nose down into a quick dive. It gives you time to turn around and attack from the rear.

That kind of thing helped. And you got to know your aircraft inside out—all it could and couldn't do.

On a typical day we'd be up and on the airfield before first light—aircraft ready, engines warmed up and ready to go. Because we had radars to warn us of an incoming raid in our sector, we were usually on fifteen-minute alert. But in late August and early September—when they were hitting our bases—sometimes several times a day we would be on "cockpit alert"—sitting in the cockpit, guns loaded, engine running, just waiting for the signal to launch, what direction to head and what altitude they were coming in on. Those were very long days—and very short nights.

Had we lost, and been invaded, Germany would've controlled the whole of Europe. There would have been no stepping-stone for the U.S. to come to our help. That was something we thought about a lot in those days.

By the first week of September 1940, RAF Fighter Command was reeling from the effects of the Luftwaffe assault on its string of bases. Hitler, still hoping for some kind of accommodation from Churchill, had ordered that London not be attacked—and the British capital had been largely spared the wrath of the German bombing campaign. Though aircraft plants, munitions factories, and shipyards had been hit—with attendant civilian casualties—the Führer reserved for himself any decision on attacking London's closely nestled residential areas. But on 7 September that all changed. For the first time, massed formations of Luftwaffe bombers headed not for the beleaguered RAF Fighter Command stations, but straight for the British capital.

For fighter pilots like London-born Billy Drake, the shift in German tactics was a reprieve. By that first grim week in September 1940, the twenty-three-year-old fighter pilot had already been shot down and wounded over France, evaded capture, and made his way back to England to rejoin his mates in the desperate battle.

BILLY DRAKE, RAF PILOT
London, England
31 August 1940

I took my first flight in a bi-plane at a circus when I was fourteen and became a pilot in 1936. I used to read a magazine called *Flight,* and there was an advertisement saying that the Royal Air Force wanted pilots. And I told them that I wanted to join a fighter squadron

The first time I saw a Hurricane was about 1938. We'd already been briefed by the British air attaché in Berlin, about the capabilities of the Messerschmitt 109. And the Hurricane was an airplane that had been produced to compete against the 109 with its eight guns, a proven engine, and it looked like a proper airplane. At the same time we saw the Spitfire. It had been produced at about the same time. We were certain that with these two aircraft we could take on anything that the Germans wanted to throw at us.

In those days there were no two-seat trainers. A test pilot would sit us down and tell us about the airplane, so we weren't completely in the dark. But we had to teach ourselves how to fly it.

After the Germans invaded Poland we flew to France and were posted to a French air base and settled down to wait for the Germans. We were at this place for about nine months, until May, when the Germans invaded France.

While we were in France we had no radar, like we had back in England—so we had no advance warning of any movement of the German air force. The only indications we had was when we saw these condensation contrails in the sky. But of course we had no communications so we didn't know if they were ours, French, or even German airplanes. So we had to intercept them to find out. The first time I saw a German airplane was when I intercepted one of these condensation contrails—and it turned out to be an RAF aircraft doing photographic reconnaissance. I was following him when I looked down and saw a German Me-109, coming up to intercept this recon airplane. So I paid a compliment for this German's interest by taking a shot at him.

He saw me first, dived away, and I followed him. It took me about ten minutes before I got closer to him—but I still couldn't get within range to fire. He dove again, trying to lure me into some high-tension cables but I saw them in time. He pulled up to see if I hit them and crashed, but as he pulled up—which slowed him up—it gave me an opportunity to get within range and I shot him down.

On the second day of the German invasion, my own personal airplane—which I'd had for about three years—was being serviced, so I got into another plane. When I got to 18,000 feet I realized the oxygen wasn't working. So I called the flight leader and said, "I have to return to base— my oxygen is not working."

The pilot flying the point said, "Okay... push off. We'll see you later."

As I was flying back to my base at about 12,000 feet, I saw three Dornier 17s and went straight in to attack. I shot one down, and as I was getting into position to shoot down a second one, a Messerschmitt 110—the twin-engine German fighter—got behind my tail, and repaid the compliment, setting my airplane on fire. I was panicking, and decided to get out with my parachute, and did all the necessary preparations. But when I tried to jump, I hit my head against the canopy—which probably saved my life because the flames were all around me and I was covered in petrol. If I had I opened the cockpit hood at that time, the flames would have come inside and enveloped me. But as it was, I was able to roll the plane upside down, the flames were swept in the opposite direction, and I fell out.

The parachute worked, but I'd hurt my back and my legs getting out of the aircraft—I thought I'd lost my leg, it was hurting so. Somehow I made a safe landing, but as I was climbing out of my parachute harness, five or six French peasants confronted me with pitchforks and scythes. They thought I was a German. I showed them my RAF wings, and then they couldn't have been more helpful.

They got me on a motorcycle and took me to a medical clearing station. There were no doctors there, just orderlies—and they had run out of anesthetic. Before they started to dig away and to extract the bullet fragments that were buried in my back, they gave me morphine. They said, "Do not worry about your leg, it is still there. There was only shrapnel doing all the harm in your leg."

After digging out the metal from my back, they got me into a car, and took me to a train that took me to a French hospital at a town called Chartres.

About five of my squadron mates were killed during the period that I was laid up. When I made it back to England, the medical authorities had a good look at me and said, "He's fit enough to fly." By now the Battle of Britain had started, and all I wanted to do was to get back into a fighter unit.

The Germans shifted tactics and started to bomb our fighter airfields. If they had kept it up—and gone after the radars—they might have knocked Fighter Command out of the skies over England. But then Hitler suddenly shifted tactics again and started to bomb London and ignored the fighter airfields. It was a big mistake for their air force. It gave Fighter Command a chance to recover—to replace planes and pilots and repair our air stations.

Because we had radars and a very good early warning network, we could launch our Hurricanes and Spitfires just in time to intercept the bombers as they were lining up to make their bomb runs over London— when they have to stay straight and level.

After a few weeks of heavy losses the German air force turned to night terror bombing—just trying to kill as many civilians as possible. Night attacks made their bombers harder to find, but it also meant that they weren't going to have as many Me-109s with them—and after a few weeks, we all got pretty good at night flying. I was credited with shooting down twenty-four and a half German planes—the half was because somebody else had already put some hits into one of them.

We encountered some French fighter pilots flying for the Germans. They would occasionally come over the Channel to test our defenses. I intercepted one over the Channel one day and indicated that he should come back with me, and land. But he indicated "no." So, I had to get behind him as he turned, and shoot him down. That wasn't a very pleasant task, but a very wise officer once told me, "An order is an order and not an excuse for discussion." That's the way it was in the war. If we were told to do something, we did it. That's how we did our jobs—we did them to the best of our ability.

For the people of London, Hitler's shift in strategy meant that *they* were now the targets for the waves of German aircraft. Starting on 7 September, hundreds of Heinkel and Dornier bombers, escorted by scores of Me-109s and Me-110s, poured high explosives down on London's factories, offices, and homes.

Over the capital were 1,500 barrage balloons—trailing long cables to snare Luftwaffe propellers. In and around the city were more than 2,200 medium and heavy caliber anti-aircraft guns.

For those on the ground, the air raids followed a pattern that became almost a ritual: first the wailing of air raid sirens, then the roar of the approaching bombers, followed by the snarl of fighters snaking through the bomber formations, guns blazing. Next came the blasting of anti-aircraft cannons from batteries set up in parks and on rooftops around the city. Finally—if the RAF pilots and anti-aircraft gunners couldn't turn the raiders away—came the crash of bombs.

For Chrissy Quinn, a London factory worker, it was a terrifying experience.

CHRISTINA QUINN
London, England
15 September 1940

I was born in the East End of London. Everybody was poor in those days, so we weren't any poorer than other people, and my dad had a bad illness in 1934, so he never got a job again. But my mum went to work as a tent finisher. I had two brothers that worked and they used to give mum a pound a week, and she used to buy their clothes out of that. Dad died when he was sixty.

I won a scholarship, to go to high school—we got one pound and eight a month as a grant. I learned dressmaking at school, and I went to work in a factory making brassieres for a German man who was interned as soon as the war started. His factory was closed that morning—but that afternoon I went to work as a sewing machine operator in factory making army overcoats in the East End of London.

I was just nineteen when the war came, and was engaged to a nice boy but he was called up right away. Pretty soon, all our boyfriends left. Lots of them never came home. They died in France or North Africa or at sea.

We thought that was as bad as it could get, but then the Germans started the bombing here at home. At first it was far away—in Plymouth or Portsmouth, Bristol, Birmingham. But then they started coming after London.

Our factories were all bombed. Some days we headed off to work to find that the factory had been hit during the night. Once we were sent to Kent, to pick hops in the fields. It was a beautiful autumn day and then we heard the German bombers high overhead, heading for London. We couldn't see the planes—just the vapor trails they leave—hundreds of them. They told us to get in the ditches and from there, lying on our backs, we watched as our fighters climbed up to meet them.

The fight went on for a long time, right overhead and it was terrible, really terrible—but you couldn't stop watching overhead. I can still see the parachutes coming down—I don't know whether they were ours or theirs—but there were a lot of them.

Another time, in London, my sister had just had a baby, and we were at the market when the air raid warning went off. So, we ran home, went in the Anderson Underground station shelter, and stayed for hours. We were terrified. When we came out, the bombing was finished, but everything was ablaze. For miles along the docks, ships and everything was alight. And, of course, those who had lost their homes were milling about, trying to recover some belongings and get to a shelter.

Late in the fall, I guess it was the end of September, the Germans pretty much stopped coming in the daylight and started just bombing just at night. All of England was under a strict blackout—meaning no lights could show. If we had a night shift at the factory, we had to walk in the middle of the road and let the moonlight guide us. It was frightening, walking in the blackout. If it was a moonlight night, we knew the Germans would be coming to bomb. If it was a *rotten* night, they usually wouldn't come. But if it was a nice moonlight night, we thought, "Well, tonight's the night they'll come."

The worst thing was when our own house got bombed. The air raid warning must have been late so as the siren went off we raced for the shelter and the sky was already full of planes. We could hear our Spitfires and

Hurricanes right over our neighborhood and then *bam, bam, bam,* the anti-aircraft guns were all going. We were all terrified.

When we came out the shelter, three houses were completely bombed, and there was a man, who had been standing on the step watching the air raid. He was a bit of a cripple, a tiny little man. And he was blown to smithereens. As we come out the shelter, you could see bits of him lying about. But the chap next door who had hid under the stairs, he was saved. Our house was badly blasted and we had to move to another place that the council found for us.

The people really pulled together. Everyone tried to help each other. If someone had a shop that got bombed, they would try to open up again right away. "It's business as usual," we'd say, and even if everything was bombed, shops opened up to carry on. We were more worried about our fellows in the army.

We never thought the war would finish. Wherever you went, somebody was being killed. But somehow or other we seemed to take it all in our stride. And we got on with our work—*if* we had a place of work to go to the next morning. I mean, we lost everything, me and mum. I also lost a brother in the war. But we were defiant.

Defiance was a vital quality for the English people during the Battle of Britain and the subsequent "Blitz" against the island's population centers. Ron Dick was a schoolboy living on the outskirts of London when the war started. The daily melee in the sky above his homeland made an indelible impression.

RON DICK
Outskirts of London
11 December 1939

When the war started I was nine and was told that we were all getting shot at, because we were British. People were expecting to be raided by the Luftwaffe. We had a choice of two sorts of shelters from the government for our flat. One of them was called the "Militant Shelter." It was a large steel box, which was erected inside the house. It had a very strong steel frame with steel mesh sides. You raised the sides of the mesh, put mattresses and the like inside, and the family slept there. If the house collapsed during a bombing raid, it would fall around you—but you'd eventually be dug out. And that kind of shelter did save a lot of people.

My family didn't go for one of those. We went for an "Anderson Shelter," which was a corrugated steel arch delivered to your backyard. Then you dug a hole, placed the arch over the hole and poured concrete over the arch. It was sort of garden shed made of corrugated steel and concrete. Once set up, you'd put as much earth as you could on top of the thing and install a blast door on the front. After that you put bunks inside. We slept in that from the start of the air raids, until the spring of 1941. For the whole of the winter of 1940–41, we slept outside in the corrugated shed during the air raids.

The early daylight raids were pretty obvious. This air raid siren would sound and we were all supposed to take cover. Sometimes we just stood about outside the Anderson Shelter watching to see if anything would happen. Eventually, you'd see the Luftwaffe fly over us on their way to the London docks. And once they started bombing we had to take extra care—we lived close to the target, so we were in the line of fire all the time. And we got heavily bombed during the Battle of Britain. During the daylight raids, you'd see these large formations coming over. I don't know, they were up ten to fifteen thousand feet, I suppose. We could see the Spitfires going after the German fighters and the Hurricanes were mostly aiming at the bomber formations. And then we'd hear the gunfire: the machine guns and the heavier *thump* of the Me-109s' cannon.

And when our fighters were out of the way, there was a lot of anti-aircraft fire. That was the noisiest element of the whole performance, because we had anti-aircraft batteries all around us, and they made a tremendous racket. And at that point you more or less had to take cover because now there was shrapnel falling from the exploding anti-aircraft shells.

It was a popular activity for schoolboys like me at the time, after a raid, to go rushing around the streets looking for these little pieces of metal, putting them in a cardboard box and collecting the shrapnel.

There was a discussion between my mother and father about whether I should be evacuated safely out of the city. There were two evacuation options for British children. One was to evacuate to Canada. That was particularly attractive early in the summer of 1940, when a German invasion was a definite threat. A lot of people decided that they wanted their children safe overseas. The other choice was being evacuated to the English countryside where it was a lot less likely that the children would be killed in a bombing raid. Tens of thousands of young British children were relocated under this program but my parents finally decided they didn't want to do that to me because I would become somebody else's child. So, thankfully, I never left. I was there for the whole of the Battle of Britain and the "Blitz" afterward.

The sound of an air raid has stayed with me. Although, the funny thing is, I suppose nine-year-old boys are very resilient creatures. I don't remember being very terrified by any of this stuff. It was all a big adventure.

By the autumn of '40, the Luftwaffe commenced regular night raids—which meant that we were getting bombed twenty-four hours a day. During that period there was one particularly heavy night raid when we were all in the Anderson Shelter. It was the early hours of the morning—pitch-black night. There was a tremendous racket with all the anti-aircraft guns firing, but terribly ineffective. But the fact they were making a lot of noise made us feel better.

I could hear the droning of the German aircraft going overhead and the continuous screams of bombs, making sort of a whistling, rushing noise. And then, when they got very close, a tremendous whistling roar. There was this one load of bombs, four of them, that hit very close—and I could hear each bomb scream and then the explosion as each the bomb hit the ground.

Immediately after the first explosion I heard the second bomb—and another huge explosion, this one bigger. Then the Anderson Shelter rocked when a third bomb went off. It felt like the Anderson Shelter was actually at sea. Finally there was a loud thump, but no explosion. And we sat there.

The raid went on and on and eventually petered out. Dawn came and we ventured out of the shelter to see what was going on—the shelter was just behind our house. In front of our house there was a large hole in the ground. A bomb had gone into this hole but hadn't gone off. It was just sitting there. The civil defense people were roaring about trying to clear the area. My father grabbed our family and said, "Get some bedding; we're off to Number 12 up the road."

When I had a look at the street—a typical suburban 1930s street with the houses joined together in townhouse style—there were places where the three previous bombs had carved great holes in the street. There were two or three houses missing. We were still clutching the bedding and walking up the street. And now the daylight raids had just started. Sirens went off again. And we could see a big German formation coming over the top of us.

We were about five houses away, when there was this enormous explosion. And it felt like the oxygen had been sucked out of the atmosphere. I whipped around in time to see the front of our house fall. The initial reaction was they must be bombing us again. But then I realized that that the bomb that had landed in front of our house had just gone off— it obviously had a delay fuse. It blew the front of our house away.

The RAF fighter pilots during the Battle of Britain were our heroes. When I was a boy, they were knights in shining armor. One of my heroes was Douglas Barter, the "legless ace." Though he lost both legs, he still served as a fighter leader throughout the Battle of Britain.

All of this influenced my desire to become a Royal Air Force officer. I joined the Cadet Force as a schoolboy—the equivalent of the American Civil Air Patrol—and as soon as I turned eighteen, I joined the RAF and made a career of flying fighters for my country. I guess there were many of us who were patriots in those days.

Prevailing in the Battle of Britain and the Blitz that followed required not only dedication and patriotism, but a highly sophisticated air defense network. The RAF "chain home" radars were connected to a system of ground observers and air raid wardens who fed information into an integrated warning and control center headquartered at Uxbridge, just west of London.

The British also organized a remarkably effective civil defense structure to mitigate the effects of the German bombings. The fire brigades, rescue squads, medical personnel, air raid wardens, and explosive ordnance disposal units deployed in Britain's cities often made the difference between living and dying for those on the ground.

Nineteen-year-old Charles Leah wanted to enlist in the army—but with his three older brothers already in the military, his mother pleaded, "I've given up three sons... and that's more than any mother should be allowed to suffer." So instead Leah volunteered to be an air raid warden in his hometown of Coventry, ninety-five miles north of London.

CHARLES LEAH, AIR RAID WARDEN
Bellgreen, Coventry, England
30 September 1940

I was born and brought up in Bellgreen, on the outskirts of Coventry. In 1938, everybody in England expected the war with Germany. Prime Minister Chamberlain went over to Munich and came back waving a piece of paper and said, "Peace in our time!" which nobody believed. But it gave us a bit of time to prepare anyway.

My three older brothers all joined the forces—one went to the Navy, two in the Army. When the war started in 1939, I was going to join but my mother appealed to me to stay home so I joined the Air Raid Precautions organization. She thought my only job was to watch over a section of our neighborhood, the streets around our area.

But I didn't tell my mum what an ARP warden does during a raid. If bombs come down, the ARP has to log where they fall. If they're already exploded—it's not a problem. But if they are unexploded, or have a delay fuse, it can be a bit dangerous. My mum thought that all I did during the war was to make sure people observe the blackout, and not show any light.

In the summer of '40, the German bombers came over the Channel, over Kent, Norfolk, and the coastal areas. That's where most of the dogfights took place in the attempt to stop them from getting in over our cities. And, of course our anti-aircraft guns would try and shoot them down, which they did often.

In August of '40, I was by the Jaguar Standard Motor Works and this solitary plane flew over. Nobody realized it wasn't an English plane until it was about quarter mile away and it suddenly dropped two bombs onto the motor works. One bomb hit the paint shop, and there was an explosion and this huge plume of black smoke. The plane went off flying low, to get away, but an AA battery shot him down.

National Archives

Londoners taking shelter in the Underground.

We'd get a bit worried with the anti-aircraft guns shooting into the air because everything comes back down again, in little bits and pieces of shrapnel, and they would hit your helmet like rain. Late in the summer a German bomber dropped a load of incendiaries not far from my home and the public library burned down.

In September of '40 the Germans started what we called the "Blitz"— going after civilians in our cities. Then we had raids practically every night—the sirens would go and planes would come, and drop their bombs and head off again.

In one of them, on November 14, I was at a place called Tile Hill. I had to walk to my home, and then down to the ARP station, about three miles. On my way to the ARP post, I came across a neighbor, Mr. Gough, who was leaning against a fence and groaning. Obviously something was wrong. I asked him, "Are you all right?" And then I said, "Come on, I'll take you down to shelter." But when I picked him up, he groaned, and died in my arms.

One night the phones were down so I sent my runner to find out why. It's a very old-fashioned way of doing things, but it works. He was gone for some time so I decided to go out and look for him. About three hundred yards from the ARP station, I heard four bombs coming down, so I dove into the gutter, where there was a little bit of cover. One of the bombs landed on the other side of the hedge where I was.

Further down the street I found that the second bomb had killed Gordon, our seventeen-year-old runner. A third bomb had come through the center of three connected houses and wrecked them. I went inside one and found a father and his little girl—dead of course. I lifted the man out of the wreckage and laid him on the kitchen floor. Then I went and fetched the little girl, and laid her alongside daddy. And then I got the wife out—all of them dead.

A few minutes later I heard the last bomb explode. It had landed on the bay of my parents' house, where I also lived. It had a delay fuse. The Germans did that so they could kill as many rescue workers as possible. When this bomb went off it pushed out the bay, and the center wall fell, and everything was piled in the back. The ceilings were all falling down into the bedrooms—there was nothing holding them up.

I went around to our shelter, and thankfully my parents were inside. They asked, "What is it like?" They had heard our house had been hit, but didn't know how bad. I said, "Yeah, it's pretty bad." But we were all safe and alive.

I think everybody was proud of the RAF, and what it did. Imagine, kids of nineteen or twenty going up in a Spitfire, facing hundreds of German planes, with only a couple, a weeks' training in some little trainer. Yeah, it took guts—especially in light of some terrible losses.

✪ ✪ ✪

Hitler's deeply flawed decision to shift from bombing the RAF Fighter Command bases to terror bombing of British cities in September of 1940 is the turning point in the Battle of Britain. Though no single document survives to explain his rationale, most historians surmise that it was the consequence of a navigational error.

On the night of 24 August 1940, a ten-plane flight of He-111s, aiming to hit the piers on the lower Thames, overshot their target and dropped their bombs on the center of London, killing scores of civilians. The next night, RAF Bomber Command launched an eighty-plane raid on Berlin—the first against the German capital. Five days later, the Führer lifted his ban on "terror bombing" and urged Goering to "destroy" London.

Within a week of this decision, the Blitz was on—and Hitler was preparing to abandon Sea Lion, his plan for the invasion of England. On 14 September—the day after Mussolini launched the invasion of Egypt from Italian bases in Libya—Hitler postponed Sea Lion and on 12 October, he permanently cancelled the operation. By then, the RAF had recovered sufficiently to inflict horrific losses on the Luftwaffe bomber crews conducting daylight attacks and in November, Goering ordered that all major cross-channel raids would be conducted at night.

In describing the role of the RAF in this bloody contest, Prime Minister Winston Churchill told the House of Commons on 20 August, "Never in the field of human conflict was so much owed by so many to so few."

They were few indeed. By the end of September, RAF Fighter Command had lost more than 850 fighters knocking down 600 German bombers. Fewer than 2,500 RAF fighter pilots—among them a handful of Canadians, Australians, New Zealanders, Poles, Free French, Czechs, South Africans, and Americans—had handed Hitler his first defeat.

Thanks to their courage, by the winter of 1940–41 Churchill no longer had to worry about a German invasion. Instead he began to focus on how to turn his island nation into a springboard for a joint British-American return to the Continent.

Hitler, thwarted in his hope for a neutral or defeated England, turned his attention to a new adventure: crushing the "Bolshevik menace" by means of Operation Barbarossa, the invasion of the Soviet Union.

CHAPTER 3
THE EASTERN FRONT
1939–1941

Hitler's 12 October 1940 decision to cancel Operation Sea Lion—the invasion of England—was predicated on the inability of the Luftwaffe to gain air superiority over the British Isles. But even before his conclusion that a cross-channel operation was impossible, the Führer had already begun exploring other options and opportunities. In mid-August he had raised the prospect of taking on the "Bolshevik menace" with his military commanders—suggesting that a campaign against the Soviets would be necessary in order to secure Germany's eastern frontier.

On 2 September he signed a new Tripartite Pact with Italy and Japan—in which they all pledged to aid one another in the event of an attack on any signatory. Eleven days later, Mussolini launched an assault into Egypt from Italian bases in Libya—prompting Hitler to meet with Il Duce on 4 October at the Brenner Pass in the Alps. There, the two fascist dictators concocted a plan for bringing Franco's Spain into the Axis—and seizing all British territories in the Mediterranean from Gibraltar east to Suez.

Hitler took *Amerika,* his specially configured "command train," for the meeting with the Spanish dictator on 23 October. But Franco was unimpressed—and rejected the idea of allowing the Wehrmacht to transit

Hitler launched nearly four million Wehrmacht troops into Russia
in Operation Barbarossa on June 22, 1941.

Spanish territory in order to attack Gibraltar. Frustrated in his grand design
for turning the Mediterranean into an Axis-controlled lake, Hitler returned
to Berlin—only to learn that Mussolini, without consulting anyone, had
invaded Greece.

By the first week of November 1940, Adolf Hitler was on the sidelines
of world events for the first time in three years. Mussolini's Italian "Legions"
were charging pell-mell across the Egyptian desert toward Suez, and
his "Alpine Army" was promising to seize Athens by the middle of the
month. The Russians were moving more troops into Estonia, Latvia, and
Lithuania—as they were permitted to do under the 1939 Molotov-Ribbentrop Pact.

In the United States, FDR won an unprecedented third term and became
increasingly bellicose in his comments about the Axis in general and Germany in particular. Meanwhile, Hitler was relegated to nighttime air raids
on English cities and hoping his U-boats and surface raiders could sink
enough merchant vessels to strangle the British Isles into submission.

On 12 November, Soviet foreign minister Molotov arrived in Berlin for
meetings with Ribbentrop and Hitler. The Führer hoped to co-opt the Sovi-

ets into helping him despoil the British Empire. Hitler needed access to coal, iron, tin, bauxite, and other raw materials from the Balkans and oil from Romania. In exchange for ceding control of the Balkans to Germany, Russia would be given a free hand in Iran, the "Stan" states, and unspecified British territories in Africa.

Molotov wanted nothing to do with Hitler's deal. Instead, the Soviet official—one of Stalin's closest confidants—demanded that Russia be allowed to annex Finland and be guaranteed free access to the Baltic and transit rights into the Mediterranean from the Black Sea. Ribbentrop's efforts to convince Molotov that the British were on the ropes were not helped by British air raids that forced the two foreign ministers to conduct their final meetings in an air raid shelter.

By the time Molotov left the German capital on 14 November, Hitler had no doubt as to what his next steps were going to be. He instructed his generals to complete plans for invading the Soviet Union in the spring of 1941. On 5 December, the first draft of the war plan was presented to the Führer at the Reich Chancellery. He called it Operation Barbarossa—after a twelfth-century Teutonic emperor—and directed that "nothing interfere with com-

Wehrmacht soldier

pleting all necessary preparations for an invasion by 15 May 1941."

But on 7 December, the British counter-attacked against the Italians in Egypt—forcing one of many "interferences" in preparations for the biggest invasion in history.

Il Duce had been in need of Hitler's help even before the British Western Desert Force launched their Egyptian counter-offensive. On the night of 11–12 November, British aircraft from the carrier HMS *Illustrious* attacked the Italian fleet moored at Taranto, sinking three battleships and a heavy cruiser with aerial torpedoes. And by the end of the month, the poorly equipped Greek army had driven the Italians out of Greece and back into Albania.

In Berlin, Hitler found opportunity in Mussolini's military reversals. In February 1941 he ordered General Erwin Rommel to North Africa to shore up the Italians and start pushing the British back into Egypt. In the Balkans, his plans for "peacefully occupying" territory that the British might use to attack Germany from the south were contravened by a coup in Belgrade, Yugoslavia, on 25 March. Using the coup as a pretext, Hitler ordered the simultaneous invasion of Yugoslavia and Greece on 6 April.

As it had in Poland and then Western Europe at the start of the war, the Wehrmacht blitzkrieg proved unstoppable. Yugoslavia, compromised by internal discord and antiquated arms, capitulated on 17 April. Though three divisions of British troops rushed to aid the Greeks, they too were forced to surrender to the German onslaught five days later. On 27 April 1941, the Nazi swastika was hoisted over the Acropolis in Athens.

The late spring thaw in northeastern Europe allowed time for Hitler to postpone the start of Barbarossa and launch Operation Mercury—the world's first airborne invasion—against the British garrison on the island of Crete. Though the Germans eventually prevailed, the 20 May–1 June operation proved costly—rendering the elite 7th Airborne and 5th Mountain Divisions combat ineffective.

Crete was certainly damaging to the British. More than 2,000 soldiers—most of them New Zealanders—were killed and 12,000 were taken prisoner. Meanwhile, the Royal Navy successfully evacuated 18,000—but the British Mediterranean Fleet lost eighteen ships sunk or badly damaged in the campaign. It was the costliest engagement for the Royal Navy in WWII.

By the end of May 1940, it appeared to many observers that Hitler was once again unstoppable. German conquests in the Balkans, Greece, and on Crete were being matched by Rommel's Afrika Corps in North Africa. On the eve of Barbarossa—other than the bizarre defection of his principal deputy Rudolf Hess to Scotland on 10 May and the loss of the battleship *Bismarck* on 27 May—there was no doubt that the Führer was in absolute control of events. There were no indications that his enormous military machine was being stretched.

The Wehrmacht's 180 Infantry, twenty Panzer and twelve motorized divisions now numbered five million strong, the Luftwaffe 1.7 million, and the Navy 420,000. Twenty-five percent of all German males were now in uniform. Hitler replaced them with slave labor in agricultural production and eventually even in manufacturing war materiel.

Though Hitler's military campaigns of 1939–41 had produced the most effective and experienced military force in the world, German losses and the occupation commitments they generated were not insignificant. Operations in Poland, Norway, France, the Low Countries, the Balkans, and Greece had cost 66,750 German dead and missing, and a near equal number wounded. Over 4,000 German paratroopers and elite mountain troops perished on Crete, and several thousand more were wounded. All eighty gliders and 223 of 600 Ju-52 transport aircraft were destroyed. Too many Axis divisions were required for occupation duty in Poland, Western Europe, Greece, and Yugoslavia and Crete. But in North Africa, Rommel was demanding more troops, tanks, and planes to reinforce his 5th and 15th Panzer Divisions.

Yet none of these losses or commitments deterred final preparations for Barbarossa—finally set for 22 June. Hitler and the German General Staff were convinced that the forces they had assembled for Barbarossa would overwhelm Stalin's Red Army. Hitler was certain that the operation could be completed before the first snows whipped in from Siberia. They had good reason for optimism.

While the Red Army in the summer of 1941 looked formidable on paper—235 infantry divisions, fifty armored divisions with 24,000 tanks, twenty-five mechanized divisions, and an air force of 10,000 aircraft, and overall, more than 7.5 million in uniform—it was essentially a hollow force thanks to the purges of its leader, Josef Stalin. Between 1937 and 1939, nearly three quarters of the Red Army's officers were shot, jailed, or exiled to Siberian gulags.

The resulting chaos in the ranks of the Soviet military seriously degraded Russian readiness to fight as evidenced by the abysmal showing of Red Army in Finland during the "Winter War" of 1939–40. Stalin responded by ordering yet another purge—and finally, much-needed reforms.

But improvements and promotions were slow in coming through the cumbersome Communist Party political apparatus that Stalin had inherited from Vladimir Ilich Lenin in 1924. At the brink of war, none of Stalin's *Stavka* (general staff) or his field commanders had anything close to the military acumen, experience, or skill of their German counterparts.

In the spring of 1941, most of the Red Army's mobility still depended on horses. Few of its tanks or aircraft could be considered equivalent to Hitler's, and the Russian divisions arrayed on the western frontier were poorly disposed for any kind of a defense in depth. Perhaps most importantly, Stalin himself did not believe any of the multiple warnings he was being given about an impending attack.

Though both Roosevelt and Churchill distrusted Stalin, they both repeatedly sought to warn him of Hitler's intentions. In March 1941 U.S. undersecretary of state Joseph Grew passed to the Soviet ambassador in Washington the gist of a decrypted German cable outlining the planned attack. On 19 April, Churchill sent the British ambassador in Moscow to see Molotov with a similar intercept. In May, Richard Sorge, a Soviet intelligence agent in Japan, warned that Hitler was preparing to invade Russia with nine German armies.

Stalin's willful disregard for the realities of the German buildup even extended to ignoring his own commanders. From the first of June onward, Soviet units on the western frontier filed near daily reports of German reconnaissance over-flights, cross-border patrols by Germans dressed in Russian uniforms, and the selective jamming of tactical radio nets. Instead of mobilizing, the Soviet dictator instructed his field commanders to avoid "provocations" and ordered that Soviet state-run businesses deliver to Germany their full quotas of oil, foodstuffs, and bulk ores that had been agreed to in the Molotov-Ribbentrop Pact.

When 7,200 German artillery pieces opened fire across the Russian frontier at 0316 the morning of 22 June 1941, the last trainload of Russian oil and wheat, paid for in German gold, had just crossed the frontier into Nazi-held Poland. By dawn, more than 3,350 tanks and nearly four million German troops were moving eastward—beneath the air cover of 900 Luftwaffe bombers and 600 fighters. Within hours, more than 1,200 Soviet aircraft were destroyed—most of them still on the ground.

That night, in a radio broadcast, Prime Minister Churchill pledged British support for "Russians fighting for their homeland." But there was scant aid he could deliver given the rapid pace of the German advance. At the end of the first week of Barbarossa, more than a *half million* Russian soldiers had been killed, wounded, captured, or simply gone missing. On 3 July Stalin, in desperation, announced a "scorched earth" program—telling the Soviet people to burn their homes, factories, barns, and crops—to "leave nothing behind for the fascists to eat or use." It proved to be a cruel but effective policy.

By 9 July, two weeks into the battle, Hitler's General Staff estimated that it had destroyed more than half the Red Army divisions confronting the Wehrmacht advance. But German field commanders were already beginning to experience shortages of fuel, tank parts, and food. And though they would eventually receive personnel replacements—divisions of Finns, Hungarians, Slovaks, Italians, and even the "all volunteer" Spanish "Blue" Division—the supply situation would only get worse.

By August 1941, Hitler's armies were at the gates of Leningrad in the north, aimed at Moscow in the center, and headed for Stalingrad in the south. By then more than *five million* Red Army soldiers had been killed, wounded, or captured. Of the nearly three million Russian prisoners of war, over half a million would be dead by winter's end.

Russian POWs weren't the only ones suffering at the hands of the conquerors. Civilians in the "Occupied Zone" were treated with barbarity unseen on the Western front. Behind the advancing Panzers and German infantry, came the *Einsatzgruppen*—SS "killing units" under Hitler's orders to systematically kill "partisans, Bolsheviks, and Jews" in the conquered territories. During the first month of the invasion nearly 150,000 Jews were murdered. By the time the killing was done, fewer than 300,000 of Russia's nearly three million Jews would be alive.

For Stalin, the catastrophe of losing his army and the brutality to which his population was subjected were secondary matters. By 9 August, as Roosevelt and Churchill commenced four days of meetings at Placentia Bay, Newfoundland, that would result in the Atlantic Charter, Stalin was simply hoping to hold on until help arrived from his "allies." The British and Americans had *promised* him aid—but while he waited he *knew* he could count on help from Russia's most reliable and consistent ally: winter.

American wartime assistance to the Soviet Union would prove to be even more difficult to deliver than either FDR or Churchill imagined. Much of it would have to be convoyed through the U-boat-infested North Atlantic to the Russian port of Murmansk. Some could be delivered from Alaska through Siberia. To ensure that there would be at least one "fair weather" route, Russian and British forces—in their first joint action of World War II—occupied Iran.

But there was a further complication to delivering the aid that Stalin so desperately needed. The vagaries of the Lend-Lease act, passed in March 1941, permitted direct aid to Britain—but not to the Soviet Union. Though Roosevelt had been emboldened by his re-election the previous November, he realized that isolationist sentiment in the U.S. was still strong. A Gallup poll taken in June 1941 showed that 83 percent of the American people were still opposed to entering the war.

To help keep the Soviets in the fight, FDR engaged in something of a shell game. American trucks, tanks, machine parts, and foodstuffs would be loaded in U.S. ports—earmarked for delivery to Britain. Once the vessel arrived in Liverpool or Scotland, Churchill's people would decide what they needed—and ship the rest on to Murmansk.

For the delivery of aircraft—which Stalin needed more than tanks—he turned to a handful of young Army Air Corps officers. One of them, Lieutenant John Alison, was already in London when he received secret orders to go to Moscow.

LIEUTENANT JOHN ALISON, USAAF
The Kremlin, Moscow, USSR
12 October 1941

I was sent to London during the Battle of Britain, to assist in training RAF pilots. We had secretly set up a mission there immediately after the Lend-Lease Agreement was signed in September of 1940—even though no aid could theoretically be delivered until Congress passed the Lend-Lease Act in March of '41. Our job was to make sure that the RAF pilots and mechanics knew how to fly and maintain the aircraft we would be sending under Lend-Lease.

When Hitler invaded Russia in the summer of '41, President Roosevelt started making plans right away to help keep Russia from being knocked out of the war. FDR correctly anticipated that sooner or later, *we* were going to be involved. Immediately after the Germans started Barbarossa, the president sent Harry Hopkins, probably FDR's closest advisor, on a secret mission to Moscow. Hopkins took me with him, to help him find out from the Russians what they really needed and to offer Lend-Lease aid to the Soviets.

We left London in the middle of the night aboard a five-car train and we were the only passengers. This train went from London nonstop to northern Scotland. There, we boarded an RAF flying boat. Twenty-four hours later we were in Archangel, just south of the Arctic Circle. It was 30 July 1941.

The Russians met us with motor launches and took us ashore. A Russian general and a colonel were our hosts. I met with the Russian generals and Hopkins met with Stalin. But the Russian generals didn't want to tell me anything. I tried to find out about their tanks—whether we could improve on what they had. Their flat answer was, "No, we have a good tank."

And they did. Their T-34 was based on an American design that our military had rejected. They eventually made tens of thousands of them.

I asked about artillery pieces—they replied, "We have good artillery." Airplanes? "We have good airplanes." But they knew that they didn't have any fighters to match the Me-109—or that could climb fast enough to take on the German bombers. They finally agreed that we'd send P-40 aircraft to Russia. I think there were forty-eight airplanes to be in the first shipment to Russia. Then we had to figure how to get them there.

I was in Moscow in when the Germans got to the city and we had to evacuate with the rest of Stalin's government. The provisional capital had been moved from Moscow toward the Caucuses, and right about the time we were moving there, the Japanese attacked Pearl Harbor.

Washington then decided that we were losing too many ships trying to get cargo across the North Atlantic and into Murmansk and Archangel. The German U-boats were sending so many to the bottom that the aid just wasn't getting through. I was told to find a different way to get the planes delivered to our Soviet "allies."

Somebody back in the Washington decided that the best way to deliver airplanes was for American pilots to pick them up at the factories and fly them to where they were needed. By the winter of '41–'42 that's how we delivered planes to the British—up through Newfoundland, Greenland, Iceland, Northern Ireland—then to England.

But the best route for deliveries to Russia would be to fly them to Alaska and then across the Bering Strait into Siberia. Well, that just wasn't realistic because the Russians weren't about to let American pilots land in Siberia. As a rule they wouldn't even let Americans into the *country*—they were too suspicious.

But Washington wanted to know what airports were available and what facilities were there so that they could plan getting the planes to Russia. We went over to the Russian foreign office and met this very suave

Russian colonel. We told him the message we got from Washington and said, "We want to get this information."

The Russian colonel said, "Well, we're at war and this will take a little time." The Russians stalled as the wires went back and forth between Washington and the Russian capital. Finally, someone figured out a way to do it. If the Russians wouldn't let our people fly the planes into Siberia—let's have the Russian pilots pick up the planes in Alaska.

And it worked! One afternoon in September '42, a P-40 fighter landed in Moscow. By October, there were P-39s, B-25s, and A-20s flying in—we really flooded them with equipment. The Russians wouldn't allow Americans to fly into Russia, but American ingenuity found a way to get the planes to 'em anyway.

Eventually, 7,926 aircraft were transferred to the Soviet Union through Fairbanks, Alaska. Dubbed Operation ALSIB—for the secret Alaska-Siberia route—it was a way for American pilots to ferry planes from factories throughout the U.S. to Great Falls, Montana. From there, aircraft destined for the Soviets headed north across Canada to Ladd Field in Fairbanks. There, Soviet pilots took possession of the planes and flew them across the Bering Straits, back to the USSR.

By 1942, nearly all of the planes that the Russian received at Ladd Field had arrived there courtesy of American women. Not only did a labor force that contained millions of women build the planes—but also the aircraft often began their journey to war with an American woman at the controls.

Though female pilots were barred from flying military aircraft outside the continental U.S. during World War II, more than 1,000 WASPs—Women Air Service Pilots—ferried planes from factories to airbases around the United States. Within hours of installing the last rivet, WASPs would take off—sometimes on a 3,000-mile transcontinental delivery trip.

One of the largest airplane manufacturers was Bell Aircraft. At its Buffalo, New York, plant, Bell manufactured the P-39 Airacobra. This maneuverable single-seat fighter with its nose-mounted cannon and wing-mounted machine guns became a favorite of the Soviet pilots. Thousands of them were flight-ferried from Buffalo to Great Falls by WASPs like Betty Shea—who loved the challenge of piloting fighters with Russian markings 1,600 miles across America.

BETTY SHEA, WOMEN AIR SERVICE PILOT
Bell Aircraft Factory, Buffalo, New York
24 November 1941

Flying had been my dream since I was a little girl. The government started the CPT—the Civilian Pilot Training program—in 1938. I got in during '39 while I was in college and got my private pilot's license. As soon as I could, I signed up for the WASP program, took a test, and was accepted. It was perfect for me—I was from Buffalo and I had been around Bell aircraft since I started flying.

I was only in my very early twenties when I became a ferry pilot. We weren't trained in formation flying so we generally flew on our own. I was a loner and liked to have that airplane—with a red star, the Russian emblem, on it—out there by myself. The plane was essentially ours until we got it to Great Falls—about a twelve- to fourteen-hour flight—depending on the weather. A typical route: Buffalo to Niagara Falls to South Bend to remain overnight—then the next day to Bismarck and on to Great Falls, where the men would take them to Alaska for turnover to the Russians.

Once, one of the girls crashed and burned at Bismarck. There was a lot of suspicion that it was sabotage. The FBI, the Flight Safety people—everybody came to Bismarck to try and figure it out. I was pretty sure that the airplanes were all right but there was a lot of apprehension. I guess that's understandable after a friend goes down and nobody can find out why. It's a terrible thing.

A few weeks after the crash, I was in a flight of two—about twenty minutes out of Great Falls. I was tucked under the wing of my flight leader and he had just called me on the radio to tell me that there was thunderstorm activity in the Great Falls area—when my engine suddenly quit.

Afterwards, someone asked me, "Weren't you afraid?" The answer to that is no. It gets your attention pretty fast, but we were well trained in emergency procedures, and in that kind of a situation, you just start doing what you have to do in the cockpit. I was working trying to get the engine restarted but it just didn't catch. I didn't want to lose the plane so by trying to start it I ended up waiting a little too long to get out.

Just before bailing out I grabbed ten bucks out of my purse and jammed it in my pocket. I also had a little compass in my purse, but it was left in the airplane.

When I was a little girl, my uncle, a pilot, had told me, "If you have to bail out, after you jump, count to three—one thousand one, one thousand two, one thousand three. Then pull your ripcord. That way your parachute won't get caught by the plane on the way down."

I remember jumping out of the airplane and counting, "one thousand one, one thousand two," and some inner voice said, "Pull it!" So I pulled the D-ring on the parachute. It deployed and I swung once and came down in what is now a lake outside of Hobson, Montana, at six o'clock at night on June 19. I got out pretty late, but safely.

I was down in this big crater, so I picked myself up, rolled up the parachute, climbed up to a road, and waited for someone to come by to take me into Hobson, Montana, and then to Great Falls.

As to my airplane, it could have been sabotage. Flight Safety investigators said that it looked as if someone had put impurities in the gasoline. But I was flying again a week later.

The aircraft delivered by the ALSIB "backdoor route to Russia" would soon become a critical component in wartime aid to the Soviets. But in the winter of 1941–42, the 2.5 million Russians surrounded in Leningrad had to fend for themselves.

To shore up the Leningrad defenses—and prepare for a counter-attack in the spring, Stalin sent forty-six-year-old Georgy Zhukov to hold the line against Wilhelm von Leeb's Army Group North. Stalin had relieved the politically reliable and competent Zhukov as chief of staff because he had recommended the evacuation of Kiev before the garrison could be surrounded. By the time Kiev fell, a *quarter of a million* Russian and Ukrainian soldiers were dead—and more than 650,000 others were prisoners of war.

To ensure that the Leningrad did not suffer the same fate, Zhukov mobilized the population to dig more than 600 miles of earthworks, 400 miles of anti-tank ditches, and thousands of bunkers. In November 1941, 10,000 of Leningrad's residents died of starvation. In December the number was 50,000. And by January 1942, with temperatures falling to 40 degrees below zero, the *monthly* toll reached a gruesome 120,000 dead. One million civilians ultimately perished in the long and bitter siege—but Zhukov's defenses held.

As the siege of Leningrad began, Hitler issued Führer Directive No. 35—reinforcing Fedor von Bock's Army Group Center—and ordering that all available resources be used to advance on Moscow in what he called Operation Typhoon. When Russian pilots reported that German Panzers were closing on the capital, panic ensued. On 10 October, Stalin recalled Zhukov from Leningrad and ordered him to repeat for Moscow what he had done in the north.

Though more than a million Muscovites had been evacuated to Stalin's "provisional capital" at Kuibyshev, 500 miles to the east, Zhukov organized the remaining population. In an extraordinary feat of manual labor—most of it performed by women with picks and shovels, often under air and artillery attack—they planted nearly a half-million mines and dug hundreds of miles of trenches, tank traps, and bunkers.

As at Leningrad, Zhukov's defenses held. By the first week of December, the German offensive against Moscow was spent—and the exhausted Wehrmacht soldiers, still clad in summer uniforms and forbidden by Hitler to withdraw, began to dig in and prepare as best they could for the dreaded Russian winter.

National Archives

Hitler shaking hands with Fedor von Bock.

By 7 December 1941, the day that the Japanese bombed Pearl Harbor, the German army held a front that ran in a nearly straight line from Leningrad on the Gulf of Finland due south to the Crimea on the Black Sea. At that point, German troops controlled more than 40 percent of Russia's population, a near equal percentage of Soviet agricultural production, and more than half of the USSR's coal and steel capacity.

Yet, once the ground froze, the winter-ready Red Army was able to launch a series of limited counter-offensives. Zhukov pushed Army Group Center back from the gates of Moscow—prompting Hitler to fire von Bock and a host of his generals—including Brauchitsch, his army commander in chief. Also among those relieved was Heinz Guderian—father of Germany's Panzer blitzkrieg tactics.

Hitler appointed himself commander in chief of the army, and as his troops froze in defensive "hedgehogs" along the 1,100-mile front, he began concocting a revised grand strategy for 1942. His goals were mind-boggling. First, to finish off "the Bolshevik menace" for good in 1942—before the

Americans, against whom he had declared war on 11 December—could open a western front in Europe. Second, capture the oilfields, mines, and rich agricultural lands along the Volga River and the ridges of the Caucasus—all the way to Baku on the west shore of the Caspian Sea. And third, in concert with the Italians, seize Egypt, Palestine, Syria, Iraq, and the oilfields of Saudi Arabia.

Heinz Guderian

National Archives

The first major action after the spring thaw—the destruction of a Red Army counter-offensive at Kharkov— gave Hitler reason for optimism. By 1 June 1942, the Wehrmacht had captured nearly 240,000 Russian troops and destroyed over 1,200 tanks. But regrettably for the Axis soldiers who had to carry out the rest of the scheme, Hitler seriously underestimated the effect American industrial, agricultural, and military mobilization would have on his adversaries. By 28 June, when the ground was finally dry enough to launch his southern offensive—codenamed Blue—massive quantities of food, clothing, ammunition, aircraft, and trucks from America were already reaching Russia.

And after the offensive was already well under way and Wehrmacht troops were bounding southeastward at twenty to thirty miles a day, the Führer made another strategic blunder. He decided that seizing a single city—Stalingrad—named for his Soviet nemesis—was more important than any other part of his offensive.

On 23 July Hitler ordered Army Group B—now commanded by General Maximilian von Weichs—to seize Stalingrad and force a crossing of the Volga. The resulting exhaustive campaign, which lasted from 21 August 1942 until 30 January 1943, would pit nearly two million Germans and their Romanian and Italian allies against 3.5 million Russians in the bloodiest battle of World War II.

Maria Faustova served in the Red Army Signal Corps during the merciless engagement. She was one of a handful of survivors in her unit.

MARIA FAUSTOVA, SOVIET SOUTHERN ARMY
Stalingrad, Russia
2 February 1943

I wanted to become a teacher of Russian language and Russian literature and dreamed of becoming a literary scholar. My family and I lived in Stalingrad—it used to be called Tsaritsyn—but it had it had been renamed. One of my grandfathers lived in Moscow and I planned on going there to continue my studies. But when the Germans invaded, those dreams were over—and so was my youth.

I first learned we were at war on the morning of June 22, 1941. We heard it on the radio and there was a call for volunteers. I told my parents that I wanted to help defend our country and so on July 23, a month after the war had started, I signed up. I was given a month of training with other new recruits and assigned to the Signal Corps as a radio operator.

During the fighting of 1941 and early 1942, I didn't see any action, though we all followed the news of what was happening to the people of Leningrad and Moscow. But in the spring of 1942, the Germans came for us.

There were a few bombing raids in the winter, when the Germans tried to knock out some of the factories along the Volga River, but starting in July of '42 it got very bad, with many air raids. The bombing went on day and night, every day—not just on the factories and military installations—but on the apartments where we lived. The attacks were terrifying—but not as bad as what came next.

In August, the Germans broke through our defenses and into the city. Many civilians were killed—and the Stukas strafed them as they tried to get across the river. The battles were horrible.

I was a radio operator for a rifle regiment and one afternoon in September, an enemy tank unit broke through our front line and started coming down the street toward us. We were in the basement of a wrecked building and didn't have any place to hide. The Germans surrounded us, but after dark we were able to go through the cellars from one smashed building to another and move our headquarters to the basement of another bombed-out building.

We were trying to hold the center of the city, but almost no one was left. The Germans bombed and shelled us every day, trying to bring the buildings down on our heads. There were only walls of the buildings, and we hid in basements. It was like hell. All the people around me were dying, one after the other.

By winter it was terrible for everyone. There was no electricity, no way to stay warm. Many days we had no food. Some of the wounded froze to death waiting for treatment. The civilians who couldn't get away hid in the basements with us, and it was even worse for them. My grandfather died of starvation and cold in January. My mother and sister were starving as well. Whenever I could I would bring them some of my Army rations—mostly bread.

The fighting was brutal—from one basement to another. I don't think that there was a single building that wasn't badly damaged. The city was turned to rubble—and we lived in it like rats.

Often we had no idea where the Germans were. If you went inside a building, the Germans could be in the basement. That's how we lived— right alongside the enemy.

It seems like every day we would have to move—and always there was the roar of gunfire, mortars, rockets, bombs, and artillery. It was our artillery and Katusha rockets that finally saved us.

By January, we had more than 7,000 guns and thousands of Katusha launchers firing around the clock. That's how we fought our way back into the center of the city—behind a wall of fire from the rockets and artillery. By the time that the Germans surrendered at the end of January, we had been merged into the 35th Guard Division because everyone else was dead. We only had 124 people left—out of 15,000—but we had beaten the Germans.

Russian losses on the Eastern Front were staggering. But by the time German field marshal Friedrich Paulus surrendered the 91,000 survivors of his 6th Army on 30 January 1942, more than 145,000 of his soldiers lay dead in the rubble of Stalingrad. The Red Army had also destroyed Hitler's 4th Panzer Army, the 3rd and 4th Rumanian Armies, and the 8th Italian Army—inflicting on the Wehrmacht and their Axis allies nearly 1.5 million killed, wounded, prisoners, and missing.

Field Marshal Friedrich Paulus

National Archives

Adolf Hitler's dreams of world conquest died in the rubble of Stalingrad. The German army would never recover from its first major defeat. And Hitler's worst nightmare had come true: America was now in the war.

CHAPTER 4
PLUNGED INTO WAR
1941

E very American born before 1930 that I have interviewed for *War Stories* remembers exactly where they were and what they were doing when they learned that the Japanese had bombed Pearl Harbor. They recall the date—Sunday, 7 December 1941—who they were with, and that on the radio President Roosevelt called it "a day of infamy." They all also recollect knowing that, whether we wanted to be or not, America was now at war.

Yet, for those already fighting in the great cataclysm of World War II, the day passed like so many before and after. The fact that the United States was now a combatant didn't alter the agony and bloodshed a bit. Few of the combatants already engaged were even aware that the attack on Pearl Harbor had happened—nor could they foresee what it would mean for the outcome of the struggle.

For Wehrmacht and Russian soldiers locked in a frozen death-grip at Leningrad, the date of 7 December 1941 was just another day of pounding each other with artillery and hoping to survive sub-zero temperatures. At the center of the Eastern Front, despite Red Army losses of nearly two million dead and an equal number taken prisoner, Zhukov's 1st Shock Army

Even before the U.S. entered the war, FDR and Churchill were preparing a strategy
to defeat Hitler when they met off Argentia, Newfoundland, in August 1941.

was in the second day of a two-week counter-attack through snowdrifts that
would keep the Germans from storming the gates of Moscow. In the
Crimea, Army Group South were moving their unit into position for
another failed assault on Russian defenses at Sevastopol.

It was much the same for participants in every other theater of war. In
the North Atlantic, a Royal Canadian Navy corvette escorting a convoy from
the U.S. to Britain collided with a merchantman in the midst of a German
U-boat attack—sending twenty-three sailors to an icy death. In North
Africa, Erwin Rommel's 240-day siege of the Australians at Tobruk was in
its last horrible hours as Field Marshal Claude Auchinleck's British armored
columns smashed into the Afrika Corps in Operation Crusader. And in
China, Chiang Kai-shek's battered and poorly equipped army—barely holding the Nationalist Chinese "capital," Kunming—was under relentless air
attack from other Japanese bombers.

But if "Pearl Harbor Day" was unremarkable to the soldiers, sailors, and
airmen already fighting, bleeding, and dying in Europe, Africa, Asia, and the
North Atlantic—it was anything *but* routine to the leaders of those coun-

Ships bombed at Pearl Harbor.

tries. Though it would take Congress another full day to declare war on Japan, Canada did so that very afternoon.

Hours before the U.S. declaration on 8 December, Churchill's government in London and the rest of the British Commonwealth, already at war with Germany and Italy, decided for war against Tokyo. Then, on 11 December, Hitler and Mussolini declared war on the United States—to which Congress reciprocated that afternoon. Churchill's great hope—that the U.S. and Britain would become "co-belligerents against Fascism"—was finally realized.

But in the days immediately after the Japanese surprise attack, it became apparent that despite all the warnings, America's military was still woefully unprepared for war on a global scale. The Selective Service Act had narrowly passed in 1940, but it wasn't until 12 August 1941 that Congress extended the term of service beyond twelve months and authorized the movement of U.S. personnel overseas. The bill passed the House of Representatives by a single vote.

Though building larger, more effective U.S. fighting forces languished while war consumed Europe, America did begin to expand and improve its

National Archives

U.S. tanker struck by German U-boat.

intelligence and counter-intelligence capabilities. Unconstrained by restrictions that isolationists in Congress imposed on the military, FBI director J. Edgar Hoover began a quiet expansion of "the Bureau" shortly after Hitler invaded Poland in September 1939.

Hoover had read with alarm the reports of espionage and sabotage operations being conducted in Europe by Hitler's *Abwehr*, the intelligence department of the German Armed Forces. He correctly assumed that if war came, Hitler would attempt similar operations in the United States and Latin America—and he wanted the FBI to be ready. Hoover set out to recruit as many bright new field agents as he could squeeze into his budget. One of those "early hires" was Ken Crosby, a young lawyer in Atlanta. Crosby would help crack one of the biggest German spy rings of World War II.

KEN CROSBY, FBI
Washington, DC
15 December 1941

On 2 September 1939, I was working in a law office in Atlanta, Georgia, when I read the news of Germany invading Poland. On one of the inside pages was a little squib that said simply that in view of the unrest in the world, Congress had appropriated an increased budget for the FBI to hire more agents. The article noted that FBI applicants had to be lawyers, and I was a lawyer. I put the newspaper down, walked straight to the FBI office, applied, and three months later—in December 1939—I was FBI agent number 831 in Washington.

In early 1940 I finished my training. The FBI "Academy" was then in Washington, DC—at the Justice Department. From there, I went to Boston for my first assignment and then in early 1941 I was selected to work undercover in counter-espionage out of the New York field office.

The unit I was assigned to was already working against the Abwehr—Hitler's intelligence service. The Germans clearly anticipated that the United States was going to get in the war. They were trying to steal all the blueprints, details of armaments, shipping information, the names of the ships, the cargo of the ships—and conduct as much spying as they could—*before* the U.S. became a combatant. They also wanted to prepare for sabotage operations in the U.S. once we entered the war. And they were doing a lot of their preparations in Latin America.

The Germans had couriers going back and forth on ships, passing along all the information they could about Lend-Lease supplies, war production, our armaments industries, shipments to England, and the like. Often they relied on German immigrants and American citizens of German descent.

The office I was assigned to had been doing undercover work in connection with the Duquesne spy ring—the biggest espionage case in our history. When investigation of the Fritz Duquesne case started in 1940, leads were developed in Latin America that indicated there were German intelligence agents operating inside the United States.

William Sebold was key to breaking the spy ring. Sebold had been born in Germany, served in the Kaiser's army in World War I, but had immigrated to the U.S. in 1921 and become an American citizen. In 1939 he returned to Germany to see his mother. While he was there, the Abwehr pressured him into spying for them by reminding him that he had family in Germany. They actually blackmailed him into serving them.

But before returning to the U.S., Sebold secretly told a U.S. consular officer in Cologne about the Abwehr threats and the training they had given him. When he arrived in New York on 8 February 1940 he showed the FBI agents from my unit everything that his German "controller" had given him: a watch with a secret compartment, coded messages and communications procedures, a big pile of money and micro-photographs he'd been given to pass on to other German agents working in the U.S. and Latin America.

We set him up in an office under the assumed name they had given him and even built a clandestine radio transmitter/receiver, just as they had instructed him. He really was very bold—and very brave. I was one of the agents who worked with him almost every day.

We manufactured bogus information for him to transmit and started watching all of the people he had been told to contact. Sebold was so convincing that his Abwehr controller in Germany began directing all of their other agents in the region northeast to Sebold's office to pass on their intelligence. By the time we shut it down after sixteen months, Sebold was the U.S. "controller" for thirty-three German agents.

The office that the FBI set up for Sebold was constructed with a mirror in the hallway—and it had special two-way glass in it. From Sebold's side, it looked like any other mirror—but we always had agents with cameras on the other side—looking into the room so that we could film and photograph the German agents who came to meet with him.

Fritz Duquesne was one of the most senior German intelligence operatives in the United States. He was operating from a "front company" in New York called "Air Terminals Company" and one afternoon in the spring of 1941, I was "behind the mirror" when Duquesne walked into Sebold's office to pass on a report. Duquesne was known to be very cautious, suspicious of everything. He looked around the room awfully carefully—clearly checking for monitoring equipment. And then he walked up to the mirror and stares right into it—like he's looking straight at me.

I thought, "Can this guy see me? Maybe this mirror isn't working right. If he sees me, I'm in real trouble—I've blown the whole case." Duquesne put his face within twelve inches of my face behind the mirror—as though he was looking me right in the eye. My heart was beating so loud, I was sure he could hear it. I was ready to collapse! Then, he pulled out his pocket comb and started combing his hair!

I don't think I took a breath until he finished and walked away. When he did, I was soaked in sweat.

Shortly thereafter, on a Sunday night, my FBI unit carefully orchestrated the arrest of all thirty-three members of the spy ring. We had great evidence under the Espionage Statute—which had to be complied with in order to get a conviction—and all of them were convicted and went to jail.

In a way it's too bad we shut it down when we did. The Espionage Act provides for execution in time of war—so if we had waited until after Pearl Harbor was bombed before making the arrests, Duquesne and most of his agents probably would have been hung.

Crosby's assessment about the sentence that Duquesne and his cohorts would have received is correct. On 13 June 1942, eight German saboteurs were apprehended after being put ashore by U-boat—four on Long Island and four more on the coast of Florida. At Hoover's insistence, and with the support of Attorney General Biddle, all were tried in secret military tribunals and in August—just two months later—six of the eight were executed. The remaining two—named as "cooperating witnesses" in the trials—were sentenced to life in prison. The trials would set a precedent for dealing with non-military enemy combatants that would be used throughout the war for prosecuting spies and saboteurs and is still cited today for dealing with terrorists.

This new process for dealing with spies reflected other changes in U.S. counter-espionage, intelligence collection, and "special operations" capabilities precipitated by America's entry into the war. Shortly after Pearl Harbor, Hoover reorganized the FBI, creating a permanent office for counter-intelligence and counter-espionage. U.S. "offensive intelligence" capabilities were also transformed following the declaration of war.

On 27 May 1941, concerned about Japanese moves in the Pacific, President Roosevelt had declared a "State of Emergency" in an effort to accelerate preparations for hostilities. Using his emergency powers, FDR appointed Brigadier General William Donovan—a World War I hero—as the Coordinator of Intelligence on 11 July. Donovan's appointment created immediate friction—within the War and Navy Departments as well as with the FBI—and slowed his plans for building U.S. covert action capabilities.

In June 1942, Donovan's organization was renamed the "Office of Strategic Services"—the OSS. The following month, the War Department activated the First Special Service Force, and placed it at Donovan's disposal to conduct "espionage, sabotage, intelligence collection, and support for internal resistance" behind enemy lines. The OSS—often in cooperation with the British Special Operations Executive—would go on to conduct some remarkably successful espionage and intelligence operations.

The transformation in U.S. counter-espionage and intelligence capabilities brought about by our entry into the war reflected the changes taking place in every other part of American life. The expansion of industrial production—ships, planes, tanks, weapons, and ammunition—that had begun as a consequence of "Lend-Lease" now accelerated dramatically. Unemployment, which had hovered near 10 percent through most of 1941, now dropped dramatically as millions of men responded to calls for military volunteers and draft notices. American women—who had never thought of joining the labor force—now found opportunities in the Armed Forces, government service, war production plants, and shipyards.

American mobilization couldn't happen overnight, however. Britain, Russia, and China may have gained a powerful new ally against the Axis Powers—but the immediate effects were hardly positive. In the closing days of 1941 and the opening months of 1942, the Allies were subjected to a series of disasters. On Christmas Eve 1941, after a heroic fight, the U.S. Navy and Marine garrison on Wake Island finally succumbed to the Japanese. The following day, Hong Kong fell. And on 15 February 1942, Singapore was captured—along with 135,000 British, Indian, and Australian troops.

On 8 March Rangoon, Burma, was seized by the Japanese and the next day the Dutch government in exile surrendered the entire Netherlands East Indies. On 9 April, 80,000 U.S. and Filipino soldiers surrendered to the Japanese on Bataan and on 6 May 1942, the island fortress of Corregidor in Manila Bay was captured—ending all but guerilla resistance in the Philippines.

The Japanese juggernaut continued unabated for more than four months until their first defeat in a dramatic engagement, 3–6 June 1942, off the tiny island of Midway. Though American morale was raised by the lopsided victory—the U.S. lost 307 men, 150 planes, and one carrier while the Japanese lost 3,500 men, 325 aircraft, and *four* carriers—it did nothing to improve the situation in the European theater.

By the summer of 1942, as the Wehrmacht renewed its offensive against Russia, German U-boats were operating with impunity off the east coast of the United States—jeopardizing the delivery of war materiel, food, fuel, and clothing that were essential for keeping Britain and the Soviet Union in the fight against Hitler. During June and July 1942—the worst months of losses in the North Atlantic—U-boats sank more than a million tons of Allied and neutral shipping.

These losses prompted American planners to quietly reassess the "Europe First" war strategy that Roosevelt and Churchill had secretly decided at their conference at sea off Argentia, Newfoundland, in August 1941. Without the assurance that massive numbers of troops and huge quantities of supplies could be *safely* moved across the Atlantic, a "Second Front"—so desperately wanted by Stalin—would be too costly.

German U-boat successes in the Atlantic had climbed significantly after they established "home ports" on the Bay of Biscay, following the fall of France in June 1940. But improvements in British radar, sonar, and convoy procedures had diminished losses of Allied ships and cargo in the months immediately prior to Pearl Harbor. On 4 September 1941—three months before the U.S. and Germany were at war with each other—a U.S. destroyer, the USS *Greer*, alerted by a British patrol plane out of Bermuda, had attacked a German submarine off the U.S. east coast, prompting FDR to declare an expanded U.S. "neutrality region" and announce that U.S. ships were authorized to "shoot first" at Axis warships inside the zone. Then, while escorting a convoy to Newfoundland on 17 October—still six weeks before the U.S. declaration of war—the USS *Kearny* was hit by a German torpedo. The U.S. Navy destroyer, with eleven dead sailors aboard, managed to make it back into port—but the action created a firestorm in the

American press. To avoid further provocation, Hitler ordered Admiral Karl Dönitz to move his "wolf packs" of submarines further away from the U.S. coastline.

But once the United States was in the war, all restrictions on U-boat activity were lifted. When the U.S. moved crucial naval forces to the Pacific and geared up for war on two fronts, German U-boats moved in—hugging the east coast and operating with impunity in the Gulf of Mexico.

For eight months after the attack on Pearl Harbor—until the assault on Guadalcanal in August 1942—the U.S. "played defense" against the Axis powers. After the fall of the Philippines, the U.S. Navy had to carry most of the burden. One of the participants, Philadelphia native Charles Calhoun, was aboard the USS *Sterett*, helping shoulder the load.

LIEUTENANT (JG) CHARLES CALHOUN, USN
USS *Sterett* DD-407
16 November 1942

After 1939, the American people began to pay attention to what was going on in Europe. Many U.S. citizens were either immigrants from there or descendents of Europeans—and they were increasingly concerned about Hitler. There was a lot of news about his aggression—and it was alarming.

That's one of the reasons why a lot of us entered the service before the U.S. was in the war—that and the Depression. When our military started to grow—very slowly at first—a lot of young men saw it as an opportunity to get a decent job. The military didn't pay much, but it was work.

I came into the Navy because my father had been a merchant mariner during World War I. He was killed in an accident in 1918. I got a commission in the Navy as a communications officer and was sent to a brand-new destroyer—the USS *Sterett*. She was launched in 1938 so she was one of the newest ships in the fleet. She was initially sent to Hawaii as part of the Pacific Fleet, but in June of '41 she was reassigned to Bermuda to enforce the U.S. neutrality zone because the German U-boat threat had gotten worse.

German U-boat attacks against British merchantmen had begun in September of '39—shortly after Hitler invaded Poland. By the summer of '41 U-boats were sinking almost 500,000 tons of merchant shipping a month. The *Sterett* did anti-submarine patrols between Bermuda and the east coast from June to December of '41—but shortly after Pearl Harbor, we were ordered to escort convoys to Iceland and England.

Duty on a little destroyer in the North Atlantic is tough. A lot of it is in frigid, terrible weather—and a lot of the guys get seasick. Sometimes it was worse to be at the mercy of the weather and the sea than to get into a fight. On one very stormy transit, in March–April of '42, we had a rear admiral aboard—John W. Wilcox—and in the midst of this rough weather, there was a signal sent that a man had been sighted in the water. We were told to hold muster, and after we took roll call, everyone was accounted for. The officer of the deck told the admiral's orderly to inform the admiral that they had conducted a muster, but found no one missing. But when the orderly went into find the admiral, he wasn't there. *He was the one who had gone overboard!*

The "big ship" that we escorted in that convoy was the USS *Wasp*—a carrier. She was transporting aircraft to the British. By then we knew that carriers were a number one priority for Dönitz. Shortly after the Dunkirk evacuation the British carrier HMS *Glorious* had been sunk by German cruisers and later on, in November '41, just a few weeks before Pearl Harbor, a U-boat sank the carrier HMS *Ark Royal* in the Mediterranean. Then in December, a week after the Japanese sneak attack, a U-boat sank HMS *Audacity,* an escort carrier on convoy duty in the North Atlantic.

German U-boat commanders were incredibly audacious throughout the war. In October 1939, the U-47 slipped into Scapa Flow—the Royal Navy's principal anchorage—and sank the battleship HMS *Royal Oak* and then got away! When we pulled into the anchorage, we could see the superstructure of the *Royal Oak* sticking out of the water—just like with our sunken battleships at Pearl Harbor.

At Scapa Flow we came under the command of a British admiral and served with their "Home Fleet" for three months. Toward the end of our deployment, we were part of a big British convoy to Malta. We raced through Gibraltar into the Mediterranean with the *Wasp* to resupply the British garrison on the island and deliver Spitfire aircraft. That trip turned out to be easier than we expected. The Germans apparently never knew we came in. We ran within 300 miles of Malta and launched the Spitfires without incident.

By May we were back in New York, where they slapped radar aboard—we had no idea what it was, or how to use it. I'm not even sure they gave us instruction books. But we figured it out by the time we got through the Panama Canal and up to San Diego, which was where the 1st Marine Division was embarking for combat in the South Pacific. Our job was to get them there.

Guadalcanal, in the Solomon Islands, was the first American offensive of the war—and the battle to take and hold Guadalcanal lasted from 7 August 1941 until February 1943. We had several big engagements during that time frame—the toughest of which occurred between 12 and 16 November against the "Tokyo Express"—the Japanese air and surface action groups that came down "the slot" between the islands to pound the Marines trying to hold Henderson Field on the northeast coast of Guadalcanal island.

We were in action every night and every day. At night it was against Japanese transports, destroyers, cruisers, and battleships and in the daylight it was against Japanese air attacks. The area between Savo Island and Guadalcanal had the wrecks of so many ships in it that we called it "Ironbottom Sound."

On 13 November 1942, the *Sterett* was credited with shooting down two Japanese torpedo bombers—and an "assist" on two others. One of the damaged Japanese planes hit the *San Francisco* that afternoon, in the after-fire control tower, and killed thirty of their crew.

By the time that battle was over, the crew of the *Sterret* had done it all—"neutrality" duty before Pearl Harbor, anti-submarine patrols off the

U.S. east coast, convoy duty in the North Atlantic, service with the British Home Fleet, escorting a carrier in the Mediterranean, and fighting Japanese surface ships and aircraft in the Pacific. It shows the kind of stuff Americans are made of.

The USS *Sterett's* dramatic entry into World War II—and subsequent service in two theaters of the conflict—may not have been altogether typical, but Charles Calhoun's experience demonstrates the remarkable transformation the U.S. Navy made, once war was thrust upon us. The same thing happened in the U.S. Army. One who was there when it happened was another son of Philadelphia, Charles Hangsterfer. Like Calhoun, he too had "signed up" before the attack on Pearl Harbor.

FIRST LIEUTENANT CHARLES HANGSTERFER,
US ARMY
1st Infantry Division, England
16 November 1942

I went to Gettysburg College after high school because my eyes weren't good enough to get into West Point. I'd always wanted to be a soldier—and going to college near where a great battle had been fought less than eight decades before just reinforced the idea.

During the Depression a military career was a pretty good deal. Back then there were relatively few jobs available and duty in the peacetime Army wasn't bad at all—or so I thought. I had a chance to go on active duty under the Thomason Act. That law allowed the Army to take a thousand college graduates from ROTC, and select a hundred for a regular Army commissions.

After receiving my new gold bars as a 2nd lieutenant, I was sent to the first communication officers' class at Fort Benning, Georgia. From there I was assigned to the 16th Infantry, then stationed at Fort Jay, on Governor's Island in New York City.

By the time I got to Fort Jay in early 1941, the war in Europe was on in earnest. But we were doing very little to prepare for the kind of mechanized warfare the Germans were fighting. For several weeks we went to Edgewood Arsenal in Maryland for amphibious training along the Gunpowder River. Since we had no landing craft, we used *rowboats*. Unfortunately, most of the soldiers were from New York City and I don't think they had ever seen a rowboat—much less knew how to row one through the water.

By the summer of '41 it was apparent that people in Washington were getting serious. We moved to Fort Devons, Massachusetts, and started building barracks and training ranges, then went on maneuvers in North Carolina and finally to Puerto Rico for *real* amphibious training—this time with Higgins boats—*real* landing craft. I was in Puerto Rico when Pearl Harbor was bombed.

We returned to Fort Devons for a few months—and the 1st Division was fully "fleshed out" with thousands of new recruits and all kinds of new equipment. That summer the officers were told that we would be deploying overseas and I was sent over with the advance party to Tidworth Barracks in England, to get the place ready for the division. The rest of the division sailed from New York aboard the *Queen Mary* on 2 August 1942.

Training at Tidworth and later in Scotland was very realistic. We had some very good, experienced British instructors. All of them had seen action and many of them had been wounded. We did a lot of long hikes, conditioning exercises, marksmanship training, practice with artillery and air—and the senior officers were almost always there. Our division commander, Major General Terry Allen, and the assistant division commander, Brigadier General Theodore Roosevelt Jr., were both well-loved by the men. By the time we sailed for North Africa and Operation Torch in November of '42, I was in the 3rd Battalion, 16th Infantry and the 1st Division was ready to take on the Germans

During peacetime, the U.S. military had been all male. The onset of war brought hundreds of thousands of American women into the Armed

Forces. No woman could be subject to conscription, but they didn't have to be: they volunteered so fast that many had to be told to return weeks or months later, after uniforms were made and facilities to house and train them were built. One of those young American women who volunteered early was nineteen-year-old Pearlie McKeogh from Minneapolis, Minnesota. After Pearl Harbor, she and her boyfriend decided to enlist together.

PEARL MCKEOGH, WAAC
St. Paul, Minnesota
13 November 1942

When Japan attacked the U.S. at Pearl Harbor, I was in business college but planned to join the Navy. Then I found the Navy wouldn't let women serve overseas, so I switched to the Army. I wanted to do something different—get away—I had never been out of Minnesota. My boyfriend at the time said, "Let's both sign up." So we did. But he was rejected—I was accepted.

My oldest brother went into the Coast Guard. One brother was a farmer in North Dakota and didn't enlist. Another brother worked for a manufacturing plant in Milwaukee and my fourth brother was a minister. Both my sisters were teachers.

Within a few days of being accepted as a WAAC—Women's Army Auxiliary Corps—I was sent to Fort Snelling, near Saint Paul, for basic training. From there I was sent to a camp outside of Des Moines, Iowa.

In the camp at Des Moines they took the roster and they divided it in three. To one of the groups they said, "You're cooks and bakers." To another they said, "You're secretarial." And to the third group they said, "You're drivers." I ended up in the office because I had just finished business college, but they quickly figured out that I didn't know anything about typing.

So they put me in the motor pool, where I wanted to be—driving a jeep and a two and a half ton truck. We had girls out on that range that had never driven before, but the Army taught them how to be good drivers.

After learning how to drive and maintain jeeps and trucks, we went to Florida for more training and then in late December of '42 we were ordered to Brooklyn, New York, to await shipment overseas.

In early January '43, I was one of 196 WAACs loaded on a troopship for deployment overseas. We had our own compartment on one deck, and there were soldiers above and below us.

We had no idea where we were going and the weather was terrible. We ended up in Algiers, in the middle of the night, in the middle of a German air raid. We loaded up on trucks—I was in a truckload of women. Because of the blackout, the driver of our truck got lost, so we were the last ones to arrive at our billet. We were billeted in a home operated by the Daughters of Charity. It was rough—there was no running water, no amenities.

A couple of days later, I was told to report to the 1st Army Headquarters to see if General Eisenhower wanted a woman driver. Not many generals did, but General Eisenhower said to Colonel Lee, the Headquarters Commandant, "I'll take one, and if she works out, the rest them can also work in the motor pool." So I was picked as the test case and it evidently worked out, because the rest of the women went to work in the motor pool.

When I got to Algiers, I didn't know what a general was. The highest rank I had seen up to that point in the Army was a colonel, back at Des Moines. He was in charge of the training center. But, the first day that I went to work Colonel Lee in Algiers he said, "Pearlie, take the general to the airport." I didn't know where the airport was but I said, "Yes, sir!"

One of the other drivers, who knew where the airport was, jumped in the jeep with me. That was my first day on the job as General Eisenhower's driver.

What Private Pearlie McKeogh didn't know—but would soon find out—was the general she was assigned to drive was fast becoming one of the most successful officers in the U.S. Army. Dwight D. Eisenhower had been a colonel, serving in the Philippines on the staff of General Douglas MacArthur. He was just completing four years with MacArthur when Hitler started his blitzkrieg across Europe.

After eight years of desk duty, Eisenhower was glad to return to the U.S. in January 1940 to help organize the training for a slowly growing U.S. Army. Eisenhower established himself as a master logistician and planner during the Louisiana exercises in 1940. By the time the Japanese bombed Pearl Harbor, he was a general, one of General Marshall's most trusted and highly regarded subordinates.

At the Arcadia Conference in Washington in December 1941, Churchill had pressed Roosevelt for an operation in North Africa. Marshall resisted the idea—urging instead that the Allies gather necessary troops and materiel in England for a cross-channel invasion of France. By April 1942, when the U.S. and British military chiefs met in London for further strategic talks, it was increasingly clear that a "Second Front" in Europe in 1942 or '43 was simply too risky.

Months later, from 18–27 June 1942, Churchill again visited Washington. This time his arguments for attacking Hitler's forces in North Africa as a second front persuaded Roosevelt. The decision made, Marshall set a date—the first week of November 1942—and appointed Eisenhower to command the first U.S. offensive in the European theater: Operation Torch.

CHAPTER 5
AMERICA GOES ON THE OFFENSIVE
1942

E very Allied military planner hoped that Operation Torch could be carried off without pitting a green, untested U.S. Army against the Wehrmacht. Accordingly, the landing beaches selected for the operation were well to the west of the combat-hardened German and Italian troops of the Afrika Korps—led by one of Hitler's ablest generals, Erwin Rommel, nicknamed the "Desert Fox." Nothing, however, could change the fact that the operation would take place in some of the most inhospitable and difficult terrain on the planet—the largely barren, trackless North African desert.

Senior U.S. officers in London and Washington pointed out that raw American soldiers—some just weeks out of recruit training—and their inexperienced leaders were unprepared to go up against the Vichy French in North Africa, much less the Axis powers. Some feared that if the operation went badly, it could well lead to postponing or even canceling plans to force a landing on the European continent until 1945 or '46.

George Marshall, the U.S. Army chief of staff—and one of Roosevelt's most trusted advisors—was utterly opposed to the North African endeavor, arguing that it would sap personnel and equipment needed for invading the continent. The operation's strongest proponent—Winston Churchill—remained adamant that a "Second Front" had to be opened in Europe to help relieve pressure on Stalin and the Red Army, and he strongly believed that North Africa was the place. Roosevelt resolved the matter after Churchill's visit to Washington at the end of June 1942.

FDR informed Marshall of his decision to proceed with Torch on 25 July. The next day, Marshall appointed General Dwight Eisenhower as the Allied commander in chief of the American-British expedition. Though he had never led so much as a platoon in combat, Eisenhower was now going to command an entire army.

National Archives

Rommel, the Desert Fox

For the next three months, Eisenhower and his staff engaged in a furious round of planning. The goals of Torch—although ambitious—were relatively simple: first, to deny the use of air and naval bases in northwest Africa to the Axis, and then—by driving the enemy out of Mediterranean North Africa—create secure sea-lines between Gibraltar and the Suez Canal. If all went as planned, Rommel's German-Italian army would be caught in a pincers between General Bernard Montgomery's British 8th Army on the east and the forces landed in Torch moving in from the west.

To achieve these ends, Eisenhower assembled a fleet of more than 100 troop and cargo vessels, 200 U.S. and British warships, 500 aircraft, and 107,000 troops to force an entry in North Africa. Though Tunis was his ultimate goal, Eisenhower deemed that it was too far from his Gibraltar-based air cover—and too close to enemy air bases in Sicily, Sardinia, and Italy. He therefore selected three landing beaches well to the west, all in Vichy French territory.

A Western Task Force, commanded by General George Patton, would sail directly from the United States and seize Casablanca, Morocco. The Center Task Force—comprised of the U.S. II Corps—would sail from England to seize Oran, Algeria. And the Eastern Task Force of British and Americans—also deployed from England—would capture the Algerian capital.

Eisenhower hoped that the French colonial forces holding these port cities would quickly renounce fealty to the Vichy regime and aid the Allies in throwing the Nazis out of Africa. Weeks before the invasion, he commenced a series of sensitive, covert negotiations with French colonial officials—military and civilian—trying to ensure that the Vichy troops in North Africa would not contest the landings. On 21 October Eisenhower dispatched Brigadier General Mark Clark by submarine to Algeria for an abortive clandestine meeting with French officers thought to be opposed to the Vichy regime.

It was all for naught. By 5 November, when Eisenhower boarded a Flying Fortress in London for a secret flight to his forward command post inside "The Rock" at Gibraltar, he and his commanders expected to have to fight their way ashore against as many as fourteen French divisions. Duplicity, intrigue, anti-British resentment going back to Dunkirk, personal rivalries and antipathy toward Charles de Gaulle among French officers—all doomed Allied hopes for a "gentle welcome" to North Africa.

Yet, as the convoys closed in on their landing beaches on the night of 7 November 1942, there was still reason for optimism. The hundreds of ships steaming from England, Scotland, Ireland, and the United States had made their transits without being attacked by enemy aircraft or submarines. Scores of bombers and fighters assembled at Gibraltar—the only Allied airbase within range of the Torch landings—were unscathed and ready. And in the east, Montgomery's 8th Army had broken the long siege at El Alamein, Egypt. On 23 October his combined British, New Zealand, Australian, South African, Indian, Free Polish, Free Czech, and Free French force had smashed through Rommel's lines and was now driving the battered Afrika Korps and their Italian comrades westward toward the Libyan border.

Few of the young Americans preparing to land before dawn on a hostile shore were aware of these details. Some of them knew that FDR would broadcast an appeal to the French just before the landings: "The sons of those who helped liberate your fathers from the Germans in 1918 are coming to free you from Hitler... do not fire upon them."

But for most, like Lieutenant Robert Green, in the 1st Infantry Division, the hours before the assault were consumed with final preparatory details, a letter home—to be left on the ship, just in case—and perhaps a prayer for what was to come in the morning, just before dawn.

FIRST LIEUTENANT ROBERT GREEN
1st Infantry Division
Arzu, French North Africa
12 November 1942

I was in ROTC at Penn State when the war started. I took my commission as an infantry officer and was shipped to England to join the Big Red One— shortly after finishing infantry officers' basic training at Fort Benning. In August 1942 they assembled us at Glasgow, in Scotland. There, we got onboard the ships, practiced doing amphibious landings, and then we sailed for the Canary Islands. We were there for a few weeks, and then suddenly we turned and went in through Gibraltar on the night of 5–6 November as part of an enormous fleet of blacked-out ships. The weather was terrible— but even so, everyone was worried about air attacks from Sicily.

The night of 7 November we all wrote letters to our family and left them on the ship to be mailed. We landed the following morning, before dawn, west of Oran, in Algeria—as part of the Center Task Force. Amphibious landings always appear chaotic. Though it was dark, my rifle platoon landed where we were supposed to, on the proper beaches.

The plan was to let the French know that we were Americans. Shortly after we landed, the French sent up a flare and called out in French to our troops over a bullhorn. Then they opened fire at us and we had a number of casualties. Our response was a few mortar shells sent their way on the beach and they shut that up real quick.

After landing we were ordered to bypass Arzu, which we finally did. We were to envelop Oran from the rear, which the enemy wasn't expecting. The French garrison at Oran was still proclaiming loyalty to the puppet Vichy government—and therefore they were collaborating with the Nazis.

They had a big naval installation at Oran and there were a lot of ships in the port. Naval guns protected the place, and we encountered them later. We moved down the road towards Oran, and I had established a command post for the regiment, not far off the beach.

As we were setting up the CP and the men were digging in, an American, who was a member of the French Foreign Legion, was escorted up to the command post. He had turned himself in, so he wasn't considered a prisoner of war—but he was wandering around the area and he said to me, "Your men are very brave. The bullets come in here and your men have nothing to stop them."

My men had started to dig in behind a hedge of cactus, so I said, "They're not as brave as you think. They think that they're behind a stone wall—when they find out differently—they'll dig quicker." And they did.

The French naval personnel in the port opened up on us as we moved toward the city. The troops that were firing at us weren't Germans—they were French. I was very nearly killed there by a Frenchman firing a machine gun. Fortunately our mortar platoon opened up on him and when the mortar rounds got close, he took off.

It took us three days to get into Oran. Throughout the whole time we were taking heavy shellfire from some of the big naval guns on the ships in the port. On the third day, while we were trying to move forward, I noticed a bunch of signal flags being hoisted up a pole on top of a building to our front. It suddenly dawned on me that their forward observers were using the signal flags to adjust the naval gunfire.

My driver and I used the machine gun to shoot up the flagpole—and we stopped taking fire. The French gave up easily after that but we had already taken a lot of casualties from the people we had come to liberate. Later that day, instead of their ships joining the Allied cause, they scuttled their fleet.

The armada that landed Lieutenant Green and his comrades in North Africa consisted of both U.S. and British ships. The landing force included the entire British 78th Division. But because of French bitterness toward the British, every effort was made to convince the Vichy naval and ground forces that Torch was an exclusively American operation. In the Eastern Task Force that landed at Algiers, more than half of the soldiers going ashore were British—but they all wore an American flag sewn to their shoulders.

Seven hundred miles to the west, the 35,000 soldiers of Patton's Western Task Force had their own problems with the Vichy French. Shortly after midnight on 8 November, the 3rd and 9th Infantry Divisions and the 2nd Armored Division landed across three Moroccan beaches—Safi, Casablanca, and Port Lyautey. Though taken completely by surprise, Vichy units at Port Lyautey put up a spirited defense against a "green" American infantry, inflicting dozens of U.S casualties before surrendering two days later.

On 10 November, Admiral Darlan, the senior French commander in North Africa, signed an armistice with General Mark Clark, Eisenhower's representative in North Africa. Vichy troops laid down their arms—but that didn't end the fighting.

Hitler, outraged at the surrender of the Vichy forces in North Africa, immediately occupied the rest of France—and started reinforcing Rommel's battered army, now retreating west toward Tunisia through the Libyan desert. The first German reinforcements flew into Tunis on the night of 10 November, and seaborne deliveries of troops, supplies, armor, and artillery from German garrisons in Sicily, Italy, and France began flowing to North Africa within days.

To ensure that the German reinforcements wouldn't be able to move west, Eisenhower committed his paratroopers. Between 12 and 16 November, the British 1st and 3rd Parachute Brigades and the U.S. Army's 509th Parachute Infantry Regiment made the first Allied airborne assaults of the war—seizing airfields along the coast and vital passes through the Atlas Mountains along the border between Algeria and Tunisia.

From mid-November on, the Americans who landed in Torch wouldn't be confronting dispirited Vichy troops—they'd be fighting the battle-hardened Wehrmacht and Luftwaffe. By the time Patton's armor and infantry started moving east from Marrakesh, on 17 November, German bombers from France, Sardinia, and Tunisia were operating in the skies over the entire Torch battle area. And very soon thereafter, Rommel's reinforced Desert Army—and the weather—would create unforeseen challenges. Private First Class Jefferson White, from Tallahassee, Florida, was there for all of it.

PRIVATE JEFFERSON WHITE, US ARMY
2nd Armored Division
Morocco, French North Africa
28 November 1942

My father was a farmer who died when I was a baby, forcing my mother to take over and run the farm. The Depression was a tough time for everyone. Because we lived on a farm we always had food—none of us went hungry or had to stand in bread lines. But during the '30s, farm labor only made just fifty cents a day, working from sun up to sun down. That's why I dropped out of high school and joined the army in March 1941, at age seventeen.

I remember December 7 vividly, because it put us on a state of alert. We had just returned from the Louisiana maneuvers—where Eisenhower had first made his name. He was just a colonel in those days, but he really knew how to get things done and everyone was impressed by him.

We started getting in a lot of new soldiers right after Pearl Harbor, and in the late spring of '42 they sent us to Tennessee, on more maneuvers. From there we went to North Carolina, at Fort Bragg, where we spent most of the summer and the early autumn. Then one night, they backed up a freight train, loaded us up, and took us to Newport News, Virginia. There, we loaded up onto transport ships. Everyone was really concerned, because the German submarines were very active out in the Atlantic at that time.

No one told us where we were going. We all thought that we were headed for the South Pacific. All the war news was about the battles going on there—so that's where we figured we were heading. But, of course, we were wrong.

After we had been out at sea for several days, Captain Whitfield came on the intercom system, and invited everyone to come up to the deck. It was early in the morning, but every direction you looked there were ships. We were told that we were part of the largest convoy that had ever been assembled. There were aircraft carriers, cruisers, destroyers, and battle-ships—all surrounding the troopships—to protect them.

Now, given the weather and the temperature, it was pretty clear that we weren't in the South Pacific, but we still didn't know where we were headed—because the weather was so terrible you couldn't see the sun or the stars. Some guys guessed that we were headed to England through the North Atlantic because the waves were so rough. It was so bad that it broke the chains on some of the tanks that were secured in the hold. One of the tanks broke loose and killed a man.

Late on the afternoon of November 7, we were told to muster for haircuts and then a nice hot meal—that would be our last real food for some time. That's when we were told that we would be landing on the coast of North Africa.

Patton, our commander, was a very colorful character and a good leader. He was a genius in tank warfare and demanded the very best of every-one else who served under him. Later, Patton got the nickname of "Old Blood and Guts." But he really cared about his men and we all respected him.

My tank platoon landed at Safi shortly after midnight on the morn-ing of 8 November 1942. We were surprised that there weren't any enemy soldiers on the beach to fight us. When we came ashore we had been told to expect to be opposed by the French garrison in the port and we were all pretty anxious. But none of them showed up so we didn't have to fight them. The invasion was really a walk-in. We could've just pulled up to the docks and unloaded.

Early the next morning we were told to move up the road toward Casablanca. For the next few days, the only danger we faced was from mines that had been planted on the roads.

But then everything changed—the Germans figured out we were in Morocco and we started to get attacked by their air force and as we moved east, toward Algeria, we ran into their patrols. One day we were in a convoy of half-tracks, tanks, and trucks and a shell hit the right side of our line. General Patton came up in his light tank and stopped right where the shell had hit. And he says, "Go get 'em."

So we did, but then, a few minutes later, a twin-engine plane flew over. The Germans had been strafing our convoy, so everybody was shooting at the plane and it landed in the desert. We sent a patrol out there to check and it turned out to be an Italian major general that had come to surrender. That was our total experience with the Italians in North Africa.

In December, some of us from 2nd Armor Division were sent to reinforce units in Algeria because the Germans were going to start a winter offensive. That's when we found out about the German Tiger tank. It was said to be the best tank in the world, with an 88 millimeter anti-aircraft gun—a rapid fire weapon. But it couldn't "lob" shells like our guns—and it wasn't as mobile in that terrible terrain. North Africa may be a desert—but it's a mud-hole in winter. The Tiger was so heavy that in soft ground it often got stuck.

The Germans I saw were good soldiers. But they needed somebody to tell 'em what to do, how to do it—and when. The Americans—we were mostly farm boys. If we couldn't whip you one way, we'd whip you another. We had guys inventing things and coming up with practical ideas. One soldier invented a gadget that mounted on front of the tanks to clear mines. Then someone did the same thing with the half-track—using heavy log rollers and chains to cause mines to explode in front of the vehicle instead of under it.

We might have been green troops when we landed, but we quickly learned everything about our equipment—what it could do, and what it couldn't do. We learned warfare "on the job" as it were. For example, one of our machine-gunners switched out the rounds in the belts of .50-cal ammunition so that one round was standard ball, the next was armor piercing, then a tracer. That way we could shoot by eyesight, not by gunsight. Those kinds of innovations kept a lot of American soldiers alive.

When Eisenhower moved his command post from Gibraltar to Algiers on 23 November, he hoped to press the attack toward Tunis in a matter of days. But his army, plagued by logistics delays, inadequate numbers of trucks, and the lack of sufficient air cover, quickly found itself confronted by the realities of winter in North Africa.

Monsoon-like rains quickly turned roads into muddy tracks. Airfields became swamps. And despite the best effort of his senior air officer—Major

General Bernard Montgomery in North Africa.

General Jimmy Doolittle, the man who had led the B-25 raid on Japan just seven months before—German aircraft were more prevalent than those of the Americans in the skies overhead.

On 9 December, a month after the Allied landings, Hitler sent Jürgen von Arnim to take command of the 5th Panzer Army—and put Rommel in overall command of Axis troops in North Africa. By the end of December, Rommel's desert force, under relentless pressure from Montgomery's 8th Army, had retreated more than 500 miles west from El Alamein. Meanwhile, Eisenhower's 1st Army was threatening the Axis rear in Tunisia with American and British units spread from the Mediterranean coast, up into the Atlas Mountains, south of Tunis.

In order to make a final push that would close the trap on the Desert Fox, Eisenhower sought—and was granted—fresh troops to bring his units up to full strength. Eventually, some 80,000 U.S. and British replacements and reinforcements would be sent to North Africa. One of the first to arrive was PFC George Perrine, a young soldier from the Appalachian Mountains.

PRIVATE GEORGE PERRINE, US ARMY
2nd Armored Division
Casablanca, Morocco
29 December 1942

I grew up in the mountains of Kentucky and southwestern Virginia—just a Snowy Mountain boy, from start to finish.

In 1939 when the war started in Europe, I was a senior in high school and was out looking for work when the Japanese bombed Pearl Harbor in December '41. I figured that I was probably going to be drafted so I volunteered.

I enlisted in the Army April 1, 1942—and shipped out for armor basic training at Fort Knox, Kentucky. They were opening schools for everything—tracked vehicles, cooks and bakers, gunnery specialists, radio operators, and technicians.

I was one of 600 men sent for technical training. The school lasted for ten weeks, but we didn't get anything except the basics. Believe me, we were green as grass. The Army knew it, so we were divided up among units that had already been trained, figuring that we could always call on someone with more experience for help.

In December of '42, we shipped out of New York harbor aboard the SS *Argentina*—headed for North Africa. We landed on Christmas Eve, 1942, at Casablanca. On Christmas Day there was a German air raid on the harbor. We were sitting out there, in the open, watching it. That's how "smart" and "well trained" we were. We hadn't dug foxholes or taken cover. At night, when they came back to bomb the harbor again, we were still sitting there.

You can see—we were a young, inexperienced army in many ways. We hadn't developed as much as the Germans soldiers had.

Our cantonment held three separate battalions—Engineer, Medical, and Reconnaissance. I was assigned to the Reconnaissance Battalion. My new platoon commander told me, "You've got the easiest job in the army."

I asked, "What in the world are you talking about?"

He says, "All you have to do is find the enemy. Then all you have to do is stay alive to get back to tell us what you found. Otherwise, it won't help us."

That was my introduction to reconnaissance. But it was the truth—in a brutal sort of way.

Our CO, General Lucian Prescott, told us that a soldier carrying a field pack and weapon should be able to cover four miles in fifty minutes. He called it "the Prescott Trot." It really wasn't a walk—and it wasn't quite a run. It just about killed us to start with, but in time, and after lots of training, we could run *five* miles in fifty minutes. By January we were able to do four miles—take a ten-minute break—and then do four more. That's how we learned to assault a ridge—take your equipment and run to the top and flop down in position all out of breath. Believe me, we might have been in the armor, but we learned to cover a lot of ground on foot.

By the time we left Morocco and headed for Algeria and Tunisia, we were in really good shape. And that was a good thing, because the Reconnaissance units spent a lot of time in the Atlas Mountains—looking for the Germans—while they were looking for us. And one thing was for sure, we had thought the Germans were good—but they were really no better than us. They just had more experience.

The Germans also had a better gun on their tanks than we did—and they knew how to use 'em. What they did, they did well. But they couldn't do anything on their own. They didn't try and figure out things the way we do, and they weren't innovative. Despite our inexperience, we were quick to learn—and we were smart enough to know what we still needed to learn. If we persisted in doing well and learning well, we were really going to be better than the Germans.

On 14 January 1943, President Roosevelt and Prime Minister Churchill began a ten-day conference at Casablanca—on ground that had been in

National Archives

FDR and Churchill at Casablanca on January 22, 1943.

enemy hands only a little more than two months before. Although the city was still subject to Luftwaffe air attacks, the two Allied leaders and their staffs worked around the clock. It was at Casablanca that they decided to demand the unconditional surrender of the Axis Powers and agreed to postpone an invasion of the European continent until 1944. They also concluded that Sicily would be taken as soon as North Africa was secure.

Both FDR and Churchill were sanguine that Operation Torch was nearly completed. The day that they convened, Rommel's desert legions, having conducted a seventy-two-day retreat from El Alamein, were trying to hold against Montgomery's 8th Army east of Tripoli, Libya. By 23 January, the day before the Allied leaders completed their strategy session, Rommel's Afrika Korps was in retreat again. This time he wouldn't stop until 4 February—deep in Tunisia, behind the "Mareth Line," a series of defensive positions erected by the French before the war started.

Though he had no doubt about the eventual outcome, Eisenhower was far less certain than his leaders about the timing of a victory in North Africa. In briefing the president, prime minister, and the Joint Staff, he noted that German reinforcements were now flooding into Tunis and that preparations for an Axis counteroffensive appeared to be under way.

He didn't have to wait long. On 14 February, in weather so bad that it grounded the air forces of both sides, Rommel sent the 10th and 21st Panzer Divisions smashing into II Corps lines guarding the Faid Pass in Tunisia. General Fredendall's II Corps, consisting of the U.S. 1st Armored Division, and the 1st and 34th Infantry Divisions, was inadequately prepared for the Panzer assault and the poorly trained Americans fell back in disorder, more than fifty miles through the Kasserine Pass.

The German advance was finally halted on 20 February by the British 6th Armored Division, supported by the U.S. 9th Division's artillery—but not before 5,275 American GIs were dead, wounded, prisoners of the Reich, or missing in action. Corporal Duane Stone, a Browning Automatic Rifleman in the 34th Infantry Division, was one of them.

CORPORAL DUANE STONE, US ARMY
34th Infantry Division
Faid Pass, Tunisia
18 February 1943

I started my training in March 1941, but we didn't even get rifles until May. Later I went to Fort Dix, New Jersey, for some real training and from there, I was sent overseas on a British passenger liner that had been converted into a troop ship—along with about 1,700 other troops that were just as green as I was. We landed in Liverpool and started doing amphibious training, getting ready for an invasion—though nobody told us where. We assumed it would be some place in Europe. By July we were training for landings on beaches that were laid out exactly like the ones we'd see in North Africa on Operation Torch—but we didn't find that out until later.

In October the word came down, "We are going to take a boat trip." Everyone in my BAR squad—all three Browning Automatic Rifle teams—knew then that we were headed for war. I think they told us we were going to North Africa three or four days before we actually landed. Our objective was to take the western part of the city of Algiers.

After we landed on 8 November, we marched twenty-plus miles before we were under fire by a Vichy French battalion. The actual battle, as far as we were concerned, was over in about two and a half hours.

Things were quiet for a few days but then, about the third night, while we were in Algiers, the Luftwaffe started bombing us. Every night thereafter the Germans would spend three, maybe four hours, bombing the ships and piers at the harbor and our camps around the city. They had plenty of aircraft—but we had almost none. Almost every night German Stukas would attack 17th Field Artillery. It was like that until we headed east from Algiers in December to attack the German lines near the Faid pass, up in the Atlas Mountains of Tunisia.

For most of December, January, and the first half of February of '43, we were in a series of back and forth fights with Rommel's forces up in the mountains. Our regiment was spread between the Faid Pass and Kasserine Pass—a distance of about fifty miles. Then, on the night of 13–14 of February, the Luftwaffe carpet-bombed our whole sector. Afterwards we could hear armor moving and we very quickly realized this was no probe—it was a major attack.

One of our officers passed the word that we were surrounded and had to try to break out—and would have to make a forced march to get to the Kasserine Pass. But, of course, you don't move at night, on foot, as fast as you do in the daytime.

By the night of the seventeenth we had been battling the Germans nonstop for three days as we retreated. We had no food, very little water, and were running low on ammunition. Our biggest holdup was trying to move an entire unit of 1,800 troops through enemy lines. So we were told to break up into small groups and start walking northwest toward Kasserine as soon as it was dark.

Just before dark, a column of American tanks headed toward us. They were probably four miles away and I watched 'em, through my field glasses. Even though they were outnumbered, they engaged the Germans—but there just wasn't anything they could do. The Panzers just devastated them. There were also some armored personnel carriers with 105s mounted on 'em that fired on the German tanks but the shells just bounced off—they couldn't penetrate the Panzer's armor plate.

There were probably twenty men in the group I was with and we started out after dark. There was no moon that night and we had to move very slowly because there were minefields all over the place.

During the night we passed through some German tank platoons that were held up on the road—but I estimated that we were still twenty miles behind the German front line. Before dawn, the dozen of us who were still together stumbled into an irrigation ditch and we decided to hole up there during the daylight hours and hope that we wouldn't be spotted.

But shortly after the sun came up, a German half-track with a .50-caliber machine gun mounted on it came rumbling up through the ditch. A German officer, probably twenty-four or twenty-five years old, said in perfect English, "Gentlemen, for you, the war is over. You can go and see our homeland now."

Fifteen German soldiers circled around us, took our weapons, and made us understand that we were to start marching east. After five or six hours we arrived at a barbed-wire fenced compound, and the English-speaking officer said, "You'll stay here, for a couple of days."

Eventually they sent us to a prisoner of war camp, in Germany, that held POWs of every nationality—including about 1,500 American soldiers. They were brutal to the Americans, but for the Russians it was worse. Once, they brought in a whole trainload of Russian POWs, but never let 'em off that train—for forty-two days! By the time they opened the doors of the boxcars, half of them were already dead, and the other half probably wished they had died.

A couple of American POWs hung themselves—committed suicide. But a lot more died from what the Nazi guards said were "heart attacks." I was confined in that POW camp until we were liberated—on May 6, 1945—just two days before the war ended.

The disaster that had befallen Duane Stone and his comrades began at Faid Pass and ended just a few miles to the northwest of the Kasserine Pass—the gateway through the Atlas Mountains between Tunisia and Algeria. But by 22 February, the German counter-offensive had stalled. The Panzers were running out of fuel, and the weather had cleared enough for Allied airpower to attack the German armored columns in the open countryside. Rommel knew he was about to be assaulted by Montgomery on the Mareth Line.

On 26 February, Eisenhower launched an attack on a three-division front, driving the Germans back through the Kasserine Pass and restoring Allied positions to those held prior to Rommel's offensive. The following week he relieved Fredendall, the II Corps commander, and replaced him with Patton. From then on, it was simply a matter of time and attrition until the Allied armies could finish off the Desert Fox.

On 3 March Rommel's attempt to push Montgomery's 1st Army back from the Mareth defenses failed. Three days later Rommel was evacuated to Germany for unspecified medical treatment—leaving his deputy, Jürgen von Arnim, in command of Army Group Africa.

Von Arnim's tenure in command would be brief but violent. Between 20 March and the first week of May, with Patton pressing in from the west, 1st Army from the north, and Montgomery from the south, German and Italian troops were forced into an ever tightening noose. By then the Americans had learned the hard lessons of combat. In a pitched armor battle at El Guettar on 29 and 30 March, Patton's 2nd Armored Corps mauled the numerically superior 10th Panzer Division and sent it in retreat back across the desert with half its tanks destroyed.

By April, British motor torpedo boats were regularly interdicting German resupply craft from Sicily. American and British fighters now roamed the skies at will, shooting down German transports attempting to deliver critically needed materiel to the cornered Axis troops.

Eisenhower's strangulation strategy worked. Bizerta fell to the Americans of II Corps on 7 May and the British 1st Army seized Tunis that afternoon. By the end of the following week, the Germans and Italians, their backs to the sea and no way to escape, were through. Messe surrendered the remnants of his Italian legions to Montgomery on 12 May. The next day, von Arnim conceded defeat. More than 125,000 Wehrmacht soldiers and 115,000 Italians passed into Allied captivity.

The Allied victory in North Africa came with a terrible price: 70,000 Allied casualties. But the American army was transformed—its units were bloodied, but had proven their worth in battle. The soldiers—and their leaders—had learned valuable lessons that would soon be put to the test again on Sicily. And though they could not know it then, those who fought in North Africa had ended the expansion of the Third Reich. After 13 May 1943, Hitler would always be on the defensive.

CHAPTER 6
SICILIAN HELL
1943

Planning for Operation Husky, the invasion of Sicily, began even before the Allies had secured Tunisia. Neither Marshall nor Eisenhower wanted to tie up forces that would ultimately be needed for a cross-channel offensive. But once Roosevelt and Churchill agreed at Casablanca that there would be no invasion of Europe until 1944, the two American generals relented and Eisenhower's staff commenced work on the Husky operations plan in February 1943.

As he had with Torch, Eisenhower insisted that the objectives of the Sicily operation be clearly delineated to avoid an "open-ended" commitment of his forces. After a series of acrimonious debates with the British, who were still pressing for an invasion of the continent through the Balkans—what Churchill called "Europe's soft underbelly"—the Joint Staff finally responded to his entreaties.

The issues of what was to be accomplished in Sicily—and what forces would do it—were finally resolved by Roosevelt and Churchill during their 11–27 May "Trident Conference" in Washington. Churchill himself, with Marshall accompanying, flew directly from Washington to Algiers to tell Eisenhower the goals of the Sicilian invasion. They were to secure

Mediterranean sea lines of communication; relieve pressure on the Red Army by diverting German troops and materiel from the Eastern Front; seize air bases closer to Germany for the growing bombing campaign against the Reich; and, hopefully, force Italy out of the war.

To carry out this complex and ambitious mission, Eisenhower, the overall commander in chief, would have General Sir Harold Alexander as Allied ground commander and two field armies—the U.S. 7th, commanded by George Patton, and the British 8th, led by Bernard Montgomery. Patton's forces would include the U.S. 1st and 3rd Infantry Divisions, the 2nd Armored Division, and the 82nd Airborne—all from North Africa—and the new 45th Division, sent from the United States.

Montgomery's principal 8th Army troops were the same combat hardened but weary soldiers—plus freshly joined replacements—that he had led all the way from El Alamein. He was also given the entire British 1st Airborne Division and the 1st Canadian Infantry Division, dispatched from Great Britain.

The invasion force—nearly a half-million American, Canadian, and British soldiers, sailors, and airmen—were going up against more than 325,000 well-prepared Italian and German troops occupying terrain that gave the advantage to the defenders. Getting so many troops quickly and safely ashore over landing beaches that stretched over eighty miles along Sicily's eastern and southern shoreline required ships and landing craft that were already committed for operations in the Pacific or that had been earmarked for Overlord—the invasion of France.

Eisenhower got most of what he asked for—including brand-new LSTs, "Higgins boats," and the new DUKW—"Ducks"—wheeled amphibious vehicles that could quickly shuttle troops and supplies from ship to shore and then inland. By 10 July 1943—D-Day for Husky—the naval armada numbered more than 2,500 ships and small craft. It divided into three task forces and converged on Sicily from the east, south, and west.

To confuse Hitler about where this force was heading, the British concocted a deception plan they dubbed Operation Mincemeat. The corpse of a British airman killed in a plane crash was attired as a Royal Marine major and a briefcase full of bogus maps and documents, detailing secret plans for the invasion of the Balkans, was handcuffed to his wrist. The "major's" body was planted by a Royal Navy submarine on the coast of Spain.

The ruse may well have worked. Allied air and naval bombardment of the tiny island of Pantelleria—just off Sicily's southern coast—forced the surrender of the island's Italian garrison on 11 June. But even after that furious five-day assault Hitler refused to believe that his American and British enemies were headed for Sicily.

To ensure that the Allies maintained air superiority over the landing beaches and supported the 82nd Airborne paratroop drops, more than 1,500 U.S. and British aircraft were assembled on Malta and at fields in Algeria and Tunisia. For the airborne operations during Husky, the Joint Staff allocated a flotilla of C-47 transports—some for towing 144 of the new CG-4 Waco gliders to Sicily—which carried British troops.

Eisenhower's ground maneuver plan for Husky had actually been drafted by Montgomery—some said, in an Algerian latrine. It called for night parachute assaults by the U.S. 82nd and British 1st Airborne Divisions to seize the high ground overlooking the landing beaches. Then, at dawn, after a naval bombardment, the amphibious forces would come ashore.

The balance of the British 8th Army would land north of Cape Passero, on Sicily's east coast, seize the port of Syracuse, and then dash for Messina—where the "toe" of the Italian boot is just over six miles distant. The U.S. 7th Army was supposed to seize a beachhead at Gela, and then push north and west, protecting the British left flank as Montgomery drove north for Messina—cutting off any Axis retreat.

That was the plan. But as so often happens in war, things rarely go according to plan and Husky was no exception. By the time Eisenhower moved his forward headquarters to Malta on 7 July, things had already started to go wrong.

First, Eisenhower's intelligence staff inexplicably failed to note and report to those going ashore that Hitler had reinforced the Axis garrison on Sicily with two first-rate armored units—the 15th *Panzergrenadier* Division and the Hermann Goering Panzer Division. Second, the weather in the central Mediterranean—normally calm in mid-summer—began to deteri-orate as clouds and high winds swept in from the west.

Both the unexpected enemy armor and the adverse weather would have a profound effect on the American and British airborne troops strapping into their parachutes and boarding the Waco gliders on the night of 9–10 July 1943. One of the 3,400 paratroopers in Colonel Jim Gavin's 505th Para-chute Infantry Regiment of the 82nd Airborne Division was Captain Edwin Sayre from Breckenridge, Texas. He would be among the first to see action on Sicily.

CAPTAIN EDWIN SAYRE
505th Parachute Infantry Regiment
3 Kilometers Northeast of Gela, Sicily
10 July 1943

I was assigned to the 505th Parachute Infantry Regiment on 19 April '42, and was initially a company executive officer. Less than a year later I was promoted to captain and made a company commander. We all knew we were going someplace overseas in Europe, but didn't know where. We went by train to New York, and then boarded the *Monterrey*—a converted luxury liner for four hundred passengers. But it wasn't quite so luxurious for *six thousand* soldiers. We crossed the Atlantic and landed in North Africa as part of a large convoy with plenty of destroyer escorts.

A week before D-Day, we got maps of Sicily and aerial photos of our proposed objectives. We built sand tables, and duplicated exactly what the drop zone was supposed to look like, and knew where all our checkpoints were on the approach. We all memorized the map features and rehearsed at those sand tables with our troops, again and again.

We took off from Tunisia in a large flight of C-47s, just at dark on the night of July 9. The wind was blowing hard—in training we don't jump in wind over fifteen miles per hour because high winds will blow para-troopers off their drop zone or drag them across the ground. As we got closer to Sicily the overcast and turbulence increased, but we were all in high spirits—it was our first combat jump and we were ready.

We were supposed to jump shortly after midnight but we were late because of the winds. The whole timing of H-Hour had been based on the moon and the tides. The airborne needed a little bit of moonlight and the amphibious force needed an incoming high tide.

Theoretically, we were to have moonlight as we jumped and then the moon would be setting and we'd be in complete darkness. But instead of moonlight we got pitch-black darkness; instead of low winds we got strong ones. But at this point we had to take what we could get.

I looked out the door of my plane, with my map in hand, and I saw that we were in the wrong place. So, I went up to the cockpit and showed the pilot on the map where we were compared to where we needed to be. Fortunately I was in the lead aircraft with the most experienced pilot in the formation. Not every pilot would have let a young paratroop captain tell him he needs to turn a nine-plane formation around, and go to some other place. But this pilot listened to me—even though anti-aircraft gunners on the ground were firing at us. He asked, "Do you want to circle around and try another shot at it?" I said "yes," and we circled around, found the checkpoints, and he let us out about a mile from our intended drop zone.

The wind had to be blowing 40 to 45 miles per hour. I was blown over my DZ and landed right in the middle of a grape vineyard, and couldn't see my hand in front of my face. By dawn—as the amphibious forces were landing on the beach—right on time below us, I had collected up a handful of men from my company.

We knew very little about the enemy situation and had never been told that there was a German armored division parked on the spot that had been picked for our drop zone. If the higher command knew German Panzers were where we were going to jump, that word never got to us.

Shortly after daylight, we moved into an enemy trench line that one of my squads had captured. Then, German tanks started heading our way. Thankfully, the 1st Infantry Division had given me an artillery forward observer. So I told him, "Let's get some fire out there. They're going to overrun us here in this trench. It's better for us to be hit with our own stuff, than for them to crush us with those tanks."

He got on the radio and very quickly a 155 mm artillery battery down on the beach opened up. A "one-five-five" round hit the lead tank and it caught fire. You could hear the screams of that German crew from inside that tank a half-mile away. And then the tank exploded in front of us. That kind of dismayed the rest of the Panzers.

Gavin had ordered us, "If you land somewhere and don't know where you are, just find the nearest enemy and attack." Well, inasmuch as they were shooting at us when we exited the plane, and after we got on the ground, we didn't have any trouble finding them.

We moved a few hundred yards and were taken under fire by a machine gun. After crawling forward a bit, I could see that it wasn't just a machine gun, but a whole series of concrete pillboxes. We needed more firepower.

I got on the radio and told my platoon leaders, "I'll fire three shots close together, and everybody assemble on me." We got together and checked what we had: carbines, M1s, two light machine guns, and plenty of ammunition. But we needed a bazooka—an anti-armor rocket launcher. I called a bazooka man over and I told him, "I want you to take your bazooka and crawl underneath that culvert, and put a round into that pillbox. And if any German tanks come up, you get out and shoot it in the rear."

And he said, "That's a real good plan, Captain. Only one problem— I haven't seen my ammunition man since we jumped." So of course he didn't have any ammunition for his bazooka.

I set up my mortars and machine guns to deliver supporting and suppression fires and the rest of us crawled up until we were right below the row of pillboxes. Then, we all lobbed grenades and assaulted the emplacements. It worked and we took out a whole row of fortifications.

We had killed a number of the enemy and captured ten Germans and about forty Italians. We told the Germans to pick up our stretchers and carry our wounded, but they clicked their heels together like good Germans and said, "Nein." But my paratroopers convinced them that they really should pick up those stretchers. They did, and we started moving down the plateau to link up with the 1st Division.

Mainly because of the weather and wind, 80 percent of the British and American paratroopers dropped during D-Day on Sicily landed miles from their intended drop zones. Scores of British soldiers in the 1st Air Landing Brigade drowned when their Waco gliders were cut loose too soon from their tow-planes and the powerless craft crashed into the sea. Colonel Jim Gavin, commanding the 505th PIR, landed *sixty kilometers* from his intended drop zone.

But all the Allied paratroopers had been thoroughly trained and briefed on what to do if they found themselves on the ground, away from where they were supposed to be: find a fellow paratrooper and start making trouble for the enemy. And that's just what they did.

National Archives

Allied soldiers wade ashore on Sicily.

Within hours of the drop, little groups of paratroopers were ambushing couriers and recon vehicles, cutting telephone lines, and picking fights with any enemy units that they could find. One of them was a Brooklyn native, Sergeant Timothy Dyas.

SERGEANT TIMOTHY DYAS
505th Parachute Infantry Regiment
8 Kilometers Northwest of Gela, Sicily
13 July 1943

We left America in June of '43—about a month before the invasion of Sicily. When we arrived in North Africa we immediately started practicing parachute jumps. On the night of July 9, we climbed aboard C-47s and just after midnight on the morning of the tenth, we jumped into Sicily, just like we had been trained.

I was carrying my Tommy gun, some grenades, and a knife, along with my reserve chute, helmet, equipment-pack with supplies, lot of ammo, and canteens. I probably weighed close to 200 pounds with all the equipment.

We landed inland of Gela, where our invasion forces were to come ashore after dawn. My stick must have jumped at an altitude of about 300 feet, because my chute barely opened before I hit. If we had jumped at 1,000 feet, the wind would have blown us even further off our DZ and the Germans would have picked us off as we came down. But because of the wind and the low altitude of the jump, a lot of our guys broke arms, legs, or their backs when they landed too hard.

I hit very hard and was unconscious for some time. When I came to it was very dark and there was all kind of firing going on and a lot of our transports overhead. One of our planes was hit right after dropping its stick of paratroopers and slammed into the side of a hill and burst into flames.

After I came to, I gathered about a dozen men around and tried to figure out where we were. There was no doubt that the inexperienced pilots—probably because of the high winds—had missed our drop zone by several miles.

We were supposed to set up a roadblock to keep enemy reinforcements from getting to the guys who would be coming across the beach at dawn, so we headed toward higher ground. But as we got to the top of this hill at just about dawn, a group of German tanks was coming up the other side. We didn't anticipate having to take on tanks—we didn't even know they were on the island—particularly German Panzers. It was a real shock.

We scrambled to get off to the side of the column of tanks and I got my bazooka team—Pat Sheridan and John Rubluski—and they took out the lead tank. Now it was the Germans' turn to be shocked—they didn't know we were there.

A German officer commanding the Panzer group opened up the hatch on the turret of his tank to see if he could spot us, and we fired again. The bazooka round hit right beneath him on the turret and killed him. And then another tank came along and my bazooka team destroyed the treads on that tank and brought it to a stop. I think the impact of killing the commander of the unit made a difference when the German tanks showed up. Without their leader they didn't know what to do.

In the American Army every private was a general—meaning they could adapt. This wasn't the case with the German army. When their chain of command was broken they were helpless and didn't know what to do. It took them a good two or three hours to get a junior officer to organize them. They had a much larger force than our dozen men—and they were trying to move infantry up to where we were but every time they stood up to move, we would shoot them down.

They backed off a ways—out of bazooka range—and stated to hammer us with fire from their tanks. We had to pull back over the crest of the hill and pretty soon we were pinned down in a ditch with potato masher grenades raining down on us. They would throw grenades down into the ditch and we would throw them right back up at them. This continued for a long period of time until one of the tanks came around the side of the hill and turned its big gun on us.

We were trapped, outnumbered, and had a bunch of wounded. I was the senior man so I had to make the decision to surrender to save the lives of my men. That hurt—and it still does—because we were trained to be the best and never surrender. It was a terrible feeling but our consolation was in knowing that we knocked out their tanks and killed their commanding officer. That had bought a few hours for the guys on the beach. If nothing else, our little group had created confusion and delay among the Panzers. The tanks never did make it to the beach.

Sergeant Dyas and the surviving paratroopers of his little band became POWs. They were taken to an internment camp outside Naples, Italy, and then shipped in boxcars to Germany, where they remained for the next twenty-two months.

National Archives

American troops walk through a damaged Sicilian city.

But for the paratroopers still fighting on Sicily, their ordeal wasn't over yet. Early on 11 July, in a hand-to-hand battle on "Bloody Ridge" overlooking the Gela landing beaches, the American 1st Infantry Division and small groups of paratroopers repulsed a German armored counter-attack. But in so doing, they suffered more than 1,000 casualties.

Patton decided to commit some of his reserves—two battalions of the 504th Parachute Infantry Regiment, waiting in North Africa. Since no airfields were yet available for landing in the U.S. zone of action on Sicily, it was decided that the 1,800 paratroopers would parachute inside American lines near Gela.

Tragically, the C-47 transports carrying the paratroopers passed over the invasion fleet just minutes after a German air raid had sunk an LST. Nervous U.S. Navy gunners opened fire on the American aircraft as they approached the drop zones, straight and level at 1,200 feet, downing twenty-three and damaging thirty-seven of the C-47s. Sixty pilots and crewmen, along with eighty-one paratroopers, were killed.

Though their losses were higher than any other units in Husky, the paratroopers had bought precious time for the troops on the beaches and kept them from being pushed back into the sea. For twenty-five-year-old Oklahoma native 2nd Lieutenant Ed Speairs of the 45th Infantry Division, the hours purchased by paratrooper blood made the difference on D-Day.

SECOND LIEUTENANT A. H. "ED" SPEAIRS, US ARMY
45th Infantry Division
Messina, Sicily
17 August 1943

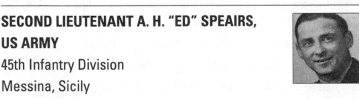

The morning of July 10, 1943, is a day I'll remember for the rest of my life. Right after dawn I went up on deck to watch the pre-H-hour bombardment. All you could see—from horizon to horizon—were gray ships. I didn't even know we had so many ships!

I'd joined the National Guard in 1938 and when we were mobilized in 1940, I was promoted to sergeant. Two years later I was a master sergeant and by the time we landed on Sicily, I was a 2nd lieutenant. That morning it was my responsibility for loading thirty-three landing craft with 45th Division troops and then guiding them ashore.

We had left the States on 3 June, escorted by U.S. Navy destroyers and cruisers. When we got to Oran, Algeria, on 22 June, we started amphibious landing exercises. It was a good thing that we'd had the practice in decent weather—because D-Day on Sicily the weather was terrible.

As we headed into the beach the wind was howling and the waves looked like they were twenty feet high. Every time we would drop down in a swell, we would lose sight of the other boats around us. We took a lot of water in and for a while I thought we might sink before we got to the shore.

Somehow I got my boats to the designated beach, but there were rocks that we didn't know about and it delayed some of the boats. Because of the wind and sea conditions it took longer than expected to start getting our tanks ashore. It's a good thing that the German Panzers didn't attack then, because riflemen are no match for armor.

For the next eighty-seven hours all I did was shuttle back and forth between the ships and the beach with my little group of boats. At the end of that time—because of all the damage—hitting rocks, bumping up against the big hulls and the like—I had just one working landing craft left, *out of thirty-three*. But by then, the ships were unloaded—and the 45th Division had gotten almost all its gear ashore intact.

On my last trip, I was told to stay ashore and catch up to my unit. They had moved inland about ten kilometers—and I was three and a half days behind them. When I got off on the beach on July 13, practically all I saw were Italian prisoners—thousands of 'em in long lines. They were all smiling, and saying, "I've got a cousin in Brooklyn." For them, the war was over—but for us it was just beginning.

There were also bodies of American soldiers on the beach, wrapped in ponchos—waiting for the graves registration guys. And, there were mountains of ammo, food, fuel drums, you name it—all waiting to be trucked forward. I caught a ride up to my unit with one of the supply convoys.

We reached Caltanissetta—a town almost in the center of the island, on 17 or 18 July. This place had been a big supply depot for the Italian army and headquarters for the Fascist Party on Sicily and it had been just about leveled by air strikes and artillery fire. There was the smell of death everywhere, and as we came to discover, there were lots of bodies of German and Italian troops in the rubble.

Patton pushed everyone very hard to keep the enemy on the run. Palermo, the capital of Sicily, was captured on 22 July—but then it became obvious that the Germans had sent in reinforcements—and that slowed everything down.

The Germans also began to use lots of mines on the roads—and to blow up all the bridges and roadways they could to delay our advance. Later on, at Cefalù, on the northwest coast, the Germans used explosives to shear off the road that had been built on the edge of a cliff over the sea. The Germans just blasted it off.

But Patton wanted us to keep pressing ahead, so our engineers came up and used bridge sections to cross the gap so that we could keep going. And they did it all while under fire—it was an incredible feat. I'm glad I went all the way with Patton.

Lt. Ed Spears' observations about Patton's pressure to keep driving forward—and the heroic acts that he inspired—were right on the mark. The 7th Army commander had come ashore on D-Day and shortly thereafter reported, "We have them on the run" and he wanted to keep them that way.

Certain that the Germans had been surprised by the Allied landings, Patton unrelentingly pressed his troops forward—before their enemy could reinforce or escape across the narrow Strait of Messina. And he almost succeeded.

Hitler *had* been totally surprised by Husky. He not only believed the inaccurate intelligence he'd received about the Allies heading for the

Balkans or Sardinia, but the Führer was also distracted by giving so much of his attention to Operation Citadel—the offensive he had launched in the Crimea near Kursk. But once Hitler realized what was *really* happening on Sicily, he moved swiftly.

On 13 July, Hitler ordered the Kursk offensive halted—it was already a disaster for the Wehrmacht—so that reserves headed for the Eastern Front could instead be sent to Italy. At his "Wolf's Lair" headquarters in East Prussia on 17 July, the Führer told his general staff, "Barbaric measures are needed to save Italy. Only by terrifying the Italian population into blind obedience, can we stiffen Italian resistance." Acting on that premise, he flew to Feltre, north of Venice, to meet with Mussolini on 19 July. The next day he ordered the 29th Panzergrenadier and the 1st Parachute Division to Sicily.

Hitler's last-minute intervention wasn't enough to save his fellow Fascist. On 23 July, Patton marched triumphantly into Palermo, Sicily's capital. And three days later, Mussolini was imprisoned.

General Patton on his way to Messina.

Patton's capture of Palermo may have precipitated the fall of the dictator, but it didn't end the fighting on the island. German reinforcements halted Montgomery's push to Messina dead in its tracks at Mount Etna. By 31 July, Patton's advance through central Sicily and along the island's northern coast had been slowed as well.

Undeterred, and adamant that he'd reach Messina before Montgomery, the U.S. Army's most famous armor tactician showed that he also had a firm grasp of amphibious warfare. Starting on 8 August, with the help of the U.S. Navy, Patton launched a series of short "amphibious hooks" along Sicily's north coast, leapfrogging his battalions beyond German strong points on the approach to Messina. Small vessels like Sub-chaser-692, commanded by twenty-four-year-old Lt. (JG) Edward Stafford, were essential to the success of these operations.

LIEUTENANT (JG) EDWARD STAFFORD, USN
Sub-Chaser SCE-692
18 August 1943

I joined the Navy because my grandfather had served in the Navy. I spent every summer with him on the coast of Maine, learning how to handle small boats and about tides and currents. I got my commission on 16 September 1941, just before Pearl Harbor and took command of SCE-692, a sub-chaser, in January of '43.

On D-Day in Sicily the weather was terrible—and the surf on the landing beaches was worse. I was nervous—this was my first experience in combat—and every one of us aboard that little ship were Navy reservists. The first class boson's mate—the senior enlisted man—was a big help, and an "old salt." He must have been thirty-three. We were the smallest class of ship to make the transatlantic crossing in a huge convoy. There were a lot of these small ships brought over for the Sicily operation—even though we were designed for anti-submarine patrols off the U.S. coasts.

On D-Day our job was to meet a wave of landing craft—five or six loaded LCVPs, Higgins boats near the transports, escort them to the line of departure, two miles off shore, and get them all on line and properly positioned for their run into the beach. Once the wave of boats started in, we'd head back out to the transport ships and pick up another wave and repeat the whole process.

But on the morning of 10 July, there was this horrible sea with ten- and fifteen-foot waves and this howling wind—and packed into each of these little landing craft are twenty to thirty soldiers all loaded up with all their weapons and equipment. I thought that someone would surely cancel the landing until the wind and sea quieted some—but I guess if we had done that we would have lost the element of surprise. That's a hell of a choice to make—and I'm glad I didn't have to decide it.

Somehow, we managed to get all our boat waves safely onto the beach but a few hours into the landing, German aircraft—Stukas and fighters—attacked us. They hit one of the 1st Division's LSTs on the beach, and she caught fire. We could see the smoke coming up from her. Surprisingly, there were very few casualties getting people ashore.

On 22 July—just twelve days after the landing—the 7th Army captured Palermo. The next day, Patton entered the city and we were the first ship to enter the Palermo harbor. It hadn't even been swept for mines when we came in.

There were wrecks all across the middle of the harbor. A ship—it must have weighed 2,000 tons—was sitting not *at* the dock, but *on* the dock. It had been blown out of the water, presumably by an American air raid, and the explosion lifted it onto the pier. We all went ashore and it was fantastic. The capital city of Sicily was a ghost town.

A few weeks later, Patton's troops were running into all kinds of opposition on the route along the north coast to Messina. The Germans had blown up all the bridges on the coast highway—and were contesting at every turn on the road. So Patton decided that he would just bypass these roadblocks and obstacles with a number of amphibious operations— smaller versions of what we had done on July 10.

Because the coastal waters hadn't been swept and the charts weren't very good, little vessels like sub-chasers and destroyer escorts were perfect for these assaults. Ships like ours were able to not only escort the landing craft into the beach but could also stay in close to provide gunfire support. That's how Patton beat Montgomery to Messina—and the little ships of the U.S. Navy helped him do it.

"Little ships" of the U.S. Navy like Ed Stafford's sub-chaser were indeed crucial to Patton beating Montgomery to Messina—by *one* day. The lead elements of both the U.S. 3rd Infantry Division and 45th Division reached the outskirts of the port on 15 August, and Montgomery's paratroopers arrived the next day. On 17 August, by prior arrangement, the Americans and the British made a triumphal entry into the devastated city. But they were too late to catch their wily Wehrmacht opponents—the Germans had escaped.

During the hours of darkness between 11 August and the night of the sixteenth, German generals Hans Hube and Frido Etterlin had safely barged more than 100,000 German and Italian troops and nearly 10,000 tanks, armored vehicles, and trucks across the narrow Straits of Messina to the Italian mainland.

Though Eisenhower was personally chagrined at the enemy's escape, Roosevelt and Churchill, meeting with the combined British-American chiefs of staff in Quebec at the "Quadrant Conference," were quick to reassure their chosen commander. But they were less forgiving of their most successful armor leader—George Patton.

During the protracted battles in central Sicily, Patton had visited a field hospital where severely—and recently—wounded soldiers were being treated. When the exhausted and emotionally drained general saw two soldiers with no visible injuries waiting to be seen by a medical officer, he confronted them, accused them of cowardice, and slapped them. The doctors and nurses who saw the incidents were appalled and the story quickly spread. As it turned out, one of the soldiers was a casualty of battlefield stress and the other had a temperature of 102 degrees—likely from the malaria prevalent in Sicily's central plain.

When the incidents were reported in the press, senior officers in Washington demanded that Patton be cashiered. Only Eisenhower's direct and personal intervention in the matter saved the tank warfare expert from professional extinction. But the two events—the Germans' escape and the general's slaps—were to have immediate consequences.

Though more than 5,000 Allied soldiers had been killed and another 17,000 wounded in the thirty-eight-day battle for Sicily, FDR and Churchill agreed at Quadrant that the momentum against Hitler required an immediate invasion of the Italian mainland. Thus, the Germans who escaped Sicily in August would face the Allies again at Salerno in September. And this time when the Americans went ashore, "Old Blood and Guts" wouldn't be leading them. As punishment for the slapping incidents, Patton was called back to England to help Eisenhower prepare for Overlord. The crusty Patton was given "command" of the First United States Army Group— which was the wholly invented army for Operation Quicksilver—to spread disinformation about the size of the American forces in England. In that role, he'd be muzzled from making his familiar outrageous remarks, and Eisenhower could quietly prepare him for the role he had planned for him in Overlord.

CHAPTER 7

BATTLE FOR THE BOOT
1943–1945

Mussolini was overthrown on 26 July 1943, in the midst of the battle for Sicily. The new government in Rome, headed by the aging Marshal Pietro Badaglio, assured Hitler that they were still allies in the Axis. But secretly, Badaglio—at the direction of the Italian monarch, King Victor Emmanuel—immediately began negotiating for Italy's surrender to the Allies.

Italian reluctance to continue in the disastrous alliance Mussolini had forged with Hitler was understandable. By mid-July 1943, nearly a quarter of a million young Italians had died in the foreign adventures undertaken by Il Duce. The Allies were holding more than a half-million Italian soldiers as prisoners of war. Although the 350,000 Italian POWs held by the Americans and British would eventually be freed, most of those who disappeared in the Balkans—and very few of those captured at Stalingrad—would ever be heard from again.

Clandestine meetings between Badaglio's representatives and Allied officials took place on Sicily and Portugal. Eisenhower even secretly dispatched Brigadier General Maxwell Taylor to Rome—at great personal risk—to confer with Italian authorities.

When the negotiations bogged down, Allied bombers were unleashed on the industrial cities of northern Italy. Then, before dawn on 3 September, Montgomery's 8th Army surreptitiously crossed the Straits of Messina, landing on the "toe" of the Italian boot—the first Allied soldiers to occupy Axis home territory since the start of the war. Badaglio agreed to Eisenhower's surrender terms that afternoon.

From the start of the negotiations, both Badaglio and Eisenhower had anticipated that once the Italian surrender became public, Hitler would react quickly and violently. Therefore, provisions for Italy withdrawing from the war included an understanding that the Allies would rapidly "intervene" on the Italian mainland to prevent German reprisals against the new government. Accordingly, as the final battles of Husky were still being fought on Sicily, Eisenhower's staff was frantically poring over maps, nautical charts, aerial photographs, and intelligence reports to determine the best points of entry on the Italian coast. The goal was to get to Rome as fast as possible.

Given limitations on shipping and the realization that 60,000 Wehrmacht troops had escaped the trap set for them at Messina, the Allies decided that the Gulf of Salerno—160 miles south of Rome—was as far north as they dared go. Codenamed Avalanche, the operation was set to commence on 9 September—only twenty-three days after Sicily was declared secure, and just hours after the public announcement of Italy's surrender.

Eisenhower had hoped that Montgomery's 3 September landing at Regio Calabria on Italy's "toe" would draw Kesselring's Wehrmacht south from Naples—but the Germans didn't take the bait. Instead, anticipating the possibility of landings at Salerno, they moved additional forces south from Rome to complicate an Allied advance on Naples.

To command the hastily cobbled-together Allied force committed to Avalanche, Eisenhower chose General Mark Clark to lead the 5th Army's assault at Salerno. Clark was given the U.S. 36th and 45th Infantry Divisions and the British 46th and 56th Infantry and 7th Armored Divisions. He also had contingents of U.S. Army Rangers and Royal Marine Commandos.

Despite the paucity of resources and the relatively brief amount of time to plan the operation, things initially went as intended.

On the night of 8 September 1943, just a few hours after Eisenhower's headquarters announced the Italian surrender, heavy air attacks were carried out on known enemy positions, bridges, and highways around Salerno. As soon as the British and American bombers were through, a combined U.S. Navy/Royal Navy shore bombardment group moved in to soften up the beaches. The following morning, Clark's 5th Army came ashore—and early that afternoon, the 1st British Airborne Division, delivered by the Royal Navy—captured the Italian naval base at Taranto, in the "arch" of the boot.

Once established ashore, Clark's 5th Army was supposed to wheel to the left and move rapidly up Italy's west coast to seize the port of Naples—forty miles north of the Salerno beachhead. Montgomery's 8th Army—operating east of Italy's mountainous central spine—was to race north as well. The Brits were to seize the airbases in the Foggia plain. If all went well, the Allies might be in Rome by Christmas.

But things didn't go well. Both Clark and Montgomery tarried on their way north. Hitler, as Eisenhower's intelligence officers predicted, reacted immediately on news of Italy's surrender and the landings at Salerno. Late in the day on the ninth, the Luftwaffe began attacks on the Italian fleet as it sortied for Malta—as required in the armistice agreement. Hundreds of Italian sailors died when the battleship *Roma* went to the bottom—sunk by a guided bomb dropped by their former Axis ally.

By 10 September, fresh Wehrmacht divisions were pouring into Italy from southern France, Austria, and the Balkans. Field Marshal Albert Kesselring, Hitler's Southwest Army commander, promptly occupied Rome, redeployed the German units that had narrowly escaped from Sicily just twenty days before, and prepared to counter-attack.

On 12 September, while Allied intelligence was preoccupied plotting the whereabouts of German units moving into the Salerno area, a team of German SS commandos—led by Captain Otto Skorzeny—parachuted into the Gran Sasso prison and freed Benito Mussolini. Hitler installed the deposed dictator as the leader of the "Salò Republic," a fascist puppet state in Northern Italy.

The following day, Kesselring's counter-attack fell upon the 5th Army in their narrow beachhead at Salerno—and very nearly succeeded in throwing the Allies back into the sea. It was a terrifying precursor of what was to come in the long, bitter battle for the boot.

Van Barfoot was a farm boy from Carthage, Mississippi. In Italy, he found himself struggling to stay alive in some of the toughest fighting, worst weather, and most difficult terrain in the European theater. He quickly learned that the topography favored the defenders—and that the soldiers he was up against were some of the toughest and most experienced in the world.

PRIVATE VAN T. BARFOOT
157th Infantry, 45th Infantry Division
Naples, Italy
03 October 1943

I enlisted in the Army in 1942 and was with the 157th Infantry, 45th Infantry Division, during the battles of Sicily, Italy, and after that, southern France. In Sicily we had some stiff opposition up on the north ridge of the island—at the place we called "Bloody Ridge." That was my first real combat experience—and some of it was hand-to-hand fighting.

We left Sicily to make the amphibious assault behind the 36th Division at Salerno, just south of Naples, on September 9, 1943. We got ashore all right and the first day wasn't so bad, but as the 36th Division began to move off the beach and head inland, contact with the enemy picked up. Starting on the thirteenth, they started taking a lot of casualties.

The Germans had reinforced their lines since the first day of the invasion and as the 36th Division moved out to the northeast, they were waiting for us. Then the Panzers counter-attacked. They pushed us back all along the beachhead and the casualties were awful.

On September 14, our regiment was told to reinforce the line being held just east of the beachhead and my platoon was ordered to move up to scout out where the Germans were and whether they were still advancing. As soon as we passed through our lines we ran into a large number of Germans. There was no doubt they were still advancing.

The sergeant leading our patrol got us up on some high ground and we called in artillery fire on the German columns. By that night, the Germans were between us and our lines. For the next couple of days and nights there were Germans all around us—and lots of artillery fire and air strikes raining down all over the place.

I think it was our air and artillery power that finally broke the German attack. We were able to link up with our battalion and as we moved forward, we passed over an area where a unit of the 36th Division had been surrounded and wiped out. There were hundreds of dead Americans. At one position it looked as though the Germans had bayoneted the wounded.

After the German counter-attack was broken, we started moving again to the north—toward Rome. On the way, our platoon was ordered to take Hill 610—a piece of terrain that controls the approach to Naples. The assault started early in the morning and on the way up we were engaged by the Germans who had dug in up on the hill. By the time we got to the top, we had killed and wounded a large number of them and captured four prisoners.

But after we secured the hill, the Germans began to use artillery and mortar on *our* position. By ten o'clock that morning, every tree on that hill was either a stump, cut off at ground level, or just pulverized brush.

My platoon leader and his runner were killed up there and so were three of our squad leaders. I was wounded by shrapnel from an artillery round—as were four other men from my squad—but at least I could still walk.

It wasn't until late in the afternoon that we were told to move off the hilltop. By then our platoon was down to eighteen of the original thirty-seven who had gone up the hill in the morning.

A few days later, we took Naples. But that didn't end the fighting. It just went on and on and on.

I never saw any of our soldiers turn back or fail to move forward during a battle. I think that's because the American soldier is a person that will stay there and fight.

The heavy Allied air and artillery attacks that helped save PFC Van Barfoot and his 45th Division comrades in the breakout from the Salerno beachhead finally had the desired effect on the Wehrmacht—forcing the Germans to fall back to previously prepared positions. But even after General Mark Clark's 5th Army linked up with Montgomery's 8th Army late on 16 September, Kesselring's 10th Army only grudgingly gave up ground as they withdrew to the north. Despite constant pounding by American and British aircraft—and naval gunfire delivered against both coasts—Naples didn't fall to the Allies until 1 October. When the Americans moved into the port city, they found it wrecked.

Naples, and the supplies that were to be delivered through the harbor, were essential to a swift Allied advance on Rome. Knowing this, Kesselring had ordered his engineers to render the port unusable—and they used the two weeks between 16 September and 1 October to destroy equipment and supplies, set booby traps, and mine the roads in and through the city. For several weeks after the Allies' arrival, there were still booby traps and delayed-fuse bombs going off in Naples.

Once again the British-American attack ground to a snail's pace. For three months, Kesselring's highly disciplined troops fought a series of effective delaying actions—mining roadways, blowing up bridges, and ambushing every Allied advance as he slowly withdrew north to his *Winterstellung*—or "winter position."

Meanwhile, SS troops began systematically rounding up Italian Jews and transporting them to Auschwitz, Poland, for extermination. The first "shipment," 1,100 Roman Jews—two-thirds of them women and children—departed for the killing center on 18 October. Only fourteen men and one woman survived. Within a month, 8,360 Italian Jews had been deported.

The Germans' meticulous records showed that 7,749 of them were murdered in Hitler's *Endloesung*—his "Final Solution."

By the time Roosevelt, Churchill, and Stalin met for the "Eureka Conference" in Tehran on 28 November 1943, supplies were flowing well through Naples, but the Allied advance on Rome was consuming men and materiel at an alarming rate. Skillfully using the terrain to the defenders' advantage, Kesselring inflicted heavy Allied casualties by contesting every hilltop and river crossing during a series of bitterly fought Allied offensives. On Christmas Day, 1943, instead of celebrating the liberation of Rome, the Allies were being held in check seventy miles south of the city, along the German's heavily fortified Gustav Line.

Anchored at Gaeta in the west and Pescara in east, Kesselring's defenses included more than 75,000 landmines, bunkers, revetments, and dug-in tanks and artillery. The German 1st Parachute Division—one of the finest units in the Wehrmacht—held Monte Cassino, a sixth-century mountaintop abbey and the linchpin of the Gustav Line. By controlling the Monte Cassino heights, they blocked access to the Liri Valley and the approaches to Rome.

On 31 December 1943, Eisenhower was officially transferred to London to take over preparations for Operation Overlord—the cross-channel invasion of Hitler's "Festung Europa"—Fortress Europe. Two days later Ike's successor, General Sir Harold Alexander, the new Allied commander in the Mediterranean, dusted off a proposal for bypassing the Gustav Line defenses that Eisenhower had earlier discarded.

Dubbed Operation Shingle, the plan that Eisenhower rejected called for a diversionary amphibious assault at Anzio—on Italy's west coast—thirty miles from Rome and fifty miles north of the Gustav Line. Ike had vetoed the operation because he believed it would consume men, materiel, and shipping necessary to both Overlord and Anvil/Dragoon—the invasion of southern France. He was also concerned that putting an Allied force so far behind enemy lines risked annihilation if the element of surprise was lost.

General Alexander, convinced by Churchill that Rome must be captured, had no such qualms and promptly resurrected Shingle. After several days of debate with General Mark Clark's 5th Army planners, General John

P. Lucas, commanding the U.S. VI Corps, was ordered to carry out the Anzio assault—not as a diversionary operation, but as a major Allied offensive.

Lucas was allocated more than 375 U.S. and British ships—including sixty LSTs and 2,600 Allied aircraft—to support landing elements of the U.S. 1st Armored Division, the U.S. 3rd, 34th, and 45th Infantry Divisions, the British 1st and 5th Infantry Divisions, a full brigade of U.S. Army Rangers, and two regiments of the U.S. 82nd Airborne at Anzio.

Seven days after coming ashore, Lucas was to link up with the remainder of Mark Clark's reinforced 5th Army—which was to have punched through the Gustav Line and headed north. The entire force was then to make a final push into Rome. It *almost* worked.

On 20 January 1944, the U.S. II Corps began its assault on the Gustav Line—with the U.S. 36th Infantry Division attacking to force a crossing of the icy-cold, fast-flowing Rapido River. Two days later, at 0200, after a very brief pre-H-Hour bombardment to preserve surprise, Lucas started landing his VI Corps at Anzio.

The Germans were completely surprised. The landings—the British on the left and the Americans on the right—were virtually unopposed. By dark on 22 January, Lucas had more than 35,000 men and 3,250 vehicles ashore and moving rapidly inland. Within the next seventy-two hours, the VI Corps had established a beachhead that was more than six miles deep and ten miles wide—but still well short of the Alban hills, the high ground that overlooked the Anzio beaches.

Then, Lucas learned that far to his south, the 36th Division had been repulsed with horrific losses at the Rapido River. Units of II Corps that were to have been charging north through a gap in the Gustav Line were in fact not able to move even a mile in the direction of Anzio.

Concerned that the link-up force from the south would not be able to break through the Gustav Line before the Germans counter-attacked his shallow beachhead at Anzio, Lucas ordered a halt to further offensive movement and directed that the units already ashore dig in. Meanwhile, under harassing attacks from the Luftwaffe, he completed his build-up of forces and supplies ashore.

Kesserling, initially stunned by the audacity of the Allied landing at Anzio, was subsequently surprised that Lucas did not exploit the situation. Noting that the lead elements of the Allied force had not advanced to the Alban hills, he began moving every available German not committed to the immediate defense of the Gustav Line to prepare for a major counter-attack against the Anzio beachhead. Among them there were the Hermann Goring and 4th Parachute Divisions—two of the best in the Wehrmacht.

By 29 January, Lucas had almost 70,000 troops, 500 artillery pieces, and 250 tanks ashore. Confident that he had landed sufficient troops and supplies to renew his offensive, he ordered the breakout from the beachhead to commence on the night of 30–31 January. The 1st and 3rd Ranger Battalions were to spearhead the attack by infiltrating German lines and seizing a strategic road intersection in the small town of Cisterna. Corporal Raymond Sadoski, a Connecticut Yankee, was among the elite Rangers committed to that operation. Neither he nor his comrades knew that the Germans were preparing a counter-offensive of their own—and would meet them in force.

CORPORAL RAYMOND T. SADOSKI,
US ARMY
1st Ranger Battalion
Anzio, Italy
31 January 1944

I was in First Ranger Battalion, a BAR gunner. We saw action first in North Africa, and then in Sicily. By the end of operations in Sicily we were guarding Italian POWs near Messina. A lot of them spoke English and one of them said to me, "Hey, how about this—we're going to the States and you're going to stay here and fight." It was kind of crazy.

On January 22, 1944, we landed at Anzio. Other than the lousy weather—cold and overcast—it was like a walk in the park. We had to cross a lot of open terrain, which I didn't like at all, 'cause the Germans could see us.

A few days after the landing the lieutenant and I went to a meeting with our battalion commander. He said that the orders had come down that we weren't supposed to take any more patrols further inland—that we were to "dig in."

We were set up just to the northeast of Anzio port. The Germans had pulled out so fast they had left a 20 mm Italian anti-aircraft gun sitting there. All our guys were horsing around, getting on the gun and the like. One of the communicators from the command post told me, "Go over to that Italian gun and get that phone wire that the Germans left behind, we can use it."

Well, instead of walking all the way out to the gun to unhook the wire, I just grabbed the wire and gave it a yank, and the whole damn gun went up in a huge explosion. The Germans had rigged that thing to blow up if anybody broke the wire.

A few nights later we were moved up to the frontlines—toward the town of Cisterna. After dark, small teams of Rangers were sent out on recon patrols in front of our position. A few hundred meters out in no-man's land we came to this road and while we were checking for mines and enemy dispositions, a German comes zipping by us on a motorcycle and almost hit one of our guys. The German stopped the bike and started to yell in German, "What's wrong with you running around like that at night? I almost killed you."

If we hadn't been on a reconnaissance patrol, we would have killed *him*! As it was, we just hit the ground and headed back to our platoon.

A couple of nights later, on the night of 30–31 January, we were ordered to infiltrate in small groups into the town of Cisterna—and to hold it until the 3rd Infantry Division arrived in the morning. On the way into the town we came across a German checkpoint alongside the road.

We crept up on them and found two guards—but one of them was asleep. We killed them both with our knives, but not before one of them—a big guy—tried to kick the hell out of my lieutenant.

After we killed the guards, we crept into what turned out to be a German mechanized unit's assembly point. It was a well-camouflaged vehicle staging area for all kinds of tanks, half-tracks, and artillery. As close as these Germans were to our lines, it was pretty clear that they were getting ready for an attack on the beachhead.

Just before dawn, one of the Ranger infiltration teams further down the road to Cisterna got ambushed and the next thing we knew, the countryside was crawling with Germans. When the shooting started, I was right beside a German revetment packed full of ammunition cases. I heaved a hand grenade into the cache and we took off running—because you don't want to stick around when you blow up an ammunition dump. They tend to go off in all directions.

You never heard such an explosion in your life! They must have had some of everything stacked in there. I got hit with an exploded artillery shell casing, but it wasn't too serious, so I crawled over into a nearby house at the edge of the town and set up the radio. By then the battle was pretty hot—and we were taking a lot of casualties.

Even though we were outnumbered, we thought we could hold on until the units from the beachhead got to us, but then the Panzer tanks started coming in. A German tank rolled right up to where we were hiding and one of my sergeants jumped up on the tank, opened the turret, and dropped a hand grenade inside it. That was one courageous, tough sergeant.

By noon it was pretty clear that we were cut off from any help or reinforcements. The Germans had us surrounded, we were almost out of ammunition, and everybody with me was dead or wounded. Col. Bill Darby told us on the radio, "Blow up the radio and then give yourselves up."

I used my last grenade to blow up the radio and waited for the Germans to come and kill us. When the Germans got to the house one of their soldiers took my .45-caliber pistol and said, "*This* is a good gun. Now put your hands on your head and give up."

We hated to surrender, but we knew if we didn't we'd all be dead.

U.S. Army Ranger Ray Sadoski was captured by the Germans during the battle at Cisterna. During the fight, 767 U.S. Army Rangers had infiltrated behind enemy lines. All but six were killed, MIA, or captured. The next day, German propaganda cameras recorded several dozen of those elite U.S. soldiers being paraded past the coliseum in Rome under the guns of their captors. They would be POWs until the end of the war.

His breakout repulsed, Lucas once again shifted to defense, while the German 14th Army continued to reinforce around the Anzio beachhead. Further south, efforts to punch a hole in the Gustav Line continued to chew up American and British units. On 11–12 February 1944, the U.S. 34th Division was driven back after a disastrous assault against German 1st Parachute Division positions surrounding the Monte Cassino Abbey. Two days later, General Alexander ordered the abbey bombed. It was one of the most controversial orders of the war in Europe—and one of the least effective for the Allies.

On 15 February, more than 400 tons of bombs dropped by 230 B-17s and B-25s turned the ancient Benedictine monastery to rubble. The 1st Parachute Division—which had until now carefully avoided setting foot on the hallowed ground—immediately occupied the hilltop, turning the wreckage into a redoubt. An Allied attack the next day by New Zealanders and Indian troops—on the heights where the monastery stood—met with disaster.

That same day at Anzio, the German 14th Army, now more than eight divisions strong, charged out of the Alban hills and smashed into the VI Corps lines protecting the beachhead. One the Americans who suddenly found himself in desperate hand-to-hand combat that afternoon was a young U.S. Army infantry captain, Felix Sparks.

CAPTAIN FELIX SPARKS
Company E, 2nd Battalion, 157th Infantry,
45th Infantry Division
Anzio, Italy
23 February 1944

Our first battle was the invasion of Sicily—that was my first time in combat. We made an amphibious landing from large ships and small boats. In our area, we lucked out because Italian soldiers occupied our landing beaches—and they didn't really want to fight us.

We lost a few men who drowned when their landing craft capsized, because the weight of their equipment took them to the bottom. Each rifleman carried two extra bandoliers of ammunition swung around his shoulders, gas masks, grenades, three days of rations—all told about forty pounds of weight not counting their rifles.

My rifle company landed with 192 men and we took very few casualties until we got to Palermo in July. That's where I was wounded in the abdomen by shrapnel and was sent back to hospital in North Africa.

The company went on without me to Italy for the landing at Salerno. Meanwhile, I recovered enough to where I could get up and walk around and was shipped to a convalescent hospital. After about a month there they classified me as Class B duty, which meant that I couldn't go back into combat.

But I didn't want to spend the rest of the war sitting on my duff in North Africa. So, in November, I went out to the airfield where I knew they wouldn't ask any questions and caught a ride on a B-17 to Naples. From there, I made my way up to the front line, where I rejoined my company. When I got there, they were stalemated at the Gustav Line.

In December my company made a couple of assaults, trying to penetrate the enemy lines. But we couldn't make it across the valley in our

sector because the Germans were dug in on the high ground and decimated our troops every time we attacked.

I was always amazed at the how the American solider responded in
combat because it was a terrible, dirty business. The weather was awful.
When you're outside in December, and only have a foxhole to sleep in, and
it fills up with water all the time—it's miserable and depressing. But our
soldiers learned very fast how to adapt.

I loved the rifle company because that's where the action was. We
were the ones who went first in any attack. But it always amazed me—why
do men do that? Every attack we made, my men knew some of their buddies would be wounded or killed. Yet, when I gave the word, they moved
forward without hesitation. They were very good, brave men and I was
very proud of them.

In January, our whole division was pulled off the line and loaded up
on amphibious ships for the Anzio landing. It was supposed to be an end-
run around the Gustav Line that would catch the Germans by surprise
and get behind them so we could press on to Rome.

The landing went perfectly. We just walked ashore and nobody fired
at shot at us. But within a couple of days, the Germans brought in troops
from Northern Italy, Austria, and the Balkans. Before we knew it, they had
us outnumbered and surrounded with our backs to the water. When the
Germans counter-attacked on February 16, my battalion, which was on
the Anzio-Rome highway, was pretty well cut to pieces by those reinforced
German units.

My rifle company was straddling the road and I had four machine
guns with each platoon. I also had two tank destroyers with me from Division. The tank destroyers had three-inch guns and when the first three
German Panzer tanks came over the hill without any infantry in support,
those tank destroyers just blew them apart at about 200 yards range.

But later in the afternoon when the German tanks came again, they
came with infantry. So, they got my tank destroyers—pretty quick—they
went up in flames. Within an hour they effectively overran the units on

either side of my company—killing a lot of my men. So, I got on the radio and called for artillery fire on top of our position because we were in foxholes and the Germans were in the open. Well, I don't have to tell you—against troops in the open, artillery is devastating.

That night, with Germans moving in front of us, on both flanks and to our rear, I got a radio message asking if I could hold out. I said, "I think I can if I had some tanks." The CP said they'd send me a platoon of tanks during the night. When they arrived there were only two tanks, but the next morning there were enough of us alive that with the tanks we were at least forcing the Germans to avoid our little position.

By the morning of the third day, I had twenty-six men left. We dug in on a small hilltop more or less on line with one of the other two rifle companies that were left. But I had an artillery radio, so I could direct artillery fire all the time. The two tanks got called back around noon so we just dug our holes a little deeper, redistributed ammunition, and hung on. The Germans, for all practical purposes, ignored us.

We stayed up there for six days—cut off from anyone else except by radio. Almost all of our battalion had been wiped out and we finally got the word that a British battalion was going to try to relieve us. Just getting up to us, the British battalion lost almost half their men. A British major told me to wait until dark and then move back down toward the beachhead and make contact with friendly lines.

We sure tried. We broke up into two squad-sized units and started moving back toward the beach but the Germans woke up to the fact that Americans were moving through their lines and they started firing on us. We dove into a ditch, crawled through the German positions, and reached our lines at daylight.

Of the dozen men following me, only one sergeant made it. We were the only two members of my entire company of 192 men to make it back without being killed or captured. Our battalion had well over 50 percent casualties; in my company, we had 99 percent casualties; and the British battalion that came to relieve us was overrun.

The German counter-attack that wiped out Capt. Felix Sparks's rifle company finally succumbed to massive American air, naval gunfire and artillery bombardments. When the Wehrmacht 14th Army finally broke off their assault on 22 February, the Germans had sustained more than 5,300 casualties. Allied killed, wounded, and missing totaled nearly 3,500. The following day, General Lucian Truscott relieved Lucas as commander of VI Corps.

But a change in commanders didn't stop the killing. Over the course of the next two and a half months the Anzio beachhead came to look like a World War I battlefield as the Germans and the Allies probed each other's trench lines and pounded opposing fortifications with air and artillery strikes. The Germans even brought up a giant 280 mm rail-mounted siege gun to blast the Allied beachhead from the safety of the Alban hills. The Americans—living in a warren of stinking, sodden trenches and bunkers—had nicknamed the gun "Anzio Annie" and made wagers on when it would be silenced by an Allied air strike. It never was.

Finally, in mid-May 1944, the American 5th and British 8th Armies launched a concerted effort to breach the Gustav Line and break the siege at Anzio. On 18 May the Polish II Corps succeeded in capturing Monte Cassino in a costly, bloody assault. On 23 May, Truscott's VI Corps broke through the German 14th Army lines at Cisterna northeast of Anzio, and two days later effected a link-up with the lead elements of II Corps, which had charged north on Route 6, past Monte Cassino.

By the morning of 26 May, the twin Allied breakouts—at Anzio and Monte Cassino—had created an opportunity for Clark and the 5th Army to either encircle the bulk of the German 10th and 14th Armies or go for a victory parade in Rome. Ever conscious of the power of the press—and knowing that Overlord would soon consume every inch of newsprint—Clark chose Rome. On 4 June, less than forty-eight hours before the Normandy landings, the 5th Army marched into the city of the Caesars.

As the Americans were rolling past the Coliseum to the Piazza Venezia, Kesselring—the master of strategic withdrawal and defense—was extricating his battered but still capable 10th and 14th Armies to a new set of defensive positions further north. By early August he was firmly entrenched 150 miles north of Rome on the Gothic Line—a continuous set of fortifications that ran from Massa on the west coast to Rimini on the Adriatic. Behind him were the great industrial cities of Italy and the Alpine passes leading to the heartland of the Reich.

For the next eight months the campaign in Italy became a classic stalemate. In August 1944, Clark had to give up seven divisions for Operation Anvil—renamed Dragoon—the invasion of southern France. Throughout the winter of 1944–45, the Allies in Italy refitted and fought the bone-chilling cold as much as they fought the enemy.

In February 1945, Roosevelt, Churchill, and Stalin met at Yalta on the Crimean peninsula to discuss the shape of postwar Europe. In March, the U.S.-British Combined Staff urged a new Italian offensive to hasten the now-inevitable German collapse. Clark, now commanding the Allied 15th Army, was provided with additional air and land forces to break through the Gothic Line, but no sealift for amphibious operations.

By the second week of April 1945, Clark had massed seventeen divisions south of the Gothic Line and set 12 April as the date to commence a new offensive. Among those troops was Bob Dole, a young second lieutenant from Russell, Kansas.

SECOND LIEUTENANT ROBERT "BOB" DOLE
Company I, 3rd Battalion, 85th Infantry,
10th Mountain Division
18 May 1945

I became a member of the enlisted reserve in December 1942 and got one of those "ninety-day wonder" commissions from Officer's Candidate School at Fort Benning, Georgia, in November 1944.

I've always wondered how I ended up in the 10th Mountain Division. I'm from Kansas, where there aren't any hills—much less mountains. The division was full of great skiers and mountain climbers—but I had never learned to ski.

At one time, you had to have at least two letters of recommendation to get into the 10th Mountain Division. The idea for such an outfit had come from the president of the American Ski Patrol—Minnie Dole. I don't think he's any relation but maybe that's why the Army sent me there.

I arrived in Italy just before Christmas, 1944, and by early January of '45 I was in a replacement depot with a whole group of 2nd lieutenants when we were told to report to the units up on the Gothic Line. Second lieutenants were sort of expendable in those days.

I was ordered to the 10th Mountain. General George Hayes, the division commander, was revered by the "mountaineers." He was a great leader. When I arrived in early February '45, the division was fighting on Mount Belvedere. The company commander in Company I, 3rd Battalion of the 85th Regiment was Captain Butch Luther, the great All-American football star of Nebraska. And a day or two after I got there I remember seeing his helmet, with a hole right between the captain's bars. He was killed and several second lieutenants were killed or wounded. Our new company commander was Captain Jerry Butcher.

Company I sustained more killed-in-action than any company in the 10th Mountain Division. Our company always seemed to be on the cutting edge when things were happening. But when you come in as a replacement you kind of feel like, "I'm the only stranger in the town here. Are they going to accept me?" Are they going to say, "This guy doesn't know anything?" Or, "You're one of these ninety-day wonders out of Fort Benning. Where have you been while we've been training at Camp Hell?"

But I needn't have worried. They were good soldiers and they accepted me as one of their own. I was assigned as a rifle platoon commander, replacing a lieutenant who'd been killed.

Sergeants Carafe and Kuschick were my two leading NCOs. They helped me get the lay of the land, ran things, and helped me along. They showed me around our lines and took me out on orientation patrol right after I arrived.

A few nights after I joined the company I was leading my own patrols. One night a week or so later, we were out on a night patrol, probing the German positions, and we ran into some Germans. In the ensuing fight, seven of us were slightly wounded. That was my first combat experience—and for weeks afterwards it was like that every night in those cold Italian mountains.

In the daytime we kept in our foxholes and tried to stay warm without getting hit by enemy artillery or mortars. At night we patrolled in the mountains and tried to keep from getting killed by rifle fire and grenades.

I remember back in the States, right after I came into the Army, seeing guys training with broomsticks when I was in the 75th Division. We weren't very well prepared back then. But these men in the 10th Mountain were well trained, experienced, and disciplined—mentally and physically.

Winter in the mountains of Italy is very cold. Our winter equipment wasn't the best—and I remember never being able to get warm the whole time I was there.

We were supposed to start a big push to punch through the German defensive line on April 12, but President Roosevelt died that day. Of course everyone was in tears and shock—we were just kids, we didn't know anything about politics—but we knew our president died, and he was our commander in chief. So that delayed everything for two days.

I've often wondered what would have happened, had he lived, and had our offensive went off as scheduled. Maybe I wouldn't have been shot, who knows? But the offensive was postponed. After a couple days to get over the death of our commander in chief, it all started again on the fourteenth of April. That day we got up quite early about 5 a.m., got everything together, and started down the road and then up the hills.

There was a hill—number 913—that's the height of the hill in feet—near a little village called Castel Diano. The hilltop was our first battalion objective. After we cleared the village and took Hill 913 we were to move on to our next objective—Hill 785—but I never made it to 785.

As we moved up on Hill 913, Company I was the point for the battalion and we began to take a lot of fire—and a lot of casualties. My platoon was in the lead for the company and my radioman, Corporal Simms, was hit first by the Germans firing down on us.

I ran to get Corporal Simms to try to get him back into some cover. As I was dragging him back toward a hole, I felt this blow to my neck and this stinging in my right shoulder. It must have been a shell fragment—too big for shrapnel from a grenade—because it broke a couple vertebrae in my neck and pretty much messed up my shoulder.

I lay there for a long time with a lot of firing going on around us—and I remember Sergeant Kuschick wrote an "M" with my blood on my forehead—M for morphine so that the medic would give me some when he got to me. Sgt. Kuschick stayed with me for quite a while before the platoon had to move on up the hill. Before he left to continue the attack, he jammed my rifle with the bayonet into the dirt beside me and put my helmet on the stock so our company medics would see it and know—somebody's there who needs attention.

I waited a long time. Finally the medics and litter bearers got to me and they started to carry me down the hill. It was very rough going and I remember being scraped along the rocks a couple of times. I just vaguely remember the sharp pain in my back. Then everything kind of went black.

I recall waking up in a field hospital where there was a whole line of wounded soldiers, all on litters. It turned out that the 10th Mountain Division suffered more casualties that day than at any other point in the war. We had a total of maybe five hundred or more killed and that day.

Despite the losses, the 10th Mountain made all its objectives that day—and went on to take Hill 785. A few days later Company I crossed the River Po. Unfortunately, I wasn't with them for all of that—or for the big celebration when it was finally over on May 2.

From the field hospital I was brought back to the Italian coast, then eventually put on a hospital ship back to the States, and ultimately got back to Russell, Kansas. I spent four years in rehabilitation. I couldn't use my left arm, and it took me about eleven months to get on my feet again. I had a blood clot in my lungs, and had tremors in my hand, for which they injected snake venom

Then I lost a kidney, and everything just seemed to be going downhill. I lost about seventy-five pounds. But then I'd look around and see somebody who was *really* sick. You think you're pretty sick, until you see them carting somebody out who died in the bed next to you.

You say, "I'm still here." But it was a long recovery. You say, "I can't be too discouraged," yet you get discouraged anyway. I couldn't dress myself. I had to ask somebody to help me with my shirt, and for a while, help with normal functions, like going to the bathroom and things like that. But once I got beyond that, I learned I could do most anything with a buttonhook. I can get dressed. I don't have much feeling in my right hand. But I've learned to adapt, and it works out pretty good.

On 14 April 1945, the day that Bob Dole was wounded, the 10th Mountain Division breached the German defensive line and opened a hole for other Allied troops to pour into northern Italy. But it came at a terrible cost. Of the 19,734 soldiers who served with the 10th Mountain Division in Italy, nearly 5,000 were casualties—nearly a third of them on the day that 2nd Lt. Bob Dole fell. His regiment lost 370 men killed in action, 1,427 wounded, and three who were captured and made POWs. But the seven-day offensive reached its goal, breaking the back of German resistance in Italy.

National Archives

10th Mountain Division in Italy.

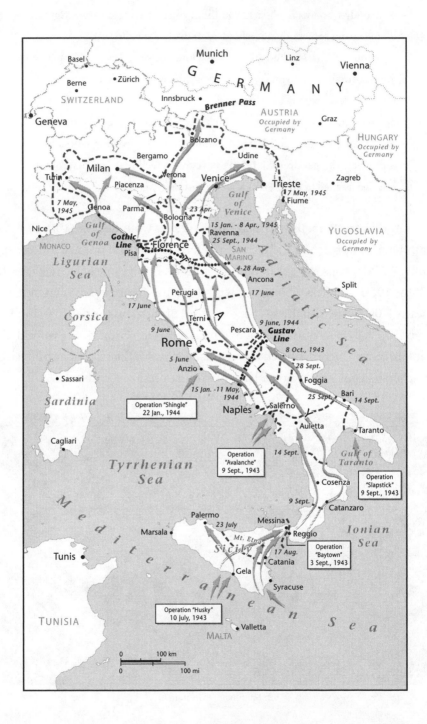

Thanks to the courage of the Mountaineers, the Allies were able to cut off a German retreat into Austria and sweep through to Trieste, Yugoslavia—where Mark Clark's army met the advance force of Marshall Tito's Yugoslav army. By then, the man responsible for so much death and destruction in his homeland of Italy was dead. On 28 April 1945, Italian Communist partisans captured Benito Mussolini, his mistress, and a dozen other fascists near Lake Como, as they were attempting to flee to Switzerland. They were all promptly executed.

The twenty-two-month-long battle for the boot had tied up—and eventually destroyed—more than a score of German divisions. Though the bloody Anzio-Cassino battles would turn out to be the most costly killing field in the European theater, the Germans who fought there could otherwise have been used against the Allies in France or later on, in Germany.

CHAPTER 8
WAR IN THE SKIES
1941–1945

In the summer of 1939, when World War II began in Europe, the entire United States Army Air Corps consisted of fewer than 1,200 combat aircraft, and the U.S. Navy had less than 900. These planes—fighters, transports, bombers, and patrol aircraft—were spread from the Philippines to the U.S. East Coast. That same summer, Adolf Hitler's Luftwaffe massed more than 4,000 combat aircraft for the attack on Poland.

The disparities in air power had been growing since Hitler came to power. By 1935, Germany's reinvigorated armament factories were turning out modern, low-wing fighters and multi-engine bombers. During the Spanish Civil War, from 1936 to 1938, hundreds of German pilots gained valuable combat experience that would benefit the Luftwaffe when war in Europe began.

U.S. military planners were not ignorant of these realities. Air power advocates were simply unable to convince isolationists in Congress to appropriate sufficient funds for building a modern air force. In the midst of the Great Depression, expenditures for military aircraft and training pilots was problematic even though the employment of aircraft in World War I—first for reconnaissance and observation, then as a means of supporting armies on the ground with bombs and guns—had galvanized the imagination of strategic thinkers around the globe.

In Italy, Giulio Douhet postulated in 1921 that future wars could be won by airpower alone, employing massive bombing attacks—not against an adversary's front lines, but against the enemy's cities and war production centers. British, Japanese, and German aircraft designers, military officers, and political leaders seized on Douhet's theories to start modernizing their respective air forces.

In the United States, the most outspoken proponent of air power was U.S. Army Air Corps Brigadier General Billy Mitchell. In July 1921, with scores of politicians and military brass looking on and cameras documenting the event, Mitchell's aircrews—flying WWI-era aircraft—bombed a group of obsolete American and captured German vessels anchored off the Virginia Capes. Though the "unsinkable" battleship *Ostfriesland* went to the bottom, the demonstration failed to convince opponents that America needed a large, independent air force.

Two years later, in a 1923 report that he described as "the masterpiece" of his career, Mitchell predicted—nearly two decades *before* Pearl Harbor—that a Pacific war would begin with a naval and air attack on Pearl Harbor at 7:30 a.m. on a Sunday morning! He was off by just twenty-five minutes.

But Billy Mitchell's unwavering and assertive manner made him more adversaries than allies. He resigned from the military in 1926 after being exonerated in a court martial for insubordination. He died ten years later—still advocating the need for a modern, independent Air Force.

Throughout the 1930s, opponents of military expenditures in the midst of the Great Depression pointed to the two vast oceans that protected the continental United States from attack by enemy bombers. But as Europe and Asia edged closer to conflagration, Roosevelt was able to convince Congress to start building small numbers of more modern fighters and bombers. That also required that pilots, aircrews, mechanics, and aircrews be trained to fly and maintain them.

By the time Hitler invaded Poland in 1939, new designs for modern fighters and bombers were coming off the drawing boards and U.S. aircraft companies were being granted small contracts for prototypes to be tested by the Navy and the Army Air Corps. Equally important, thousands of young American men were enrolled in government-subsidized civilian pilot training.

Many of those who sought to fly before Pearl Harbor were inspired by the accomplishments of solo pilots like Charles Lindbergh and the heroic exploits of World War I pilots. Articles, books, and movies about Erich von Richtoffen—Germany's "Red Baron"—and America's leading "ace"— former race car driver Eddie Rickenbacker—captured the imagination of millions.

Those who flew small, one-seat, single-engine fighters were depicted as modern incarnations of ancient knights—doing battle one-on-one. Instead of four-legged steeds, these warrior-pilots had sleek, lethal machines, powerful engines, and the ability to twist, turn, climb, and dive through blue sky.

For tens of thousands of young American men, these were alluring images in the midst of the privations of the Great Depression. Nearly all of those who volunteered—and could pass the demanding physical and eyesight requirements for pilot training—knew that Rickenbacker had twenty-six "kills" and that the Red Baron had eighty. Though few would admit it at the time, most of them nurtured the idea of becoming an "ace"—and knew that such a designation required five air-to-air kills.

In 1939 and 1940, several hundred young aviators left the United States for England, China, and Canada—not to *avoid* the war, but to test their proficiency and courage against the Germans and Japanese. Americans serving with the RAF "Eagle Squadron" and Claire Chennault's "Flying Tigers" quickly learned that the enemy aircraft and pilots they went up against were tough adversaries. Becoming an "ace" turned out to be a lot tougher than some had thought.

Robin Olds was a second-year cadet at West Point when the Japanese bombed Pearl Harbor. The son of a WWI ace, he had heard of his father's exploits in open cockpit aircraft over France—and had long ago decided to become a pilot. Second Lieutenant Olds arrived in England in May 1944, after graduating with honors from the military academy and flight school.

His first assignment was to help protect the Normandy landings from German air attack. Olds dutifully attacked ground targets, but he was at heart a fighter pilot, and looked forward to the challenge of meeting the enemy in air-to-air combat.

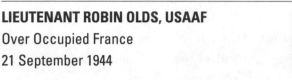

LIEUTENANT ROBIN OLDS, USAAF
Over Occupied France
21 September 1944

Dad took me up on my eighth birthday in a biplane with an open cockpit. I still get a thrill thinking about it. From the moment I felt the breeze on my face, I wanted to fly.

I remember Sunday, December 7, 1941—when one of my classmates at West Point came running up to me excitedly saying, "They bombed Pearl Harbor!"

"Who did?" I asked.

"The Japanese," he said—as though I should have known.

After graduation and flight school, I was sent to England, where our squadron flew missions over Normandy. By August, I'd been flying combat missions for more than three months and never saw an enemy airplane—but then in August, our zone of operation shifted and all that changed. Flying alone over France, I got a chance to smoke two German Focke Wulf 190s.

Just eleven days later another pilot and I, flying in P-38s, came upon a gaggle of fifty Messerschmidt 109s, and I radioed my group leader and said, "I'm going after some bandits, headed north." I could have given him more details, but hell, they were *my* bandits. I didn't want to share them with anybody.

The first one still hadn't seen me when I slid in behind him for the kill.

But just as I lined up my gun sight and was about to pull the trigger, both engines quit on my plane. I was so excited I had forgotten to switch fuel tanks after dropping my empty tanks—but I shot him down anyway. To this day, I may be the only fighter pilot in the history of aerial warfare that ever shot down an enemy airplane while flying a "glider."

After getting my engines restarted, I downed another ME-109, and then rolled into a dive. As I got closer to the ground, my controls froze. I remember saying to myself, "You're just going straight down and crash, and that'll be it."

But I managed to pull out at the last instant and just barely cleared the ground. So I said, "This boy has had it—that's enough. No more fighting now, I just want to go home."

As I started my turn for home, I looked over my left shoulder and there was another ME-109 shooting at me. And I thought, that's not fair—can't he see that I'm scared and want to go back to base? I mean—he's taking an unfair advantage of me.

Instinctively, I pulled a hard break, and that old P-38 of mine shuddered, almost turned, and stopped. The poor 109 pilot overshot my position and I just rolled the wings level—now he was right in front of me. So I took aim and shot him down. *Then* I went home.

The competition in the skies to rack up "kills" was fierce. All claims of air-to-air victories were supposed to be verified—either by another flyer who witnessed the enemy airplane go down, or by gun cameras that provided a permanent visual record of hits and kills. The squadron intelligence officers who tallied the scores would often say, "A picture is worth a thousand words."

But not all gun camera film could be recovered. Charles "Chuck" Yeager had such an experience over France. Yeager was, by his own description, "just a West Virginia farm boy." Born in 1923, he never even got close to an airplane until he was eighteen. His first flight didn't go very well.

LIEUTENANT CHARLES YEAGER, USAAF
Over Occupied France
23 September 1944

I enlisted in September of '41, just after finishing high school, and became a ground crewman on AT-6s. I was on liberty that Sunday and heard on the radio that the Japs had bombed Pearl Harbor—and that we were to report to our base.

A few days later I applied for pilot training and they took us up for a familiarization flight. As soon as we took off, motion sickness took over and I puked all over the airplane. When we got back on the ground, I said to myself, "Man, you've applied for pilot training. You've made a big mistake."

After months of pilot training in the States, I finally arrived in Europe in the fall of '43 with the 357th Fighter Group. In the spring of '44 we were given new planes, P-51 Mustangs. With the P-51 we had eight hours of endurance and could fly all over Europe—and we did.

On 4 March 1944 I was on my seventh mission in the skies over Germany, flying my P-51 Mustang—nicknamed "Glamorous Glen," after my wife, Glennis—when I spotted a German ME-109 flying alone, below me. Combat flying is a matter of self-survival. If you don't get him, he'll get you. I wanted to get him before he got me.

I pulled the P-51 up and into a big roll and slid up under the ME-109. He never saw me. I got in to about 200 yards, opened fire, and he blew up. It was my first kill, but the very next day, in a wild dogfight over France, I was on the losing end. A burst of German 20 mm shells took *me* down.

First thing I knew the prop came off my airplane, then part of the left wing, and then the canopy. So my airplane and I parted company. I came out of the plane, probably around 18,000 feet, and free-fell for awhile because it had been rumored that the Germans might strafe you in your parachute. I pulled the D-ring on my chest, the chute popped open, and as I swung by the top of a pine tree, I grabbed it and let myself down.

Now there's not a German in the world who can catch a West Virginian in the woods. So when I hit the ground, I rolled up my parachute and took off. The next day, I made contact with a French woodcutter. I couldn't speak French and he couldn't speak English. He went to get a guy who could, and he asked me, "What do you want to do?"

I told him, "I want to get into Spain. It's a neutral country."

I spent a month on the run with the French underground, before they turned me and another downed pilot loose in the Pyrenees Mountains just north of the Spanish border. It took us about four days to get across, with no food to speak of.

After nearly two months in Spain I finally got back to England—the first pilot from my fighter group to return after being shot down. Everyone wanted to know how I had evaded the Germans so long. I told them that the French resistance hid me in bordellos because the Germans weren't allowed to visit prostitutes. It was a tall tale, of course, but some of the guys in the group said that they were going to bail out the next day to check it out for themselves.

To protect the French resistance, downed pilots who escaped weren't supposed to go back into combat for fear that if they were captured they might divulge the underground's secrets. But a few weeks after I got back, I met General Eisenhower. And I told him that I didn't want to go home. He asked, 'Why?'

I told him, "It's because I haven't done my job yet, General."

As a result, on 12 October 1944, I was back in the hunt—and not long afterwards, spotted sixteen ME-109s. I came up within about 200 yards behind them and opened up on the tail end 109. He broke, and ran into his section leader—and they *both* exploded. Then all hell broke loose.

There were airplanes going every which way. One of 'em started to turn and get inside me so I let him have it. It was the kind of shot where you have to remember to lead your target—the kind of deflection shooting you do when bird hunting.

When he blew up, his wing-man cut his power back, and tried to get behind me. But when he did that, I cut my own power, skidded out, kicked right rudder, and man, just sawed him in two with those six .50-caliber guns. By then I was low on fuel and ammo but I then saw another guy headed for the deck. So I followed him down, and blew him up. There was no point going home with ammo in the guns.

Yeager's "matter of fact" narrative on how he got five kills in one day is extraordinary—but typical of the understated way in which his fellow World War II aces described harrowing air-to-air combat. A month after this engagement, Chuck Yeager became one of the first fighter pilots to shoot down an enemy jet—the ME-262.

After the war, Yeager became a test pilot. On 14 October 1947, flying another "Glennis"—the experimental X-1 aircraft—he became the first man go faster than the speed of sound. Asked what he considered his greatest accomplishment, he replied, "Probably the most *useful* thing I ever did was break the sound barrier. But the most *exciting* flying I've ever done was in combat."

That's a common sentiment among World War II fighter pilots. Most of them seem to have been born with an innate aptitude for flying—and an instinct for survival on the ground when they found themselves downed behind enemy lines. Walker "Bud" Mahurin of Fort Wayne, Indiana, demonstrated both of these qualities during the air campaign against Hitler.

Mahurin joined the Army Air Corps in 1941 and was in primary flight training when Pearl Harbor was bombed. By 26 November 1943, he had already become an ace with seven kills to his credit. That afternoon, while escorting American bombers on a raid over Bremen, Germany, he downed three German ME-110s. Now with ten kills, Mahurin ranked number eight in the Army Air Force "Double Ace" club. It was an impressive achievement—to everyone but Bud.

LIEUTENANT WALKER "BUD" MAHURIN, USAAF
Occupied France
21 May 1944

When we got into the war we didn't know much of anything about the capabilities of the German and Japanese planes. We barely knew what they looked like. We had questions like: What's their range? Can they bomb the United States? How good are their fighters? We really had very little information.

I joined the Army Air Corps in 1941 and after training I was sent to England in 1943. We were flying a lot of escort missions over France at the time. That's where I got to know the German planes really well.

The first ones I ran into over France were Messerschmidt 110s—twin-engine fighters with a gunner in the back. I brought my P-47 Thunderbolt in from above and behind, got as close as I could, and opened fire. I hit him repeatedly and he eventually went down. I pulled out from that one, turned over, and saw another ME-110. I went after him, shot him down, and then found a third, which I also smoked. And then I found one that was headed back into Germany, and I followed him a while, took a shot at it, and damaged it but he got away.

The main thing that I learned from that dogfight was that as I went by the first airplane I hit, the gunner in the back had obviously been wounded, and maybe killed. His body was caught in the wind as the airplane went down. And as I watched it I'm aware of the fact that we're chasing after other human beings, and not just a machine that's flying in the air.

Our victories and our challenges were not that impressive to me. A lot of the Royal Air Force pilots we met over there had flown in the Battle of Britain and had shot down twenty or twenty-five German airplanes. So after awhile I stopped counting.

On 27 March 1944, I was shot down over France and started my stint behind enemy lines. I had never used a parachute before but it worked as advertised and I made it safely to the ground.

I knew that I wasn't far from Orleans—but that was over 130 miles from the coast—and I was in the heart of German occupied territory. I made up my mind right then that I wasn't going to get captured.

I hid in the fields for a day—and then made my way to a farmhouse. The farmer could have turned me in, but instead, he took me to the local French resistance group. Once they were sure that I really was an American, they started making arrangements to get me out of France.

Nearly every night the group I was with would move me to a new hiding place and hand me off to a different Resistance unit. This was extremely dangerous for them because the Gestapo and the German Army were always looking for downed American and British pilots. Whenever the Germans saw a parachute coming down—or they found one of our planes wrecked but no body in it—they would flood the area with search parties. If I got caught, I'd be sent to a POW camp. But if the Resistance guys got caught, they would be executed on the spot.

During daylight I hid in haystacks, barns, farmhouses, and basements. Then at night, we would move to a new location. Finally, they made arrangements to have a light airplane fly over from England to pick me up. We went to the field where he was to land and waited but the plane didn't make it. Later on I learned that the airplane that was supposed to pick me up flew over a German airbase and got shot down.

It took five more days for the Resistance to make arrangements for another flight to come over and get me. During those five days, I lived with the Inspector of Police in the city of Orleans. He decided to hide me in plain sight.

Each day, the inspector would go into the Gestapo headquarters in the center of the city. It had a big Nazi flag hanging over the door—and German soldiers standing guard. Because I didn't speak French, the inspector dressed me up in old French farm clothing and told me to pretend I was goofy. He would go into the Gestapo headquarters for his daily meeting and I'd wait outside—right on the street in plain sight of the German soldiers, mumbling nonsense and stumbling around. If anyone tried to question me I would pretend like I was nutty—that way I wouldn't have to answer any questions.

After five days of acting crazy, another rescue attempt was made. This time the little plane made it in. The inspector and all the Resistance guys kissed me on both cheeks and I flew back to England.

Because I had seen so many of the French Resistance people and knew how the rescues were being done, I was sent back to the States for a war bond tour, and then reassigned to the Pacific.

The experiences of fighter pilots like Robin Olds, Bud Mahurin, and Chuck Yeager were typical of those of many who fought in the air against Hitler's Luftwaffe. By virtue of their courage and exceptional skill they became aces—members of a very select group of pilots from any war.

During World War II there was another very select group of American fighter pilots who were unique not just because of their daring and ability but because of the color of their skin. The tails of their planes were painted red—but their skin was black. They became known as "The Tuskegee Airmen," named for the place in Alabama where they trained to wield fighters against the best that the Luftwaffe could put in the sky.

Moton Field in Tuskegee, Alabama, was a tiny municipal airport in 1941, when war was raging in Europe and America was getting ready to fight. In July of that year a small group of Americans—all of them volunteers—gathered there to build the only all-black unit for the U.S. Army Air Corps.

In the 1940s the American military, like the rest of our country, was segregated. While the degree of segregation varied from state to state, it was strictly adhered to within the U.S. military. Mess halls, barracks, barbershops, and all other facilities were all separate.

Though black Americans had been a part of the U.S. military in every war since the Revolution, with few exceptions they were assigned to segregated, all-black units—usually with white officers. Even after the start of World War II, with the desperate need for men in every branch of the service, there were many who believed black men couldn't fly combat aircraft.

Foreseeing the likelihood of war when Hitler unleashed his blitzkrieg and invaded Poland in 1939, President Roosevelt had convinced Congress to create the Civilian Pilot Training Program. The CPT was open to all Americans—male, female, black, white—and in most cases the program was administered in affiliation with a local college or university. Among the scores of centers offering CPT there were only six all-black schools where the program was offered. One of them was the Tuskegee Institute in Alabama.

At the beginning of 1940 there were just 125 licensed black aviators. A year later, there were 231. This small evidence of progress gave these young black men hope that the U.S. Army Air Corps would let them fly. And it did.

In January 1941, FDR ordered a reluctant General "Hap" Arnold, chief of staff of the Army Air Corps, to start accepting black American pilots. Arnold formed the all-black 99th Pursuit Squadron as an "experiment," and announced that training would take place in Tuskegee, Alabama.

The surprise attack on Pearl Harbor occurred as the first cadets were training. Four months later, the first class got its wings. But the course was tough—two out of three cadets washed out. Many might well have been good enough to earn their wings—but there were only thirty-five pilot slots available in the 99th Pursuit Squadron. Lee Archer grew up in Harlem, and he wanted one of those slots.

CAPTAIN LEE A. ARCHER, USAAF
Ramitelli Airbase, Italy
21 August 1944

I was born in New York and raised in Harlem. In 1939 I volunteered to come into the service—and asked for the Army Air Corps. I took all the necessary tests and passed them easily. But then a lieutenant told me,

The dramatic rescue at Dunkirk in Operation Dynamo, 27 May–4 June 1940, saved the British Army to fight again.

Churchill inspired the people of England to weather the idea of "blood, toil, tears, and sweat."

The pilots who flew the Hawker Hurricane (above)
and the Supermarine Spitfire (below) were the heroes of the Battle of Britain.

US C-47 transports were the backbone of Allied air transport.

German air attacks against the Sicilian invasion fleet often had lethal effects.

Crew of the Liberty ship SS *Booker T. Washington* after making their maiden voyage to England.

Landing at Normandy 6 June 1944.

A U.S. soldier stops by a killed German soldier on the road to St. Lô.

U.S. troops march through Paris after it was liberated on 25 August 1944.

101st Airborne troops guide U.S. re-supply planes into Bastogne.

U.S. soldiers murdered by German SS at Malmedy 11 December 1944.

National Archives

The horrors of Nazism are exposed at Buchenwald Concentration Camp.

National Archives

Marshal Zhukov decorates General Montgomery with the Russian Order of Victory outside General Eisenhower's headquarters as the Allied leaders celebrate Victory in Europe.

Berlin came at a heavy cost, but American troops knew they were fighting for a worthy cause.

"You're not going to be called. The Army Air Corps is not going to take any colored. We never had any, we never intend to have any, and so you're out."

When I got to Camp Wheeler in Macon, Georgia, I learned about the Civilian Pilot Training program—and heard that it was open to everyone, so I applied—and got accepted. In November 1942 I was officially transferred to the Army Air Corps and sent to the special unit at Tuskegee.

I seemed to have no trouble flying. I flew solo—graded as first in my class—was cadet first captain in basic training, and cadet first captain in advanced training for the whole Aviation Cadet Corps. And I graduated number one in my class, with orders making me a second lieutenant in the United States Army Air Corps, on 28 July 1943.

The 99th Tuskegee squadron was as good as any other fighter squadron in the Army Air Corps. One of the things that made us so good was that we stayed together as a unit. Because we were all black, we didn't get moved around to different squadrons like other pilots. We trained together, lived together, and eventually fought together. We knew each other so well by the time we went overseas, you could tell who was who by the way they talked, walked, or flew.

In April of '43 the 99th was ordered to North Africa and we were given the mission to fly a lot of patrols and provide support for the ground troops—dive-bombing, strafing, and the like—a lot of air-to-ground combat. We saw a lot of action but never got close enough to any enemy aircraft to engage them.

We spent most of the summer and fall on bomber escort missions over Sicily, fending German aircraft off our bombers. Then in January 1944, during the Anzio operation, the 99th became part of the 332nd Fighter Group. We were stationed in Ramitelli, Italy, near Naples, and our primary mission became bomber escort.

About the time we got there, the bombers were just getting the new Norden bombsights. The bombardiers claimed that with this new sight they could drop a bomb in a pickle barrel from 30,000 feet—and they wanted to stick to all-daylight bombings to get pinpoint accuracy on factories, airports, oil refineries, and mines.

The only trouble with daylight bombing runs is that it's a lot easier for the enemy fighters to find the bombers. On some raids 400 or 500 bombers would be sent out on a mission and the German ME-109s would come up and just rip into 'em. We heard of one raid where we lost *eighty* bombers. On every B-24 there's ten crew people—and the B-17s had a crew of thirteen. So if we lost 80 bombers—we lost *at least 800 men.*

After trying that a few times, they decided that the bombers ought to have fighter cover for these raids. The 99th was then given the mission of escorting the bombers of the 15th Strategic Air Force. Our job was to accompany the bombers on their runs to and from their targets and protect them so that the German fighters couldn't get take 'em out.

When we got this new mission they also gave us a new airplane. One day we were flying P-39s—and the next day we were in the P-47 Thunderbolt. It was a huge airplane—with a 16-cylinder radial engine—and built like a tank. It had eight machine guns—four in each wing—and at any altitude it could fly with anyone else. Later on we got the P-51s—an even better airplane. It could go further, stay longer, and go higher.

The guys in the bombers loved us—we never lost a single bomber to an enemy aircraft while we were protecting them. Sometimes over the target there were so many planes in the sky dodging around the bomber formations that the gunners couldn't tell friend from foe. One of the guys in the squadron had the idea of painting the tails of our fighters red so that the gunners wouldn't shoot at us by mistake. It was a good idea—and the bomber crews thanked us.

It was while we were flying those escort missions that I got all my kills—five of them. That should have made me an ace—but after my fifth kill, someone "reviewed" my first kill and sent me a notice that they had decided I should only have gotten credit for "half" a kill—meaning that another pilot or gunner had also hit the Me-109 I downed. The only trouble with that is that no one else ever claimed the other half! I figure somebody up the line just wasn't ready for a black guy to be an ace.

Racism wasn't really a problem overseas. We just did our jobs—just like everyone else. But when I came back to the States we came into Norfolk, Virginia, and as I came down the gangplank there was a sign: "Colored troops to the left—white troops to the right."

I was surprised and disappointed that things hadn't changed while I was gone.

By war's end, Tuskegee had trained over 1,000 black aviators and many thousands of mechanics and technicians. Their aircraft flew over 15,000 combat missions, destroyed over 250 enemy planes, and never lost a bomber to an enemy fighter.

After the war, President Harry Truman signed Executive Order 9981 desegregating the military—more than fifteen years before the 1964 Civil Rights Act—and ensured that minorities could serve in every branch and at every level of the U.S. Armed Forces. The daring deeds of the Tuskegee Airmen helped pave the way for today's soldiers, sailors, airmen, Guardsmen, and Marines. At the U.S. Air Force Academy, the inscription on the statue dedicated to them reads:

"The Tuskegee airmen rose from adversity through competence, courage, commitment, and capacity to serve America on silver wings, and to set a standard few will transcend."

The men flying the fighters—no matter what color they were—quickly learned that there was plenty of excitement but far less romance to flying than they had imagined when hearing about it before the war. Those who flew the bombers knew that right from the start.

When America was thrust into war in 1941, the U.S. had but a handful of modern bombers. The twin-engine B-25s that Jimmy Doolittle's crews flew to raid Tokyo in April 1942 were good medium bombers, but they were limited in range and payload. The only "heavy," long-range bombers in production on the day that the Japanese attacked Pearl Harbor were the B-17 and the B-24.

Built by Seattle-based Boeing Corporation, the four-engine B-17 weighed twenty-seven tons, had a range of 1,850 miles, and could cruise at 170 mph at an altitude of 35,000 feet carrying a payload of 8,000 pounds. The B-17 bristled with thirteen .50-caliber machine guns, prompting a newspaper writer to describe it as a "Flying Fortress." The moniker stuck. Capable of absorbing incredible punishment and still remaining aloft, Flying Fortresses would drop *over a million tons of bombs* over Axis targets in Europe from 1942 through mid-1945.

Consolidated Aircraft Corporation in San Diego, California, was producing America's "other" heavy bomber at the start of the war—the high-wing, four-engine, twin-tail B-24 "Liberator." First tested in December 1939, the B-24 had a range of 2,900 miles, cruised at 175 mph, and carried an 8,800-pound payload. By the end of the war, 19,256 of them—more than any other aircraft in U.S. history—would be built and flown by every branch of the U.S. Armed Forces. Though there were twenty-two variants of the B-24 produced in five separate facilities between 1941 and 1945, most were equipped with eleven .50-caliber machine guns that proved lethal to attacking fighters. By 1944, the Ford production line at Willow Run, Michigan, was turning out a new B-24 *every fifty-eight minutes.*

With America in the war, production of B-17s and B-24s ramped up immediately. So too did the training of aircrews. Since most B-17s had a crew of thirteen and B-24s had ten, hundreds of thousands of men had to be trained to fly, fight, man, and maintain these fleets of planes.

Few of these young Americans had ever gone more than a few miles from home when they joined the Army Air Corps. Hardly any of them had ever seen an airplane close up, let alone flown in one before. Many didn't even have a driver's license.

It didn't matter. If they passed the tests to get in the Air Corps, they could be trained. And they were. Within weeks of Pearl Harbor, scores of new air bases were being built to accommodate the bombers coming off the production lines—and the aircrews that would spend nine months to a year learning all they could about these flying behemoths. Then, those assigned to the European theater would usually go to England for their final stages of training. There, most of the bombers and crews were assigned to the newly formed 8th Air Force.

On 17 August 1942, the Americans flew their first daylight bombing raid across the English Channel—striking German positions near Rouen, France. All eighteen B-17s returned safely.

On 20 August, a thirty-plane daylight attack was flown against the Luftwaffe base near Abbeville, France, in an effort to support the disastrous Allied amphibious raid at Dieppe. Once again, all the American B-17s returned safely.

Then, on 10 October, 100 USAAF B-17s launched an attack in the afternoon on German positions around Lille, France, near the Belgian border. The British followed up with an equal-sized nighttime raid on the same installations. In the Allied attacks, more than ninety German aircraft were destroyed on the ground and in the air, but only one British plane and two U.S. bombers were lost.

The success of these early attacks validated a strongly held thesis in the USAAF: that daylight bombing attacks were more accurate—and could be conducted with minimal losses. Officers in the British Bomber Command, having abandoned daylight raids almost a year earlier because of horrific losses, counseled otherwise. Over the next thirty-three months, the American "Bomber Boys" would pay a terrible price for their leaders' insistence on daylight bombing.

By the summer of 1943, American B-17 and B-24 bomber crews based in England and North Africa were striking near daily at Axis targets in France, Belgium, Italy, Austria, and Germany itself. Army Air Corps planners, convinced that strategic bombing could shorten the war, decided to try a massive raid to destroy Hitler's principal source of oil: the Ploesti refineries in Romania.

Operation Tidal Wave called for a 180-plane formation of B-24s to launch from airfields in North Africa and head north across the Mediterranean and over the Aegean Sea. After clearing the Balkans, the bombers were ordered to descend to an altitude of 500 feet or lower to avoid German radar. The B-24s would then drop their bombs on specific targets within the Ploesti oil fields and refineries, taking out the fuel supply for the Third Reich's war machine. The nearly 2,000-mile round trip was to be conducted in radio silence to preserve the element of surprise.

The challenges for the bomb groups assigned to the mission were formidable. In addition to the extremely long-range and low-altitude requirements, the American aircrews also had to avoid German fighters, hundreds of anti-aircraft guns, and barrage balloons over the target. Captain Richard Butler of San Diego, California, was a twenty-one-year-old B-24 co-pilot on the mission. Though he had already seen plenty of action over France and Germany, he volunteered to go on the Ploesti Raid.

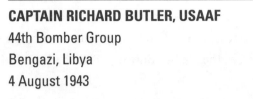

CAPTAIN RICHARD BUTLER, USAAF
44th Bomber Group
Bengazi, Libya
4 August 1943

We arrived in England in the spring of '43 and our first few missions were diversionary flights out over the English Channel. We would take off in a large formation and try to get the Germans to come after us so that a group doing a real raid would have a better chance. Several times yellow-nosed German Focke Wulf 190s out of Abbeville, France, intercepted us before we ever got to the French or Belgian coastline. They were very aggressive.

On 14 May '43 we flew our first real mission over France, where we lost a couple of airplanes. Then we were sent to bomb the submarine pens at Keogh, Germany. The mission was a disaster because B-17s flew over the target ahead of us and higher than our B-24s. So their bombs fell right through our B-24 formation and a couple of them hit our airplanes.

The B17s were also dropping incendiary bombs—clusters of four-pound sticks of explosives. As the incendiaries drop out of the airplane, bands around the bomblets break loose and all these sticks—there were about 100 in a bundle—fall and spread out. One of those incendiary sticks came through my windshield, and landed on the flight deck. Our radio operator picked it up with his leather flight jacket and threw it out the bomb bay—before it had a chance to ignite. According to the intelligence, our raid on the submarine pens put them out of commission—at a cost of seven of our airplanes.

In June of '43 we started practicing low-level flying in England—though we weren't told that we were going to North Africa until later in the month. When we got to Libya, we flew some missions over Sicily, in support of the invasion there, and several over Italy.

When we weren't flying actual missions, we practiced low-level attacks—out over the desert—flying at 500 feet or less—in formation. A couple of B-24s actually scraped the desert during those runs. Thankfully, we didn't lose anybody.

A few days before the Ploesti attack we were briefed on the mission, assigned specific targets, and told what we could expect. For example, we were told that the German 88 mm anti-aircraft guns couldn't be lowered enough to hit us at 500 feet or less because supposedly they were designed for shooting at planes at high altitude. And they told us that we didn't have to worry about enemy fighters—that if any came up, inexperienced Romanian pilots would be flying them. Most of this proved to be wrong.

On 30 July, the day before the mission, a general from Washington said, "If the mission is successful and the refineries are destroyed—but every one of our airplanes is lost—it would still be worthwhile. It can shorten the war by at least six months."

The morning of 1 August we were all up well before first light. Our group commander, Colonel Leon Johnson, said, "If anybody doesn't want to go—they don't have to go." But everybody went.

I was the co-pilot of our B-24 and Walt Bunker was the pilot. Walt was anything but a religious man, so I was surprised, as we were going out across the Mediterranean, to see Walt pull out one of the small Bibles we were issued and start reading it. I always carried mine with me and I got it out and read some Psalms. I had read from the Good Book on other missions, but I had never seen Walt reading a Bible. That kind of gives you an idea about how serious we were taking this mission.

Once we got across the Mediterranean and up the Aegean to the coast of Greece we had to pull up to clear the mountains in Greece and then Bulgaria. By the time we got over Romania, the skies had cleared, but some of the bombers in this long formation had gotten separated and off course in the clouds. Because we were flying on radio silence, some of them actually over-flew Bucharest, Romania.

Instead of hitting our targets in one long, continuous stream of bombers, we ended up with different groups of B-24s coming in over the refinery from different directions. The Germans must have known we were coming because they were ready.

As we approached our target we dropped down to about 300 feet. All of a sudden, there were all kinds of opposition. Haystacks swung open, and guns inside started firing at us. Off to our right, a train with guns on it was firing at us. We flew over a building that had a big red cross painted on top of it—and the guns on its roof opened up at us. Our B-24s were so low that the gunners were actually engaging anti-aircraft batteries on the ground.

Then, just about a mile from our target, German fighters appeared. An Me-109 came up behind our wingman on the right and blasted him out of the sky. A few seconds later, our bombardier, Henry Zweicker, called out: "Left! Left! Left!"—because he could see our aiming point, the boiler house for the whole Ploesti refinery. Our bomb bay doors were already opened or we would have over-flown our target. As it was, we hit it dead on.

Just as we crossed over the target, we hit a barrage balloon cable. We caught it right between the fuselage and the number three engine. The cable broke—fortunately. We lost number three engine and we also lost all of the instrumentation for number four engine.

Lloyd Neeper, our flight engineer, was in the upper turret. He said that our right wing came within twenty feet of scraping the ground. Well, we had one engine shut down, and some damage, but no one was injured. So we climbed on out of there and headed back to Libya. We didn't have any trouble knowing the way out. All we had to do was keep the enormous column of black smoke and fire behind us as we headed south. In a matter of minutes it was already rising thousands of feet into the air.

We had to fight the controls all the way home but we made it back to our field at Bengazi. When we landed, our fuel gauges were all reading "empty."

Richard Butler and his aircrew were among the favored few. Of the 178 B-24s that launched on Operation Tidal Wave, forty-one were lost during the raid, two collided en route home, and eight landed in Turkey and had their crews interned. Of those that made it back to Libya, many were too damaged to ever fly again. Five Medals of Honor were awarded to the men who flew this mission.

The attack on Ploesti was expected to destroy 75 percent of the refinery's capacity. Yet within two months, Hitler's engineers had restored it to full production.

Despite the loss of so many aircraft—and 481 American airmen dead or missing in action—proponents of "precision daylight bombing" continued to press their case. While the British maintained their "area night bombing" policy, the U.S. Army Air Corps mounted increasingly heavy daylight raids aimed at strategic industrial targets.

For example, on 13 August 1943, the U.S. 9th Air Force attacked the Messerschmitt aircraft plant in Austria. On 15 August, B-17s attacked the heavily defended ball-bearing plant at Schweinfurt, Germany. On 17 August 1943, 146 American bombers hit an aircraft plant at Regensburg, Germany.

A second raid on the Schweinfurt ball-bearing plant on 14 October was so bloody that the Army Air Corps dubbed it "Black Thursday." Sixty B-17s were lost, many more damaged, and 594 men were listed as killed and missing in action.

By January 1944, the Allies had wrenched southern Italy from the grip of Field Marshal Kesselring and the 15th Air Force moved to airbases in Foggia and Cerignola. Among the pilots at Cerignola was a twenty-one-year-old, South Dakota-born 1st Lt. George McGovern, who piloted a B-24 assigned to the 741st Squadron, 455th Bomb Group.

LIEUTENANT GEORGE MCGOVERN
741st Squadron, 455th Bomb Group
Cerignola, Italy
20 March 1945

In April of '42—four months after we were at war, ten of us who had been in the Civilian Pilot Training program decided to volunteer for duty as military pilots. We thought we were ready for combat. We'd all had thirty-five hours of CPT instruction and soloed in a single engine aircraft. Our only question was whether to be Navy flyers or Army flyers. We borrowed a car from the college president and another one from the dean of the school, and took off for Omaha—all ten of us.

The Army and the Navy had recruiting offices there for our area. After we got to Omaha, one of the guys picked up a rumor that if you signed up with the Air Corps, they'd give you a complimentary ticket to a cafeteria near the recruiting office. So, on the strength of that unsubstantiated rumor—for a meal that was probably worth about a dollar—all ten of us joined the Army Air Corps. That was the scientific basis we used to decide we wanted to be Army flyers.

Because there was a shortage of instructor pilots, we didn't get sworn in until February of '43. When we arrived at Jefferson Barracks, Missouri, we were put in the charge of a tough, old, hard-bitten Army sergeant. That was a rude awakening from life on the campus at Dakota Wesleyan University and I initially despised him—until we'd been in there a couple of weeks and came to realize he was trying to train us so we'd stay alive. We left there with a lifelong feeling of affection for Sergeant Trumbull.

After Basic in Missouri, we were sent to pre-flight training at the San Antonio Air Cadet Center, in Texas. From there we went to Southern Illinois University, where we learned navigation, meteorology, aircraft mechanics, and did a lot of physical training.

It wasn't until we were sent to Muskogee, Oklahoma, that we flew for the first time—in single-engine, open cockpit PT-19s. We then went to Coffeyville, Kansas, and multi-engine training at Pampa, Texas. Finally, at Liberal, Kansas, I got introduced to the B-24 bomber. The instructor was Norman Ray, the guy who had gotten me into the CPT two years earlier. He'd joined the Air Force a year and a half earlier than I had—and he was my instructor on the B-24 bomber. He was really tough on me—but I'm alive today because of Norman Ray and all those other good instructors I had.

I graduated in April of '44 and went to Lincoln, Nebraska, where I was assigned a B-24 and a crew. I was scared to death about what these guys would think. I was just twenty-one. Our flight engineer was thirty-three years old. The rest were eighteen, nineteen, and twenty.

They sent us to Mountain Home, Idaho, to the 2nd Air Force so we could all work together for six weeks—learning the plane—and how to become a team. We then went to Topeka, Kansas, for a final briefing before being shipped overseas out of Norfolk, Virginia. By the time I left for the war in Europe that summer of '44, I'd seen more of America than I'd even heard of just two years earlier. It was like that for a lot of us in World War II.

The Liberator was a good airplane, but it was very difficult to fly. We had to use every muscle in our bodies to keep that plane on course and altitude for eight, ten, or twelve hours. You had to keep it in formation in bad weather, and with people shooting at you. Later in the war, they added hydraulic controls. That was the equivalent of adding power steering to a Mack truck. I've seen 200-pound football players, solid muscle, who had to be lifted out of those cockpits after a mission—they were that exhausted. I was a little thinner and wiry, so it was easier for me to move around than some of the others. I was glad for every one of those physical fitness tests we took—because it took all of it to fly that airplane.

The B-24 wasn't heated, so when we flew at 20,000 to 25,000 feet, the temperature outside and inside would be around 45 or 50 degrees below zero. We were on oxygen from 10,000 feet on up. We had fleece-lined helmets with goggles, an oxygen mask, sheepskin-lined boots, and flak vests over a lined, leather jacket. It was very uncomfortable—particularly in turbulent air.

The Air Force had a practice when we first went into combat—we had to fly the first five missions with an experienced crew. So I went up five times in late October and early November of '44 as a co-pilot, with an "old" veteran pilot—he was probably twenty-three years old by then. He had circles under his eyes, and he'd flown about thirty missions. Those first five missions—one over Austria and four into Germany—weren't too bad—we saw some flak, but encountered no enemy aircraft.

The first mission that I flew as the pilot with my crew was to hit the aircraft assembly plant in Regensburg, Germany—a very heavily defended target.

I had thought, up until that point, that, "You know, this isn't going to be so bad. You see this flak all around you, but it hasn't hit us. So maybe this isn't going to be as bad as everyone said."

We were just pulling in on that bomb run when a piece of flak—molten metal—smashed through the middle of the windshield, hit a big steel girder right over our heads, and fell to the floor. If it'd been six inches to the left or right, one of us would have been beheaded, literally, by that piece of shrapnel. Our aircraft engineer was standing behind the co-pilot and me, leaning over looking at the instrument panel, and it went maybe an inch above his head. I turned around and his face was snow white.

We were flying at about 250 miles an hour, minus-50 degrees temperature outside—and we had to complete the mission. We went over the target, dropped our bombs, and came back. That first brush with death in an airplane sobered me up in a hurry.

Our base in Italy was cold, windy, and wet a great deal of time—lots of rain in southern Italy, where we were. But our living conditions were a lot better than the soldiers fighting at the front north of Rome.

In December of '44, we were speeding down the runway when, just as we were about to lift off, the right tire blew to smithereens. I had to make a quick decision—should I hit the brakes and try to stop the plane before the end of the runway, or should we yank it into the air? I chose the latter. I pulled up and we skimmed the ground for a long ways before we finally got up enough airspeed to climb. We missed the trees at the end of the runway by inches.

After we got some altitude, I called the tower and told them what happened. And they said, "Yes, we saw the blow-out."

I asked, "What do you think I should do?"

The tower replied, "Well, Lieutenant, that's up to you, but there are several options. You can head your plane out towards the Adriatic and bail out with your crew. Or you can go on the mission, drop your bombs, and when you get close in on your way back, bail out over the Adriatic. Or you can go on the mission, drop your bombs, and then try to land when you come back. We've had bombers come back on one wheel and land."

Since we were already in the air and getting into the formation to go attack Wiener Neustadt, in Austria, I decided to go ahead with the mission. I told the crew, "We've got a seven- or eight-hour mission ahead of us. When we get back, I'm going to land this plane. If any of you guys want to bail out before I try, you're welcome to do so. You have plenty of time to think about it and let me know." They all decided to stay with the plane.

When we got back, as I approached our field, I slowed the plane to just above stalling speed and touched down right at the end of the runway. As it turned out, it was the best landing I made during the war.

Our worst mission was probably over the Skoda Ammunition Works in Pilzen, Czechoslovakia, on our eighteenth mission in January '45. We lost an engine on the way into the target and so I advanced the other three engines to stay in formation. But over the target, right as we dropped our bombs, we got hit hard and lost another engine and got a number of flak holes in the fuselage.

On two engines we headed back to our base in Italy, but just as we reached the Adriatic—over the coast of Yugoslavia—we lost a third engine. We started losing altitude fast. I didn't want to ditch in the Adriatic because there were fifteen- to twenty-foot waves that day and figured if we hit one of those waves, the airplane would break to pieces and we'd freeze or drown in the water.

I asked the navigator, "Is there any place we can land this airplane?" He looked at the chart and said, "There's a 2,200-foot runway at the Isle of Vis, off to our left. Can you land this plane on twenty-two-hundred feet?"

I said, "Well, it's better than no feet. Let's do it."

As I lined up with the runway, I could see the carcasses of other bombers that had smashed into a hill at the end of the strip. Well, we put that plane down right at the end of the runway and my co-pilot and I both got on the brakes as hard as we could press. We were up out of our seats, jamming the brakes all the way down. She ground to a halt just a few feet from the end of the runway.

The crew was very appreciative—and gave me accolades for my skill as a pilot. It was the only time I saw that crew leap out of the plane and bend down and kiss the ground. But when you walk away from a landing like that, you don't worry too much about who gets credit for it—you're just glad to be alive. The next day they sent in a DC-3 in to pick us up.

There were two things that kept me steady during the war. One was the knowledge that every minute we were in the air, taking off, or landing, there were ten young lives that depended on me—and all ten of us would die if I failed or made a mistake.

I won't tell you that I wasn't afraid. I was afraid a lot of times. Anybody that tells you that they flew thirty-five combat missions over Germany in World War II and they never had a moment of fear, they're either crazy or they're prevaricating.

The average crew with the 15th Air Force only got to complete seventeen missions, so you can tell the casualties were heavy. We weren't fully aware of that at the time. We would see a couple of planes go down. Maybe a week later we'd see three or four more go down. What we didn't fully comprehend was how cumulative the losses became. Over a period of thirty-five missions, which was the quota for a crew, we had a casualty rate of around 50 percent.

I came back in '45, and went back to school, finished my B.A., and then went to Northwestern and got a Ph.D. After that I taught history and government for five years. I went into politics full-time in '56, ran for Congress, and to everybody's surprise, I got elected.

My friend Tom Brokaw talks about my generation being the Greatest Generation. I don't know about that. I don't think we were any greater than your generation, and others that have come along. It's just that we triumphed in a war that the country was behind.

The strip on the Isle of Vis, where Lt. McGovern landed his "Dakota Belle"—nicknamed for his bride, Eleanor—was *less than half* the length of a B-24 runway. For his skill and courage in completing the mission and safely landing his crew, he was awarded the Distinguished Flying Cross. George McGovern went on to be elected senator from South Dakota and was the Democratic Party candidate for president in 1972.

✪ ✪ ✪

By the time the war in Europe ended on 8 May 1945, more than 40,000 American airmen had been killed in action—a higher casualty ratio than that of any other branch of service in the U.S. Armed Forces during World War II. Another 80,000 were wounded in action, or in accidents or training—25,000 of them in the United States. Over 65,200 U.S. aircraft were destroyed by enemy fire, accidents, and mishaps. Nearly half of those who took off from bases in England, North Africa, and Italy to take on the Axis didn't make it back.

Though the idea that a war could be won by air power alone was invalidated during World War II, the contest did prove that air superiority was absolutely essential to victory. Whether they flew fighters, bombers, or transports—the pilots and aircrews who served in the European theater from 1941 to 1945 forged a legacy that persists to this day: that the United States could never again afford to be without the most advanced air force in the world.

CHAPTER 9
WAR AT SEA
1941–1945

It began on 3 September 1939, a little more than eight hours after Britain declared war on Germany. At 7:30 that evening, 250 miles northwest of Ireland, the German submarine U-30 torpedoed MV *Athenia*—a British-owned passenger liner, killing 118 of the 1,400 passengers and crew. They would be the first of tens of thousands to perish in what Winston Churchill called the "Battle of the Atlantic."

When Hitler invaded Poland on 1 September 1939—the event that precipitated World War II in Europe—he had only fifty-seven U-boats. They were under the command of Admiral Karl Dönitz—one of the most fervent acolytes in the Nazi cause. Within the span of a year, the number of U-boats at sea and attacking Britain's Atlantic lifeline would double—as would Allied shipping losses.

On 29 November 1939, Hitler issued Führer Directive Number 9, authorizing unrestricted attacks against vessels attempting to support the economy or military of Germany's adversaries. From then until the end of the war, Britain's 4,000-ship merchant fleet—the largest in the world—would be under attack from aircraft of the Luftwaffe, surface vessels of Germany's navy, the *Kriegsmarine* (small torpedo-firing and mine-laying

National Archives

The crew of the USCG cutter *Spencer* watching explosions sink a German U-175.

E-boats), and armed merchant raiders. But the greatest threat of all came from *Unterseeboots*—U-boats.

Hitler's goal was simple: to strangle Britain into submission. And it was not beyond the realm of possibility. The British Isles required nearly 60 million tons of imported products annually to support a peacetime economy. Food, raw materials for production, oil, non-ferrous metals, high-tensile steel, fabric for clothing, leather for boots, rubber for tires—all arrived in England via more than 10,000 shiploads per year. Karl Dönitz told the Führer that if he had 300 U-boats, Britain could be blockaded into capitulation. Hitler set out to give his loyal subordinate what he wanted.

To contend with the threat, the British first turned to the colonies of the United Kingdom—and then the United States. Even before Winston Churchill became prime minister on 10 May 1940, the Roosevelt administration was quietly doing what it could to help. Despite restrictive neutrality laws enacted by Congress, and just days after war began in Europe, FDR authorized the sale of munitions to Canada—though it was an open secret that Ottawa would simply transfer whatever it received to Britain.

U.S. convoy en route to England.

On 16 September 1939 the first large transatlantic convoy of war materiel and foodstuffs sailed from Halifax, Nova Scotia, for England. Until the U.S. entered the war, convoys of thirty to forty ships—shepherded by four to six armed escorts and equipped with "asdic" (British-invented underwater acoustic detection gear) and depth charges—would form up off Canada to make the Atlantic transit. For the next two years, convoys of ships under every flag in the British Empire, and many others "leased" by the British from "neutral" nations for the duration of the war, had to run a gauntlet of U-boats, surface raiders, and Luftwaffe attacks in order to reach or leave England.

In November 1939, Congress amended U.S. neutrality laws to permit France and Great Britain to purchase war materiel, provided that American-flagged vessels did not transport the arms. This action made essential arms and equipment more available to the democracies standing against Hitler, but did nothing to improve the delivery of these crucial provisions to those who needed them.

The problem of getting supplies to England was exacerbated even further in June 1940 with the fall of France. By July, Dönitz established submarine bases in both Norway and the Bay of Biscay—all but eliminating the problems of getting his U-boats out of the Baltic and significantly increasing their area of operations in the Atlantic. The French bases at Bordeaux, La Rochelle, St. Nazaire, L'Orient, and Brest—which Dönitz heavily fortified—halved the time it took for his U-boats to transit to their "hunting grounds." At the same time, the British were forced to recall many of their surface ships and patrol aircraft to defend against the possibility of a German invasion and to fight the "Battle of Britain" against the Luftwaffe. As the number of armed escorts and protective over-flights for convoys dropped, merchant losses increased dramatically.

The announcement—on 3 September 1940—that the U.S. would transfer fifty "obsolete" American destroyers to Britain in exchange for leases on British bases in the Atlantic was a morale builder in London, but made the immediate situation even worse. Hitler responded on 6 September by declaring that *all* merchant vessels—of *any* nation—attempting to deliver *anything* to Britain would be sunk. Dönitz and his U-boats did all they could to implement the threat.

By the autumn of 1940 German U-boats deployed from France and Norway were operating in "wolf packs" of ten to fifteen U-boats against convoys to and from the British Isles. Losses of ships, cargoes, and crews exploded. In September and October 1940 more than 125 vessels—800,000 tons of shipping—went to the bottom. Had winter weather not curtailed U-boat operations in the North Atlantic, it would have been worse.

Then, in December 1940, just weeks after his re-election for an unprecedented third term, FDR set out to change the equation. Publicly proclaiming that the U.S. had to be the "Arsenal of Democracy," he urged Congress to pass "Lend-Lease"—allowing the British to "borrow" or "buy-now-pay-later"—for arms, munitions, ships, and planes. In anticipation of congressional approval—which came in March 1941—American shipyards immediately commenced work on dozens of destroyers, destroyer-escorts, and cutters. Roosevelt also extended the U.S. "neutrality zone" east to Bermuda and all the way north to Iceland. He ordered the new U.S. Atlantic

Fleet to commence escorting convoys within this zone, thus freeing up British ships for operations closer to home.

Despite these changes, by the spring of 1941 shipping losses were again on the rise. With better weather, bigger U-boat wolf packs returned—and this time, the brand-new battleship *Bismarck*—the pride of Hitler's surface fleet—came with them.

When the British Admiralty discovered that the most powerful battleship in the world had sortied for the Atlantic, every available ship in the British Fleet was ordered to give chase, and merchant ships in eleven convoys scattered for the nearest friendly port. By the time the *Bismarck* was sent to the bottom on 27 May, the battleship HMS *Prince of Wales* had been badly damaged, the battle cruiser HMS *Hood* had sunk with all hands, and President Roosevelt had declared an Unlimited National Emergency.

In June of 1941, Hitler invaded Russia—further complicating the maritime supply situation, and bringing the U.S. ever closer to an armed confrontation. In August, the U.S. and Royal navies began escorting convoys laden with Lend-Lease supplies headed for Murmansk. On 4 September, the destroyer USS *Greer*, alerted by a British patrol plane, pursued U-652, which had been shadowing a convoy. When the U-boat fired a torpedo at its antagonist, the *Greer* responded with a depth charge attack. Then in October, the USS *Kearney* was damaged, and U-boat torpedoes sank the USS *Reuben James*. Both destroyers were defending convoys from wolf pack attacks when the attacks occurred.

By late autumn of '41, the weather in the North Atlantic once again curtailed U-boat operations. When Pearl Harbor was bombed on 7 December 1941, there were only a dozen German submarines operating along the British-Russian maritime supply routes. Though surprised by the Japanese attack, Dönitz quickly put together a plan for a massive U-boat strike against shipping lanes just off the American mainland. But on 11 December, the day Hitler declared war on the United States, he was directed by the Führer's senior staff to keep the bulk of his undersea fleet close to home.

Undeterred, Dönitz devised Operation *Palkinshlog,* or "Drumbeat"—using only five 1,100-ton, Type-9 U-boats. On the night of 23 December 1941, the five submarines deployed from L'Orient, France, for the 3,500-mile trip across the Atlantic. A week later, in a successful effort to confound Allied convoy planners, he dispatched a six-boat wolf pack of his smaller 740-ton U-boats to the waters off Newfoundland.

The operation was a stunning success—made more so by the lack of American preparedness for such an onslaught in waters off the East Coast. In just three weeks, starting in January 1942, the Drumbeat gambit sent twenty-six American vessels, 162,000 gross registered tons of shipping, and 252 American merchant seamen to a watery grave—many times within sight of land. Some called it "the Pearl Harbor of the Atlantic." The Germans called it "Happy Time."

For the next ten months Allied shipping losses were devastating—particularly along the U.S. East Coast and the Gulf of Mexico—where no convoys or protective procedures of any kind had ever been implemented. By April, U-boats had sunk eighty-seven ships—more than 500,000 tons. In May, Dönitz shifted south to the Gulf of Mexico, sinking another forty-one

U-3008 on patrol.

ships, mostly tankers. And though there were never more than a dozen U-boats operating along the U.S. east coast at one time, the worst was yet to come.

The warm waters of the Gulf Stream, just east of the American mainland, offered both lucrative hunting grounds for the U-boats and a welcome respite for German submariners who had been fighting in the cold waters of the North Atlantic for better than two years. One of those Germans who saw the U.S. for the first time from the deck of a U-boat was Peter Petersen. He was a nineteen-year-old diesel machinist when he joined the crew of U-518. Petersen had grown up near the Danish border and volunteered for U-boat service after he was drafted. He made three deployments to the U.S. coast starting that spring of 1942.

PETER PETERSEN
Machinist Mate, *Kriegsmarine*
Aboard U-518
14 November 1942

I volunteered for the U-boats because the pay was better and I thought that the guys on those boats were very brave. Our mission was simply to sink ships. My U-boat—U-518—was just one of 1,154 submarines that Germany built during the war. Each of the boats our size—and there were some larger—had a crew of about fifty-five men, and each could carry up to twenty-two torpedoes.

When we got to the American east coast in the spring of 1942, it was a shooting gallery. We found it very easy for us to sink ships there, because there were no convoys, no escorts, and no patrol aircraft at all on our first deployment. The American navy was nowhere to be seen. And the merchant ships had no idea how to handle it.

We were able to swim in the Gulf Stream during the day, take the sunlight on the deck, and listen to American music on the radio. We didn't need to operate in wolf packs because there were so many individual ships—

tankers and transports—traveling up and down the east coast without escorts. We would arrive on station off an American port like Charleston, post a lookout, and just wait for the ships to come steaming out.

Unlike the cities of Europe, American cities still had their lights on at night, making it easy to see the silhouettes of our targets. Some of them even steamed with their lights on. These slow-moving merchant ships were like sitting ducks.

On our first trip to the American coast, my boat, U-518, operated with U-123. Captain Hardegen, our leader, was a "drumbeater." He was a tough commander but a very successful one. On April 7, Captain Hardegen made an entry in his *kreigstaag* logbook, "We are marching again, tight along the land—from lighthouse to lighthouse that burn brightly as if during peace time."

I'll give you an example of a typical attack. On April 8, 1942, both of our U-boats were patiently waiting for our next kill off the coast of Georgia. Shortly after midnight, Captain Hardegen spotted an American tanker proceeding northward. It was the SS *Oklahoma,* a Texaco tanker.

Sometimes we would attack unescorted merchant ships with our deck gun, but this time, because we were so close to shore, he fired a torpedo—but it missed. We had to speed on the surface to catch up with the tanker and an hour and a half later he tried again. This time he hit his target—and the ship exploded instantly. It must have been carrying gasoline.

There were so many unescorted ships that we used up all of our torpedoes in just a few weeks and we had to go back to France to get more. This was the hard part of the trip—because we never knew when we were going into one of the bases in France if we were going to be attacked by British aircraft or ships.

Later on, after the Americans started convoys off the east coast, we took U-boats into the Gulf of Mexico. And when they started escorting down there, we moved further south—off the Panama Canal—and eventually all the way to Brazil. For those kinds of trips we would have to be resupplied and re-fueled at sea. For that, we had *"milch cow"* resupply submarines or merchantmen converted into tenders and we would replenish our fuel, food, torpedoes, and ammunition at sea.

As the war went on, it got more dangerous to be in a U-boat. The British and Americans built more ships than we could sink. Their sonar, radar, and depth charges got better and more effective. Long-range airplanes with radar were a very big threat. Boats like U-518 actually spent most of the time on the surface, because we couldn't stay down very long on our batteries. The biggest threat we faced was from airplanes that could spot us from the air with radar and drop bombs and depth charges on us and then call to a destroyer to finish us off.

When I completed my last deployment to the United States, we returned to our base in Norway. When we pulled into our base, we had been at sea for a total of 333 days. The first day ashore we could barely walk, because we had been confined to the U-boat for so long. The U-518 was a very good boat—because we made it back. Most of us didn't. Serving on a submarine in the Atlantic was very dangerous. Eighty percent of us did not come back.

Petersen's assessment of how dangerous it was to serve aboard a German U-boat is borne out by the numbers. From December 1939 to the end of the war in Europe in May 1945, Dönitz deployed 830 U-boats into the Atlantic and Mediterranean. Only 134 returned. Overall, the odds were little better. Counting those deployed in the Baltic, Indian Ocean, and the Arctic approaches to Russia, Dönitz committed 1,175 U-boats to the war but lost 781 or them. Of 40,900 German U-boat crewmen, 25,870 were killed and another 4,879 were captured when their U-boats were sunk or—in three cases—captured.

The convoy system, initiated by the British during World War I and implemented again by the Royal Navy in World War II, eventually doomed Hitler's effort to strangle the British Isles. Though Dönitz attempted to adapt his tactics and deployment patterns to counter the Allied convoy measures, he was never able to make up for losses in U-boats and trained crews as the U.S. and British improved their anti-submarine warfare capabilities. By May 1943, long-range variants of the American B-24 Liberator, Navy PBY-Catalina, and the British Wellington bombers made all but small areas of the mid-Atlantic deadly for U-boats and their crews.

German scientists invented dramatically improved magnetic and then acoustic-homing torpedoes, radar detection equipment, the *schnorkel*—air-intake devices—and even a hydrogen-peroxide propulsion system. But by mid-1943 Dönitz was losing more U-boats than German shipyards could replace, and Allied shipbuilders were launching more than six new ships for every one sunk.

National Archives

Navy PBY-Catalina—instrumental in hunting down U-boats.

Though warships were vital, so were transport vessels. The first Liberty ship, the USS *Patrick Henry,* was launched on 27 September 1941. By 1943, eighteen U.S. shipyards on the East, West, and Gulf coasts were launching "Liberty ships" as fast as they could be welded together. Valued at $1.5 million each, Liberty-class ships were 440 feet long and could carry nearly 10,000 tons of cargo at eleven knots. Over the course of the war, 2,708 Liberty ships were built—the fastest going from keel to completion in just four days.

To man these thousands of new vessels—and the new tankers and coastal freighters being constructed—the U.S. Merchant Marine put out an urgent call for able-bodied seamen. Nearly a quarter-million American men answered the call—many of them too old to be drafted, others who had been spurned by military recruiters for poor eyesight, others who were just too young. And unlike the military, the U.S. Merchant Marine service wasn't segregated.

Those who volunteered to serve in the Merchant Marines were putting their lives on the line just as much as any soldier, sailor, airman, Guardsman or Marine. Going to sea in a Liberty ship exposed a seaman to risk of being bombed by the Luftwaffe, sunk by a German surface combatant like the *Bismarck*, torpedoed by a U-boat, or attacked by one of Germany's ten surface raiders—deceptively constructed to look like a merchant ship, but every bit as lethal as any warship.

Throughout the war, the vessels most at risk of being attacked by a U-boat or a merchant raider were those that traveled alone. Though convoy operations were well underway by 1942, delays in loading, port and pier availability, and the need to deliver priority cargoes urgently were all problems that caused thousands of ships to make their transits without escorts. On 10 September 1942, George Duffy, of Newburyport, Massachusetts, the Third Mate aboard the Liberty Ship *MV American Leader,* found out just how dangerous steaming alone could become.

GEORGE DUFFY
MV *AMERICAN LEADER*
South Atlantic Ocean
10 September 1942

I had wanted to go to the Naval Academy but failed the physical exam so I went into the Merchant Marine instead. For the first six months in the classroom—learning mathematics, navigation, rules of the road, Morse radio code, seamanship—you name it. Once we got our mates licenses we were automatically ensigns in the naval reserve.

In early 1942 I was assigned as third mate on the *American Leader*, a C-1 class Liberty ship—the smallest of the four classes. It was a little over 400 feet long, had a 27-foot draft, and could carry about 10,000 tons of cargo.

We left New York Harbor on 26 April 1942, with a full cargo of war supplies for the Russians and the British forces in the Middle East. We were carrying barbed wire, army boots, steel ingots, steel plates—and nine twin-engine bombers lashed on deck with all of their spare parts in the hold.

On the routing we were assigned there were no convoys and no escorts available. All we had for protection was our high speed—we could make eleven knots—and firepower from our ten-man navy gun crew—using a single 4-inch gun and two .50-caliber machine gun mounts in case of air attack.

We headed first to Trinidad, where we filled up with fuel—enough to go 7,500 miles. We spent a few days there until we got clearance for the first leg of our run—all the way to Cape Town, South Africa. There, we took on more fuel and then got our routing—and once again, no escorts were available—up through the Indian Ocean and into the Persian Gulf.

At Bandar Abbas, Iran, we offloaded all the equipment for the Russians and took on ten tons of opium—for making morphine back in the States. We then went up the Shatt al Arab to the British offload facility in Iraq where we discharged all their military equipment. We took on some Arab tobacco consigned to Philip Morris and headed for India, where we offloaded the steel. After that we made port in Colombo, Ceylon—now called Sri Lanka—and took on 7,000 tons of rubber and drums of latex and coconut oil.

Following the British routing instructions we made it back into Cape Town on the night of the third of September and the captain went to the admiralty office to get our routing instructions for New York while we took on fuel and made a few minor repairs. The British said that there were U-boat wolf packs operating off the U.S. coast so they routed us due west to Cape Horn, up the west coast of South America to the Panama Canal where we were to pick up an escort to New York.

We had heard about two German raiders operating in the South Atlantic—but the British Admiral in Cape Town said they had been sunk or driven off. In these waters we were more concerned about raiders than U-boats. They were faster and better armed than U-boats and the raiders were pirates—flying anybody's flag they felt like. A raider looks like an ordinary merchant ship until it goes into action.

We got under way for Cape Horn on the night of 7 September. Three nights out of Cape Town we were making nine knots on a heading of 270 degrees, and all of a sudden, shortly after dark, up out of nowhere came another vessel. Without warning they opened fire with deck guns and we were on fire.

I ran out on deck and there were flames everywhere and this strange ship was still firing at us. Some of their 4-inch and 5.9-inch shells had exploded in the engine room and ruptured our fuel tanks and we lost all power. The lifeboats had been destroyed by the gunfire so when the order came to abandon ship, we had to throw the life rafts into the water and jump over the side into the oil that was burning on the sea.

While we were getting the rafts in the water, another shell burst burned me and caught my life jacket caught on fire. So when I went into the water, I was glad to find a life raft. Able seaman Ken Pride helped pull me into the raft and pretty soon there were twenty-three of us in this raft, sitting there in 56-degree water watching our ship burn.

She didn't sink right away because of all the rubber in the holds—and so this ship that looks like a merchantman—but isn't—fires two torpedoes into the *American Leader* to send her down and stop the fire, which could have attracted attention. Shortly after she sank, this big ship pulls up alongside and starts to pick up survivors. We were worried that it might be a Japanese ship—but then we heard them speaking German.

Out of a crew of fifty-eight on the *American Leader,* they rescued forty-seven of us—and that's how we learned that we had been sunk by the German raider *Michele.* We were put in the hold with almost 500 other POWs—British, Indian, South African, Canadian, and New Zealanders—whose ships had also been sunk or captured by the *Michele.* I think we were their eleventh victim.

I have to say that they fed us well and gave us very good medical attention—otherwise a lot of us would not have survived. On 29 November, the *Michele* sank another American transport, the *MV Sawokla*—but there were only nineteen survivors from that one.

We hoped that they would take us to some neutral country to be interned—but instead they turned us over to the Japanese. That's when things really got rough.

> It was quite an experience. Having started the war as a Merchant Marine officer on a Liberty ship, I got sunk by a German auxiliary raider and ended the war as a Japanese POW—doing slave labor on a railroad in Indonesia. Nobody can tell me that life in the Merchant Marine isn't interesting.

The ten German auxiliary raiders sank or captured 138 Allied merchant ships, totaling a million gross registered tons. The *Michele* was struck by a torpedo from the American submarine USS *Tarpon* on 17 October 1943, and the surreptitiously armed merchant ship that had sent nineteen Allied vessels to the bottom was sunk herself.

German raiders like *Michele* preferred unescorted merchantmen as targets. No Allied vessel in a convoy was ever attacked, sunk, or captured by a lone auxiliary raider. Forays by major German capital ships like *Bismarck* or *Tirpitz* were certainly threats to convoys—but so rare that losses in such action are remarkable only because there were so few.

Attacks on merchant shipping by Luftwaffe aircraft were likewise most effective against unescorted vessels. Though a large number of slow-moving merchantmen all within a confined sea-space might seem an attractive target, the escorting warships with effective radar and anti-aircraft guns increased the risk to the attacking aircraft.

It was the same for the U-boats. Though "wolf pack" attacks on convoys sound ominous, the numbers show otherwise. The majority of the Allied merchant vessels sunk were not in protected convoys, but were mostly single ships crossing alone.

The challenge then for the British—and the Americans after Pearl Harbor—was to find enough well-armed escorts to economically organize and protect the convoys plying the routes across the Atlantic. Battleships, cruisers, and destroyers had far too many other tasks and were too few in number to be employed exclusively in convoy duty.

The best ships for the job were smaller, lightly armored vessels, equipped with sonar, radar, and an effective suite of anti-aircraft and anti-submarine weapons. Based on a British design, the Americans called them "destroyer escorts"—and they became the guardians of the Atlantic convoys, crucial to eliminating the U-boat threat.

The dead and wounded are transferred from the USS *Menges*
after the ship was struck by a German torpedo.

The USS *Menges*, DE-320, was one of more than 500 destroyer escorts
built in U.S. shipyards between 1943 and the end of the war. Captained and
crewed by the U.S. Coast Guard, the *Menges*—with Lt. (JG) Ed Nash aboard
as gunnery officer—was assigned to convoy escort duty shortly after she was
commissioned in the autumn of '43. The experiences Nash and his ship-
mates had aboard the *Menges* were typical of the perils faced by merchantmen and the crews of the little ships that protected them.

Nash was a green young officer just out of OCS and advanced training
at the Navy School in Miami. He joined a crew of the newly commissioned
USS *Menges* in late fall of 1943, and took the ship for its shakedown cruise

out of Bermuda during the next two months. By early April 1944 he was still getting used to the rigorous life of a seaman on the *Menges,* doing convoy escort duty from the Norfolk to Gibraltar and back.

LIEUTENANT (JG) EDGAR "ED" NASH, USCG
USS *Menges,* DE-320
Atlantic-Mediterranean Convoy Escort Duty
3 May 1944

The *Menges* was just 306 feet long, had a beam of thirty-six feet, seven inches, and could make about 22 knots. We had a crew of fifteen officers and 200 enlisted—and were armed with three 3-inch guns, and three 40 mm anti-aircraft mounts—one "quad" and two twin mounts. We also had sonar, radar, depth charges, and assorted smaller caliber weapons, and of course, three-eighths-inch-thick welded steel to protect us from whatever the enemy or the sea threw at us.

Right after our shake-down cruise and some specialized ASW—anti-submarine warfare training—we were assigned to escort duty for convoys, crisscrossing the Atlantic. Depending on the size of the convoy, there would be anywhere from six to fifteen escorts—and the whole convoy could only go as fast as the slowest merchantman. Depending on where we were in the screen we would be zig-zagging constantly—usually at about twelve to fifteen knots.

If any of the ships in the screen detected a U-boat or picked up aircraft on radar, we would go to General Quarters instantly—and stay that way—with all the watertight doors dogged shut and the men in their gun mounts for six to eight hours at a time.

As soon as we got far enough east, so that we might be in range of German aircraft, we usually went to GQ as a matter of routine just before dusk. The U.S. and British air forces owned the sky during the day, but after dark, the Luftwaffe would come out hunting for unescorted merchant ships—and of course, convoys. That problem didn't get better until after France was liberated in the fall of '44.

On 30 March 1944 we were escorting a big convoy from Norfolk into the Mediterranean. At Gibraltar, ComNavNAW—Commander, Naval Forces in North African Waters—had warned us that German torpedo bombers were making forays over the shipping routes looking for targets. Sure enough, that night, just at dusk, thirty planes hit our convoy.

Two or three planes came over at very high altitude dropping flares to illuminate the convoy. This was a huge concentration of ships—carrying reinforcements and supplies for the battles in Italy—and the build-up for the invasion of southern France later in the summer.

As the flares were dropping, about ten Ju-88s came in low from dead in front of us, trying to get inside the escort screen and at the "softer" transports and merchant ships to drop their torpedoes and bombs. Only a few from the first wave made it through—but they followed up with a second and then a third wave.

We were shooting at anything we could see—and we nailed one with our 40 mm twin-mount—square in the nose of the bomber—and it crashed into the water. One of our 20 mm mounts also damaged another—so we weren't doing too badly. I wanted to use the 3-inch battery but the German planes were so low the skipper told us not to fire because he was worried that our shots might hit one of our ships.

My combat station was on the wing of the bridge, giving me an extraordinary view of the battle. It was during the third wave of the attack that one of the German planes got through and suddenly the *MV Paul Hamilton*—about 800 yards off our beam, exploded in one huge fireball. She was full of ammunition—and had aboard almost 500 soldiers from an army ordnance unit—plus the ship's crew and the navy armed guard detachment—over 580 men.

One of the escort ships behind us was sent to pick up survivors. They didn't find a soul. Three other ships suffered damage from torpedoes and bombs but none of the others went down.

We had another serious air raid on the convoy but this time we had some warning. A radar picket well out in front of the convoy picked up the inbound raid and alerted us. But even then, some of the planes got through and a Navy destroyer, steaming just ahead of us and off to port, took a torpedo amidships and went down in a hurry. We picked up 107 of her men and another Coast Guard DE behind us picked up more. We also picked up two German airmen who had survived being shot down.

By the spring of '44 we thought we had taken the worst that the Germans could throw at us—but we were wrong. On the night of 3 May '44 we were at the front of the screen, escorting a convoy of mostly empty merchantmen back to the U.S. when our radar watch saw a blip on his scope, and guessed—correctly it turns out—that it was a U-boat.

German U-boats could do up to 18 knots on the surface—but only about 6 knots submerged. They preferred to loiter about on the surface waiting for a target—and only submerge when they had to. But this U-boat was already submerged—apparently thinking that he could let the convoy pass by and then attack from the rear—where there was only one escort. But our radar operator was so good he had picked up the sub's periscope at 12,000 yards. That was the good part.

We had been warned that the U-boats were now using a new T-5 naval acoustic torpedo—guided to its target by the sound of a ship's propeller blades and engine. To counter this new threat, the *Menges* had been equipped with what's called "foxer" gear—a tremendous noise-maker that is towed on a cable about 200 yards aft of the stern. It's designed to make a real racket so that acoustic torpedoes will home in that sound instead of the ship.

We should have been streaming our "foxer" gear but the skipper didn't want me to because it interferes with the sonars on our ships—making it harder to detect a submarine. He also said he was concerned that the noise of our foxer gear would attract U-boats. Well, *that* didn't matter—*this* U-boat already knew where we were.

We went to General Quarters and immediately informed the convoy and the rest of the escorts that we were closing the contact to attack.

We were at our battle stations for about twelve minutes and making about 20 knots when it hit us. An acoustic torpedo homed in on the sound of our screws and quite literally, blew the stern of the *Menges* right off the ship.

Thirty-one of the crew were killed instantly—and twenty-five more were wounded. Some of the crewmen on the fantail were thrown into the water by the force of the explosion. With our engine room gone we quickly went dead in the water—but our emergency generators kicked on—powering up our radars, pumps, and emergency lighting. Our combat watch—still on duty even though the ship could sink at any second—spotted the sub on radar just off our port beam. So the radioman passed the sub's position to two other Coast Guard DEs—the *Pride* and the *Mosley*—and they immediately took off after the U-boat.

Amazingly, our ship held together. The seams and water-tight doors held. She didn't take much water at all forward of the engine room and our damage control parties kept her afloat. We put one of our boats in the water to rescue those in the crew who had been blown over the side and most of them survived.

Just before dawn one of the other escorts came alongside and we transferred our wounded. A short while afterward a French tug arrived, took us under tow, and brought us into Oran for temporary repairs.

Later in the day, our sister ships, USS *Pride*, DE-323 and USS *Mosley*, DE-321, hunted down the German U-boat that had hit us. Just before noon the sub fired another of his acoustic torpedoes and damaged a Free French DE, but *Pride*, *Mosley*, and two other escorts finally hounded the German U-boat so long and damaged it so badly with depth charges and "hedgehogs" that it had to surface. The sub was taken under fire immediately, causing the crew to scuttle her. The Coast Guard escorts captured about half of the crew, including the skipper and learned that our assailant was U-371.

It turned out that the captain of U-371 was just twenty-five years old—and that he had intended to fire another torpedo and finish us off. But when he heard the small motor of our lifeboat—which we had put in the water to rescue our guys in the water—he thought we were abandoning ship and he decided not to "waste" another torpedo.

The USS *Menges* was eventually towed back to the Brooklyn Navy Yard where the stern of another damaged DE was welded to her hull. She finished the war as she had started it—doing convoy duty in the Atlantic. Ed Nash was reassigned to an 83-foot Coast Guard cutter and participated in the invasion of Normandy on D-Day.

The German U-boat fleet that had been such a prominent threat to the survival of Britain earlier in the war was slowly ground down by Allied convoys, long-range patrol aircraft, and eventually, by the introduction of escort carriers and "hunter-killer" units—dispatched not to defend convoys, but to hunt down and destroy enemy submarines.

Though the U-boats sent to sea by Admiral Dönitz would attack combatants like the USS *Menges* when necessity or opportunity arose, their preferred targets were merchant ships. By the end of the war 4,786 merchant vessels flagged to the nations of the British Empire would lie on the bottom of the world's oceans, along with 578 U.S.-flagged merchant ships. More than 80,000 Allied Merchant Mariners were missing, dead, or prisoners of war. The carnage was horrific—but it was the only way to win the Battle of the Atlantic.

There is one other sad footnote to the blood-sacrifice made by the American Merchant Mariners. When the war was over, the survivors who had "delivered the tools of war" weren't accorded the status of veterans. Though they had been subject to all the hardships, dangers, and privations of any man in uniform, they were denied the benefits afforded veterans— including the GI Bill. In 1988 President Ronald Reagan finally awarded the recognition that the World War II Merchant Mariners deserved— forty-three years after the war.

CHAPTER 10
WAR ON THE HOME FRONT
1941–1945

W hen Hitler started World War II by invading Poland in the summer of 1939, America was lagging behind the rest of the western world in emerging from the chronic, decade-long economic upheaval that had begun with the stock market crash of 1929. The worldwide "Great Depression" had created massive unemployment, bank failures, and the collapse of market value for nearly every commodity. Millions of Americans lost jobs, homes, farms, and businesses as banks foreclosed on loans and mortgages in an effort to survive.

In the United States, the effects of the global economic collapse were aggravated by a severe drought that ruined agricultural productivity in the southwestern plains. Hundreds of thousands of farmers and their families lost everything in the "Dust Bowl." By the mid to late 1930s, many of these farm families had migrated west, searching vainly for jobs and a homestead.

The Roosevelt administration's response to the economic crisis may well have exacerbated and prolonged the crisis in the United States. FDR's National Recovery Administration, colossal federal spending—and debt— along with make-work programs such as the Civilian Conservation Corps, the Works Projects Administration and "New Deal" social programs were far less effective in stimulating the U.S. economy than more conventional, market-based initiatives undertaken in Britain and France. And unlike Britain and France—which both initiated economically invigorating military build-ups as Hitler became more threatening in 1936—the U.S. made no such significant investments.

In Germany, Hitler applied his National Socialist theories to mobilize the nation to his grand design. Like Roosevelt, he too created massive public-works projects—the *Autobahn,* upgraded railways, new bridges, and enormous stadiums and parade fields to showcase his Third Reich. As with military conscription, most of these projects—like the industrial expansion necessary for the production of weapons, munitions, aircraft, and ships—had an almost immediate, positive effect on the German economy.

In the U.S., Roosevelt's public works projects—the Tennessee Valley Authority being the largest—had the effect of creating upwards of 40,000 jobs. But the full economic and military benefits of these colossal endeavors on the broader population would not be realized until the 1940s.

While European nations mobilized—stimulating their economies in the process—the U.S., pacifist in its politics and isolationist in diplomacy, languished—spurning re-armament and conscription as security or economic remedies. When Hitler invaded Poland, both Britain and France mobilized completely, and by the following spring, Britain became the only western government in history to conscript women into the armed forces.

The first tentative steps toward mobilization in the United States didn't even begin until 1939. That summer the U.S. Army was authorized to increase its active-duty strength from 130,000 to 227,000—but only by taking in new volunteers or activating units of the National Guard. Congress didn't authorize conscription until the summer of 1940, after the evacuation at Dunkirk.

Industrial mobilization in the United States actually began sooner than that of the military—largely as a consequence of free enterprise. Merchant ships—desperately needed by France and Britain—were not considered war materiel under the American neutrality laws—and both countries began placing orders for vessels in various sizes and designs in early 1939. U.S. arms manufacturers—though initially banned from selling munitions directly to the combatants—*were* allowed to sell weapons to Canada, which began placing orders for planes, tanks, trucks, artillery pieces, and other combat arms even before Hitler ordered the Wehrmacht to march across the Polish frontier. The Canadians promptly shipped the American-made weapons and equipment to England—a subterfuge that persisted until Lend-Lease came into effect in March 1941.

It was Lend-Lease—and FDR's stated desire that the United States become the "Arsenal of Democracy"—that really accelerated America's astounding industrial mobilization and ended the massive unemployment that was so pervasive during the Great Depression. Within a matter of weeks after Roosevelt proposed the legislation, private sector architects and engineers were drawing up plans for new aircraft, tank, truck, and arms manufacturing plants; new steel mills; expanded electrical generation and distribution; new and bigger mines; as well as enhanced oil production and refining capacity.

Rosie the Riveter

Agricultural experts also began planning for dramatic increases in wheat, soybean, corn, beef, hog, poultry, and dairy production. By the time the Japanese attacked Pearl Harbor on 7 December 1941, America's industrial and agricultural sectors were well ahead of the U.S. Armed Forces in preparing for war.

In May 1940—as Hitler invaded the Low Countries and France—Roosevelt issued an Executive Order, activating a National Defense Council of business and labor leaders, headed by Frances Perkins, his Secretary of Labor. Charged with coordinating and prioritizing the massive requirements of feeding and equipping our allies and supplying the U.S. military with all that would be needed in the fight ahead, the NDC quickly realized that America's principal shortage wouldn't be raw materials—it was labor. Though nearly ten million American men were still unemployed when the war began, Perkins and her NDC colleagues knew that almost all of them who were fit for duty would be summoned for military service, leaving gaping employment holes in agriculture and industry.

London had solved this problem with a universal call-up of the entire adult population of Great Britain. Men *and* women between eighteen and forty-five who were fit for military service were put in uniforms. All others were sent to work in fields and factories as directed by the British government. Those too young or old to fight or work often found themselves drafted as air raid wardens, plane spotters, teachers, child-care givers, hospital aides, drivers, message handlers, or for neighborhood civil defense.

National Archives

Women assembling machine parts in an airplane plant.

Such coercive measures were out of the question in the United States. But Perkins and the NDC also knew there was a vast, untapped workforce available: America's women. Convincing them to join the war on the home front became one of the primary goals of the Roosevelt administration in 1941–42.

Spurred by the NDC, President Roosevelt and the First Lady launched a nationwide propaganda campaign encouraging women to "Free a Man to Fight." The theme of all the posters, billboards, newspaper, magazine, and radio ads was essentially the same: while American men served on the front lines, American women would have to serve on the assembly lines. The Office of War Information distributed posters and handbills promoting "Rosie the Riveter" and her "We can do it!" slogan. When necessary, reluctant union and industry leaders were none too gently prodded by the NDC into opening their factory floors and union halls to women by promoting women's war work as a "temporary" response to a national emergency.

The results were dramatic. Within a year of the U.S. entry into the war, more than a million American women had become hourly wage laborers in the defense industry. A year later it was 2.5 million. Many of these young women took jobs that had heretofore been male-only. In airplane plants they not only did meticulous work assembling fine machine parts and electric components—they were also welders and crane operators.

By 1942, American women were assembling bombs, building tanks, welding hulls, and greasing locomotives. Phyllis McKey moved from Oregon to California and joined them.

PHYLLIS MCKEY
Kaiser Shipyards
Oakland, California
22 September 1943

I was just twenty-one and a new mother, living in Oregon, when my husband and I and our new baby moved to California for his job. I had never expected to work outside the home, but there was a notice in the paper that the Kaiser Shipyard had openings for women. My sister Marian came down from Oregon to help take care of the baby and I applied for a job as a welder.

As an apprentice welder I made ninety cents an hour—which was good money. I caught on quickly and after a few weeks, I was put out in the yard where we were building Liberty ships. I think our shipyard was the first to mass-produce ships—by pre-fabricating various pieces, then bringing the parts together from all over the yard with great big cranes and welding them together right there in the dry dock.

To build the ship's deck-houses, they laid a slab of steel down and we welded the pre-cut walls to the roof while standing on what would be the ceiling. As we finished each one, a crane would come and pick it up and carry it to the hull—which was also assembled in sections. There, it would be welded to the ship's deck. After we had been at it awhile we could turn out *a ship a day*—in three shifts. All it took was some spirit, energy, and a can-do attitude.

While we would be welding beads in the pilot house, pipe fitters and electricians would move in and install all the water pipes and valves, electric wiring, and switches—so that about the time we were finished with the welding, they would be done with their work. It was an amazing process—and we all took great pride in what we accomplished.

Was a woman as good a welder as a man? Better, I think. Women did embroidery work, crochet work, knitting. For those things you not only needed to know the technique, you wanted it to be beautiful. And it was the same with welding. I could run a bead weld as good or better than any man on my shift—and that's not me talking—that's what my job supervisor said.

Was it hard work? Sure. It's hot and dirty, too. Those welding masks are heavy—so were the leather gloves, chaps, and gauntlets we wore to keep from getting burned. Sometimes a spark would roll down into a glove and there'd be little round BBs of hot metal burning your flesh. It was so dirty that sometimes at the end of a shift, my skin would be completely black. But we weren't doing this to look good—we were doing it to help win the war and feed our families.

After I had been there awhile, another sister came down from Oregon—she took a job in the Kaiser drafting department. Finally, my mom came and I took a job on a graveyard shift so that we could take turns in the bed.

I was promoted to journeyman welder, making a dollar an hour—the same pay as my husband, who was also a welder. That didn't sit well with him because he hadn't wanted me to go to work. He had expected to be the head of the household—and that I would come and ask him for money to buy things. Well, my job at Kaiser gave me independence—and that was something most women didn't have until the war.

Our marriage didn't survive—but I'm proud of what we accomplished. The women who worked in that yard built good ships that helped save a lot of lives. I never heard about any man who sailed on 'em complain about that.

Opening so many new jobs to women had not only a profound effect on the war effort, but it also had inevitable consequences on American society and culture. Before the war, less than 20 percent of women between eighteen to forty were in the salaried labor force. By 1940 it was 25 percent and by 1945 it had swelled to 35 percent. At the end of the war, with factories and shipyards running twenty-four hours a day, seven days a week, more than half of all adult American women were working outside the home. Three-quarters of the new women workers were married, most were over age thirty-five, and more than a third had children under fourteen.

The war also caused shifts in population. Americans flocked to places with military bases and defense plants; six million migrants left farms and rural areas for urban areas where defense jobs were plentiful. Often it meant taking a new job, in a new place, in a new plant, making new products—all of which required that their new employer train these new workers. Lourelei Prior was one of those who benefited from such training when she went to work for General Electric.

National Archives

Free a Man to Fight.

LOURELEI PRIOR
General Electric Aircraft Engine Plant
Fort Wayne, Indiana
5 November 1945

My dad died in 1936, the year I graduated from high school in the little town of Garrett, Indiana. My mother couldn't work and I had a twelve-year-old little brother so to support them, I went to work in an undergarment factory. When the war started, one of my good friends went into the Women Marines. I wanted to go with her to join up but my mom was really upset—that I would be leaving her and my little brother to fend for themselves.

About that time there was a story in the newspaper about jobs in defense plants opening up for women in Fort Wayne. I applied for a job at the GE aircraft engine plant and was accepted. We all moved to Fort Wayne so that I could work at the GE plant and take care of them.

When I started at GE the first thing they did was to send me to school to teach me how to read blueprints and operate a diamond-tipped lathe and a thread-mill. After the training, I was put to work making electrical armatures for aircraft engines. At this plant they had three shifts, twenty-four hours a day, seven days a week. Those gentlemen at GE treated me like a jewel. Because I had to look after my mother and brother, they gave me a day shift.

I had several different jobs during the time that I worked at the GE plant. My first job was to cut armatures from steel stock using the lathe, then wind copper wire onto the armatures. I was responsible for the whole piece, from set-up to completion. Each armature had to be made to very exact specifications—so it required a lot of attention to detail. And each one weighed about sixty pounds, so I had to be pretty strong. It was hard work, but satisfying to help the war effort and it paid a good wage and allowed me to support my mother and brother. It's also how I met my husband, Herbert.

The machines we used at GE had safety guards around them and Herb was responsible for maintaining the machinery and tools we used in my part of the plant—and making sure that the safety guards were in place to protect people. One of the other gals told him I was single and he started to come around a lot to check on my machines and safety guards. One day when the diamond tip broke off my lathe, the supervisor roped off the whole area and Herb and I and several others had to crawl around to find the diamond tip. Afterwards he asked me out.

We dated for a few months and decided to get married. This wasn't an easy time to be a new bride because everything was rationed. Only one person from each family was allowed to register for a "War Ration Book" with colored stamps in it that allowed you to buy certain amounts of food, clothing, shoes, coffee, gasoline, tires, fuel oil, coal—just about every-thing—all based on the size of your family.

As I recall, Red Stamps were used for meat, butter, fat, cooking oil, sugar, milk, and cheese. Blue Stamps were for canned fruits and vegeta-bles, juices, dry beans, soups, baby food and the like. But having a ration stamp didn't guarantee that something would be available. We all learned to use everything very sparingly and not waste anything. Even razor blades had to be re-sharpened. In almost every store there were posters with slo-gans like, "Do with less so they'll have enough," and "Pledge to save food."

One of the scarcest things was butter—and someone invented a veg-etable-oil substitute—margarine. It was white and came with a capsule of food coloring to mix into the margarine to make it look like butter.

We couldn't get stockings either—all the silk was used for parachutes and nylon hadn't been invented yet. Now, stockings didn't matter at the plant. There, all the gals wore tight clothing and pants and a hat and safety glasses—and no jewelry—because of the heavy machinery. But no gal or new bride wants to be seen in a skirt without stockings! So when I would go out with Herb, sometimes to make it look like I had on stockings, I would draw a black line up the back of my legs with an eyebrow liner pen-cil to make it look like I was wearing silk stockings.

In our house we didn't grumble about the shortages. We just thanked God for what we *did* have—and I had four brothers-in-law who were in the service. If giving up a little bit helped the boys "over there" and would bring them back sooner, it was fine with us.

Some people got scarce things on the black market and there were men who could have served but didn't. Men with children who worked in a defense plant and those who were sole providers didn't have to go. But Herb wanted to serve and we talked a lot about that and so just a few months after we were married, he joined the Merchant Marines.

While he was gone, my mother, brother, and I made do and helped the war effort as best we could. We had a "victory garden" for fresh veg-etables and we canned the extras in Mason jars for winter. We saved anything we didn't need for the "scrap drives" and recycled everything: tin cans, newspapers, magazines, cardboard, clothing, tin foil, bits of rubber, broken glass, paper sacks. The Boy Scouts would come to the door once a week or so to collect it or we would turn it in at our church.

At the GE plant we were all encouraged to buy War Bonds. We could either get stamps for a "War Bond Book" at the post office, or have the money for the bond deducted from our pay. That's how I did it—and every three months I got a new bond.

Very few people in those days had cars—and during the war, there were no new cars made because all the carmakers were building jeeps, trucks, tanks, and planes. Those people who did have a car had a hard time getting gasoline and tires. Nobody had a spare tire so everyone with a car had a tire patch kit, rubber cement, and a hand-operated air pump.

These shortages and rationing and all really didn't bother us much. I got up every morning before six—and walked to the plant to be there before seven. We got a half hour for lunch. I would usually work until five—sometimes later. There was a time—it went on for about two months—when we worked seven days a week without any days off. During the war I never took any vacation. It just wouldn't have felt right to me—taking a vacation with my husband and all those boys off at the war. They didn't get any vacation.

Before Herb left we would occasionally go out to a movie or dancing. We also went to a few of the Fort Wayne Daisies baseball games together. But while he was gone, it just didn't seem right. I figured we would celebrate when he got home. And we did!

When the war ended, there was a big parade in Fort Wayne. Herb and all the other boys came home and he went into the heating, roofing, and sheet metal business. That's when we started our family.

The war was a hard time for a lot of people—but I look back on those days and can say that we did our part. I felt like I had done something for my country and was blessed that my husband made it home. Nobody came up and said "thank you," for being a "Rosie the Riveter." They didn't have to. Herb was grateful. That's all that mattered.

With a workforce bolstered with women like Phyllis McKey and Lourelei Prior, the U.S. began to turn out massive quantities of war materiel—overwhelming Hitler and his Axis partners. American farms and industry not only fed and equipped our own rapidly growing armed forces for a two-front war, but did the same for our allies.

When the Americans, British, and Canadians stormed the beaches at Normandy, nearly 30 percent of the food being consumed by the British people originated on American farms—about the same proportion as the bombs and ammunition being used by His Majesty's military. By then, British pilots were flying American-built transport aircraft, every British armored unit was fighting in American-made Sherman tanks, and nearly all of the landing craft that would put them ashore were produced in the U.S.

It was the same for the Soviets. Though the Red Army generally eschewed American aircraft and armor, they still accepted more than 14,500

National Archives

Women kept the home front running as they became the primary workforce.

planes and nearly 7,000 tanks—along with 375,000 trucks, fifteen million pairs of boots, millions of gallons of fuel, more than 2,000 locomotives, and 10,000 freight cars.

By 1944, American shipyards—like the one where Phyllis McKey worked—were turning out Liberty ships in mere days, and warships in a matter of weeks. That same year, America's aircraft plants produced more than 95,000 transports, fighters, and bombers.

Victory gardens, like the one Lourelei Prior had, were so successful that by 1945, some twenty million of them produced approximately 40 percent of America's vegetables. Despite the shortages and sacrifices that most Americans experienced, the U.S. standard of living actually *rose* between 1940 and 1945.

Though food and other commodities were in short supply during the war, the greatest shortage was simple: men. The absence of so many men— more than twelve million were off in uniform—affected not only war production, but it also effectively shut down the American pastime. By 1942, professional baseball had lost so many players who either enlisted or were drafted into the military service that there were too few left for the games to go on. That's when women stepped up to the plate—literally.

The Wrigley family decided that those on the "Home Front" needed some respite from the day-to-day labor of war production, and created the All American Girls Baseball League. One of the teams that Lourelei Prior got to watch, the Fort Wayne Daisies, had an all-star pitcher: Dottie Collins.

DOTTIE COLLINS
Fort Wayne Daisies
14 May 1945

My dad was a big baseball fan and taught me to throw a curveball when I was a kid. I was five feet seven inches—tall for a girl in the '40s—and when the Wrigley family started up the league, one of the scouts had me throw some pitches. After I tried out, they offered me a job—pitching for the Fort Wayne Daisies.

The idea of a women's league was a good one. Because all the men were gone, there were empty ballparks all over the country. And everybody knows that being outside at a ballpark on a summer afternoon is healthy. Starting a league of women ball players seemed like a good way to get people outside in the fresh air and have some good, all-American fun. It was also a good way to use something that was entertaining to help keep up morale and raise money for war bonds at the same time.

When the league was formed a lot of us tried out and the competition was pretty fierce. Many of the girls had played in school or college, but I was the only one with a curveball. And I did all right—I had a career record of 117 wins and 76 losses with a 1.83 earned run average.

Our coaches were all professionals and told us right from the start that we were "ladies first." Of course *our* theory was, if you're going to play baseball, you can't be a lady. But in addition to practice in batting, fielding, base running, how to steal and slide—all the stuff of making a good baseball player—we also had to do things like walk with a book on our heads to teach us poise, the right way to wear make-up, and how to act like ladies. We traveled all around the Midwest and were very carefully chaperoned. When we weren't on the field we were told to use proper manners and etiquette and dress "like a lady."

The people who ran the Women's Baseball League insisted that everything we did be geared to entertainment. From the moment we arrived in town for a game, everything was carefully orchestrated. There were press conferences and lots of cameras as we got off the bus—and then out on the field during warm-up—just like in Major League Baseball. Even the way we dressed was part of the production.

Just before our first game they handed out our uniforms—they were these one-piece, sleeved dresses—that were hemmed below the knee. When we said, "How do you play baseball in a dress?" we were told, "You either wear this uniform or you don't play." Well, by the second game, most of us had shortened them—though about all we could get away with was a hem right about the middle of the knee.

Let me tell you, sliding into home plate wearing a dress can be a very painful experience. But as you might imagine, our male fans were very enthusiastic. We had a lot of fun—and in our own way did our part for the war effort on the home front.

Though continental America's "Home Front" was far more secure than that of any other combatant nation in World War II, it was not completely immune to enemy action. Both the Japanese and the Germans attempted attacks on the U.S. mainland, but only the Japanese succeeded.

On 23 February 1942, a Japanese submarine surfaced a few hundred yards off Ellwood, near Santa Barbara, California, and shelled a coastal oil storage facility. There were no casualties and only minor damage to a small shed.

The Japanese also tried attaching incendiary and explosive devices to hydrogen-filled balloons and launching them into the jet stream. Several caused nothing more than minor forest fires along the West Coast. But in May 1945, one of these "balloon bombs" killed the wife and all five children of the Reverend Archie Mitchell when they inadvertently detonated the hellish device after discovering it in a meadow during a picnic, 200 miles from the Oregon coastline.

Hitler was even less successful than the Japanese—though the Nazis claimed otherwise. On 9 February 1942, the French liner *Normandie,* in the process of being converted into a troop ship, burned and sank at Pier 88 in New York Harbor. Paul Goebbels, the Führer's loyal propaganda minister, fed suspicions that the ship was the victim of German saboteurs. A lengthy investigation concluded that the fire and subsequent sinking—by water intended to put out the blaze—were the consequence of negligence and incompetence rather than Nazi malevolence.

Yet the Germans did try—at great risk to their agents—to conduct espionage and terror operations inside the U.S. Shortly after declaring war on the United States, Hitler ordered the Abwehr, Germany's intelligence service, to land saboteurs by U-boat along the East Coast to conduct attacks on defense plants, railroads, and bridges, and to spread panic by putting time-release bombs in movie theaters and other places where the American public congregated. During May and June of 1942, two Abwehr sabotage teams were landed on the coast of Florida and on Long Island. Had it not been for an alert Coast Guardsman named John Cullen, the German agents might well have succeeded.

JOHN CULLEN, USCG
Amagansett Lifeboat Station
13 June 1942

In the summer of '42, I was just twenty-one years old and had been in the Coast Guard just six months. I was stationed at Amagansett Lifeboat Station, on Long Island. There were about fifteen of us there. We did lifeboat training, and patrolled a three-mile stretch of beach every night.

I used to walk down by the surf, where I could make better time. On the night of 13 June, I was on patrol, maybe 200 yards from the lifeguard station, when I saw two men, just above the high water line.

I called out and asked, "What are you doing?" And one of these guys turned and walked toward me. He said, "We're fishermen and our boat ran aground. We intend to stay here until daybreak."

I said, "That's hours away. Why don't you come up to the Coast Guard station, have some coffee and wait there?"

He said, "No, thanks, we'll be all right here." Then he said, "Do you have a mother and father?"

I thought, that's a strange thing to ask, but I said, "Yes I do."

The man said, "Would you like to see them again?"

I told him, "Yes, I would." Meanwhile, another fellow carrying a sea-bag came up behind me, and said something in German. That's when I said to myself, "Uh-oh—this isn't good."

The first man said to me, "I'll give you some money, if you forget about seeing us here."

"I don't want the money," I told him. "But, I can forget."

"Well . . . I'll give you 300 dollars," he told me. I only took the money to prove that I met somebody there—because I didn't think anyone would believe my story.

I didn't turn around—I backed up when I left. Then I ran back to the station, notified my officer in charge. I told him, "I got paid off by some Germans, and I don't know what they're doing, whether they're coming in or going out."

The watch officer stayed calm. He said, "We'll break out some rifles and go back—and see if we can find them." But they were gone.

We went back to the boathouse, got a couple of shovels, came back, and dug up several large cases that the Germans had buried in the dunes. Inside the cases we found the sea-bag I had seen earlier, along with German uniforms and explosives. All of a sudden, just off shore, a blinker light started going on and off. In the drifting fog we could see a submarine.

So I ran back to our station and notified another Coast Guard unit and told 'em, "There's a German U-boat out here." He notified the Army, and pretty soon, the beach was full of soldiers with anti-aircraft guns, trucks, and searchlights.

In the cases that we dug up we found four different types of incendiary bombs and when a Navy intelligence officer arrived and saw that he said, "Boy, we've got something big here." Soon the FBI came. And they took me to their office, grilled me, and then took me into New York and started showing me photos from their files. After looking at hundreds of pictures, I found one of the fellow who spoken English to me on the beach. His name was George Dasch.

For the next few days an FBI agent and I must have visited just about every restaurant, newsstand, shop, hotel, bus station, and train station in the area, trying to locate this man Dasch. He was readily identifiable by a gray streak he had in his hair.

It turned out that Dasch had gotten cold feet. He called the FBI, first from New York and then from Washington, D.C., and turned himself in on June 19. I was brought in to confirm his identity and told that I would have to testify at his trial.

Dasch revealed everything—how they had been trained, what their targets were, and the identities of all involved. By June 27, the FBI had the other three saboteurs who had landed from U-202 off Amagansett in custody—along with a second group of four that had landed from another U-boat on June 17 just south of Jacksonville, Florida.

President Roosevelt and Attorney General Biddle decided that all eight would be tried by a secret military commission. I was told that it was the first such tribunal since the assassination of President Abraham Lincoln.

I was the first witness called when the trial started on July 8. By the fourth of August, all eight had been convicted and sentenced to death. FBI Director Hoover and Attorney General Biddle appealed to President Roosevelt for leniency on behalf of Dasch and one of the others—a man named Berger—because they had cooperated. Their sentences were commuted to thirty years for Dasch and life in prison for Berger. The other six were executed on August 8.

Hitler was stunned by how quickly the Abwehr sabotage venture had been wrapped up, and he forbade risking any more U-boats or agents on such operations. In July 1944, two German spies—not saboteurs—Erich Gimpel and William Curtis Colepaugh, were transported by U-boat to the coast of Maine with the desperate mission of collecting information on, among other things, the Manhattan Project, America's secret attempt to create an atomic bomb. They too were quickly apprehended, tried before a military tribunal, and sentenced to death.

Colepaugh and Gimpel had their sentences commuted to life in prison by President Harry Truman. Eventually, the sentences of all four surviving German agents, ill-fated saboteurs Dasch and Berger and captured spies Colepaugh and Gimpel, would be reduced to time served. But by the time they were released, all that remained of the Führer and his Third Reich were ashes. The American home front that Adolf Hitler sought to sabotage and spy upon had armed and fed his enemies—and crushed his dream of world domination.

CHAPTER 11
OPERATION OVERLORD: NORMANDY
1941

Our landings in the Cherbourg-Le Havre area have failed to gain a satisfactory foothold and I have withdrawn the troops. My decision to attack at this time and place was based upon the best information available. The troops, the air, and the Navy did all that bravery and devotion to duty could do. If any blame or fault attaches to this attempt it is mine alone.

That was the kind of message no general would ever want to send. It meant that Operation Overlord—the biggest military maneuver ever conducted—had failed. General Dwight David Eisenhower penned the brief communiqué by hand on a small sheet of notepaper late on 5 June 1944, and put it in his pocket. He knew that the monumental effort to cross the channel and breach Hitler's Atlantic Wall across Normandy's beaches was that uncertain. Eisenhower was supreme allied commander and he shouldered that responsibility. He kept the note with him throughout D-Day, 6 June, and all of the next day. Thankfully, it remained in his pocket.

Overlord, a name chosen by Prime Minister Winston Churchill, had been in the planning stages for more than two years. Churchill had done

National Archives

Allied troops landing at Normandy.

all in his power to delay or even avert the operation altogether—fearing a repeat of the carnage the British army had endured in the trenches of France during World War I. Churchill instead preferred a "Second Front" against Hitler that would have been launched through the Mediterranean, against what he called "Europe's soft underbelly." The issue was finally decided in a series of conferences among the Allied leaders: Trident, in Washington, during May 1943; Quadrant, in Quebec the following August; and ultimately a meeting at Tehran with Stalin, in November.

Though the Soviets had done nothing to help the British when England stood alone against Hitler from June 1940 through the start of Barbarossa a year later, Stalin had been pleading for Churchill and Roosevelt to launch a second front that would relieve the pressure on his Red Army. Overlord was the answer he had been hoping for.

The decision to invade Fortress Europe across the beaches of Normandy had not been easy. The point of entry had to be within the operational radius of the British Spitfire—the most plentiful but short-range Allied fighter. The beach gradient had to be such that amphibious ships and landing craft could pull in to discharge their cargoes and then quickly withdraw.

"Sea room" offshore had to be sufficient to allow battleships, heavy cruisers, and destroyers to maneuver safely while delivering shore bombardment. And there had to be a major port or ports in the area to enable the offload of millions of tons of supplies and equipment to support a rapid buildup—and then effect a breakout from the beachhead.

Pas de Calais met all these requirements. It was a shorter dash across the English Channel—and far closer to Berlin—but the city had formidable German defenses. Eisenhower, Montgomery, and the Allied planners all agreed that Normandy's beaches weren't as well defended, and that the nearby ports at Cherbourg, Deauville, and Le Havre would suffice—if they could be captured early. Just in case, the Allies prepared two artificial harbors to be towed into position once the invasion beaches were secure.

These two "portable ports" were comprised of sixty-five vessels that would be sunk to create a breakwater, enormous concrete and steel caissons, piers that would rise and fall on the tide, and nearly one hundred floating concrete sea-walls—all of it codenamed "Mulberry." It was all frightfully expensive, but well worth the cost—for the Wehrmacht intended to hold the Channel ports.

Against an expected Allied assault, Hitler arrayed ten armored and fifty infantry divisions organized in two army groups, B and G—all under General Gerd von Rundstedt, the Führer's senior commander in the west. Notwithstanding the nominal size of this force, the Germans were in fact stretched thin by the need to defend a 2,000-mile long coastline that ran from the Baltic to the Pyrenees.

In November 1943 Hitler had issued Führer Directive No. 51, ordering that the Atlantic Wall be strengthened. The following month he dispatched Erwin Rommel to command Army Group B and invigorate improvements in the defenses.

Over the next five months Rommel supervised a frenzy of construction. On potential landing beaches his engineers built thousands of "Belgian gates"—ten-foot-high steel structures topped with mines that were invisible at high tide. Long posts with mines affixed to them were dug into the sand at low tide. Tens of thousands of steel tetrahedrons—called "hedgehogs"—were placed at the water's edge to rip open the hulls of landing craft.

Press-ganged Frenchmen and slave laborers were used to string hundreds of miles of barbed wire, pour concrete for gun emplacements, construct fortifications, and dig anti-tank ditches. By the end of May 1944, the beaches of France were isolated by rows of barbed wire and some *six million* land mines. For miles back from the beaches, open fields that could be used to land paratroopers or gliders were mined, flooded, and booby trapped with sharp steel spikes to impale airborne invaders.

By late spring, Rommel was convinced that his beach defenses were adequate to slow, but not stop, an Allied landing. His many painful encounters with the Allies in North Africa convinced him that if he also placed his Panzers well forward, he could achieve another Dieppe—or Dunkirk—and push the invaders back into the sea.

Positioning the German armor to repulse the invasion was crucial, and it became a major point of contention between von Rundstedt and Rommel. The Desert Fox, knowing personally the effectiveness of Allied air power, wanted his Panzers as close to the invasion beaches as possible. Von Rundstedt insisted that the armor be held back from the coast until the Allies were ashore, and be used to launch a massive counter-attack.

Hitler resolved the dispute the worst way possible—by placing most of the Panzer and mechanized units in a central reserve and under his personal command and control. Then, compounding his error, he positioned these mobile forces north of the River Seine, close to where the Allies were expected to come ashore at Calais.

That the German high command believed Calais to be the most likely invasion site is testament to Operation Fortitude—the remarkably effective deception and disinformation campaign that the Allies had been conducting for more than a year. To convince Hitler that the invasion would indeed come across the Channel narrows, a fictitious First U.S. Army Group—FUSAG—ostensibly commanded by General George Patton—"formed up" in Kent and Sussex. Empty tent-camps, plywood trucks, rubber tanks, inflatable artillery pieces, dummy landing craft, and phony radio transmissions were employed—along with some less benign measures.

As they had prior to Operation Husky in Sicily, Allied counter-intelligence put false documents showing plans for an invasion across the Dover Straits on the body of a dead Briton and planted the corpse on the French coast. In January 1944, Abwehr agents in England—they had all been caught and "doubled"—began filing "intelligence reports" with controllers in Berlin about the Allied build-up along the Dover Straits. For weeks before D-Day, bridges, road intersections, and rail lines in and around Calais were bombed far more heavily than similar targets in Normandy. And though they did not know the true invasion site until the last minute, French resistance cells were repeatedly told to collect detailed intelligence on German dispositions near Calais.

Adding to German uncertainty was their lack of aerial or naval intelligence. Although nine *Kriegsmarine* E-boats managed to torpedo three LSTs—and kill 749 U.S. soldiers and sailors—during an Overlord training exercise at Slapton Sands on 29 April, the German naval command at Cherbourg didn't connect the event with preparations for an invasion at Normandy.

The Luftwaffe was likewise flying blind when it came to what was taking place just across the Channel. The build-up for Overlord would have been impossible to miss from the air: 6,500 ships and landing craft jammed into every port and anchorage from Falmouth in the south to Brighton in the north; more than 125 airfields—many of them brand-new—swarming with 12,000 Allied aircraft; nearly 500 miles of new railroad track jammed with hundreds of thousands of packed freight cars; and nearly a million American, British, and Canadian troops crammed into cantonments all over southeastern England.

All of this would have been visible from the air. But the Luftwaffe, with only 475 combat-effective aircraft left in France, had long ago been driven from the skies over England. From January 1944 to D-Day, fewer than thirty-five German aircraft survived the flight from France to England and back again.

National Archives

General Eisenhower addressing troops before Operation Overlord.

Unwilling to trust deception and surprise alone, Eisenhower ordered that the approaches to the beachhead be sealed off just before the landings. Starting ninety-six hours before D-Day, thousands of American and British fighters and bombers swept over the French countryside, attacking every train, truck, bridge, or vehicle they could find. Though the Germans had by June become masters of camouflage, the aerial attacks were devastating.

By 4 June 1944, Gen. Eisenhower, Gen. Montgomery, Lt. Gen. Omar Bradley, and Gen. Miles Dempsey—the senior Allied commanders—had visited every assault unit scheduled to land at H-Hour in Normandy, a total of more than 160,000 troops. Their visits were an encouragement to those about to undertake one of the most difficult operations in history: an amphibious attack against the most heavily defended coastline in the world.

The British 3rd and Canadian 3rd Infantry Divisions—along with the 40th and 48th Royal Marine Commandos—would land on the far left at Juno, closest to Caen. Gold Beach would be assaulted by the British 50th Infantry Division, while the 56th Brigade of Royal Marine Commandos would attack near Arromanches. The American 1st and 29th Infantry Divisions and the 2nd Ranger Battalion would take Omaha beach, and Utah would be seized by the 4th Infantry Division—followed by the 9th and 90th in order to seal off the Cotentin Peninsula.

High winds and seas and low clouds forced the assault—originally scheduled for 5 June—to be postponed for twenty-four hours. General Erwin Rommel, convinced by his meteorologists that the weather was too poor for any kind of action on the coast of France, left for a short leave in Germany. He brought with him a pair of French shoes for his wife's birthday on 6 June.

Montgomery and Eisenhower spent the last hours of 5 June with those who would secure the flanks of the beachhead and be the first to meet the enemy: the paratroopers of the British 6th, and the U.S. 82nd and 101st Airborne Divisions. Bernard Ryan, a physician from upstate New York and a graduate of Harvard Medical School, would be among those first Americans to hit the ground on D-Day.

CAPTAIN BERNARD RYAN,
MEDICAL CORPS, US ARMY
506th Parachute Infantry Regiment,
101st Airborne Division
Cotentin Peninsula, France
6 June 1944

In February of '43, I was a brand-new resident at Bellevue Hospital, and decided to volunteer for service before I got drafted. I volunteered for the paratroops because I thought it would be more exciting than the Army Air Force. It was certainly exciting.

After initial training at Carlisle Barracks, Pennsylvania, then parachute training at Fort Benning, Georgia, we formed up as a Parachute Infantry Regiment shipped out of New York for England on 5 September 1943.

We trained in England from then until D-Day, doing field exercises, training, and five or six practice parachute jumps. On field exercises we'd head out at night and march thirty-five miles or so—and it was good that we did—it kept us in shape.

While we were in England all our mail was censored. My mother was a widow and worried about me as her only child. She thought I ought to have my head examined for joining the paratroopers.

About a week before D-Day, our battalion was sent by train down to an airfield near Exeter, on the south coast of England, where we were put behind barbed wire enclosure. No one could come or go. That's when we were briefed on where we were going right down to the smallest detail, with maps, aerial photos, and sand tables. Each unit was assigned a mission and various objectives.

The battalion I jumped with was supposed to seize two bridges across the Douve River and stop the Germans from bringing their armor against Utah Beach. They told us we'd only be in combat for a week. That turned into six weeks.

At about five o'clock on the afternoon of the fifth, General Maxwell Taylor, the Division Commander, told us that we were going that night. Our battalion commander gave us a pep talk, said a prayer, and we broke up to pack our gear and draw our parachutes. We got down to the C-47s at about seven o'clock and spent the next few hours getting buckled up, arranging our jump equipment and boarding the planes. Like everyone else, I was carrying about 100 pounds of equipment—in my case, medical gear, food, water, and a canteen of medical alcohol.

We took off about ten-thirty at night and circled awhile, so that the twenty-four C-47s carrying our battalion could get into formation and then head south over the Channel. The weather was okay that night, and a lot of the men were sleeping, some smoked cigarettes, and of course, most of us were pretty scared.

It was a quiet flight until we hit the coast of Normandy. Then, all hell broke loose. The anti-aircraft and small arms fire from the ground was tremendous.

Our planes were supposed to stay in formation at an elevation of 500 feet, but these pilots were green and started to take evasive action by flying in all different directions. And instead of slowing down when they approached our drop zones, they speeded up. And, we were being thrown all around the plane while we were flying over this flak. After a half hour of this we were all very anxious to get out.

The jump master is supposed to turn on a red light when the pilot tells him we're approaching the drop zone—so that we can stand up and hook up our static lines and then turn on a green light as the signal to jump. Well in this case it seemed like there was less than a minute between the red and green lights and we went out at between 400 and 500 feet going very fast. It occurred to me that I was one of the "old men" on that jump. My birthday was June 1—I was twenty-eight years old.

When I came out of the plane, there was a terrific opening shock as the parachute popped open because we're going so fast and carrying so much equipment. The ground fire was so bad that I pulled up my feet to dodge the tracer bullets coming up. It was an inferno beneath us and in the thirty seconds or so it took to hit the ground, I thought I was going to get killed right off the bat.

I landed in a flooded field about two miles from where our drop zone was supposed to be. Some of the guys were dropped as much as twelve miles from where they were supposed to land. I came down in water up to my hips—in an area that the Germans had flooded since our last aerial photographs had been taken.

I was worried about drowning—and then about being spotted by the Germans. I was in such a hurry to get out of my chute, that I cut my hand with my trench knife. After wading around for a few minutes dragging my wet equipment, I found three other men from my outfit.

We headed toward a fire in the distance, thinking it was a burning plane—but it turned out to be Germans and they opened fire on us. We all flopped back into the water and got separated. I spent the next three days trying to get back to where my battalion was supposed to be holding these two bridges—but I had to cross this elevated road that ran between Cherbourg and Carentan. There was a lot of German traffic on it and I had to hide out, using my little "cricket" clicker—which all of us had—hoping to link up with anyone from my unit.

On the morning of the third day, the 4th Division broke through to where I was and I finally got linked up with about 115 of our men who had made it to the bridges we were to hold. That's all that made it out of 700 men in the battalion.

Our casualties were very high. Our battalion commander and executive officer were both killed on the jump. All four of our company commanders and all four first sergeants were either killed or captured. The other medical officer was captured. So, it was a very bad situation.

We were further away from the beach than anybody and we had landed right in the midst of a German Parachute Division. Then we were attacked by Panzer Grenadiers. If General Bradley hadn't reinforced us with some tanks from 2nd Armor Division, none of us would have made it back. At the end of the tank-infantry fight, "Bloody Gulch" was littered with American and German wounded and dead.

After we were relieved at Carentan, we moved back down to the beach, loaded on an LST, and returned to England. There we re-fitted, got replacements, and trained some more. Our next combat operation was the daylight jump into Holland for Operation Market Garden in September. We also fought at Bastogne during the "Battle of the Bulge" in December. We took a lot of casualties in all of those battles.

By the end of the war, Bernard Ryan was one of the most highly decorated medical officers in the U.S. Army. His two Silver Stars—the nation's third highest decoration for bravery—and two Purple Hearts for wounds in action indicated the kind of combat he and his fellow paratroopers endured taking on the Wehrmacht.

Though many of the U.S. parachute infantrymen failed to hit their assigned objectives in Normandy, the airborne assault succeeded nonetheless. The 13,000 American and 4,300 British paratroopers blocked roads and bridges that the Germans would have to use to launch a counter-attack. Though casualties among the follow-on glider-borne troops were high,

Medics treat the wounded after the invasion.

most survived the crash landings of their Horsa and Waco gliders. And for many hours after the landings, the dispersion of the airborne and glider-borne troopers confused German commanders about where—and how many—there were.

This was not the case for the amphibious forces closing in on the Norman coast. Remarkably, given the magnitude of the operation and the marginal weather, things were generally on time—and most units landed reasonably close to where the voluminous Overlord Operations Plan ordered them to go.

- **0100** U.S. and Royal Navy warships in the van of the Allied armada called all hands to General Quarters as a flotilla of tiny minesweepers began clearing sea lanes into the invasion beaches.

- **0200** The first Allied bombers took off from bases in England to pound targets around the beachheads.

- **0300** Thousands of British and American troops aboard Horsa and Waco gliders began descending on fields and roads up to ten miles inland to reinforce the paratroopers.

- **0309** One of the few German radars that was still operable detected the invasion fleet off Le Havre. Field Marshal von Rundstedt, comfortable in the chateau he occupied at Saint-Germain outside of Paris, declined recommendations by his staff to start moving Panzers toward Normandy.

- **0330** Agents of the French resistance *"Centurie"* network were at work cutting both civilian and German military telephone and telegraph lines, sowing confusion among various levels of command in the Wehrmacht.

- **0400** Word was passed aboard the thousands of Allied ships now gathered off the assault beaches: "Prepare to land the landing force," the signal for 150,000 British, Canadian, and American men to start moving to their disembarkation stations and their landing craft.

- **0515** The battleships *Texas, Nevada*—a Pearl Harbor survivor—and *Arkansas* opened up on Omaha and Utah beaches from 11,000 yards offshore. Joining the old battlewagons closer in, the heavy cruisers *Tuscaloosa, Quincy,* and *Augusta*—along with more than two dozen destroyers and gunboats—began blasting German fortifications emplacements ashore.

- **0530** The naval bombardment paused for fifteen minutes for waves of heavy bombers to pass overhead for the only scheduled air strike on the beach defenses. Unfortunately, because of the cloud cover, most of the 4,400 bombs dropped on Utah beach by 276 B-26 bombers fell short and into the water. At Omaha beach it was even worse. Not a single one of the 480 B-24 Liberators dispatched on the mission hit even close to the beach or the coastal defenses. All the bombs fell well inland.

- **0630** H-hour on the American beaches—the men of E Company, 2nd Battalion, 8th Infantry, 4th Division, landing on Utah beach became the first U.S. soldiers to come ashore at Normandy. Though the wind and tide had pushed them almost a mile south of their target, they encountered little opposition. By nightfall, more than 21,000 troops, 1,700 vehicles, and 2,000 tons of supplies would be ashore on Utah—at a cost of fewer than 200 casualties.

On Omaha beach it was an entirely different story. The German fortifications covering Omaha between Port en-Bessin on the left and the cliffs of Pointe du Hoc on the right were largely unscathed by the pre-H-Hour bombardment. Enfilade fire from 88 mm guns mounted in concrete casements cut to pieces the assault waves of the 116th Regiment of the 29th Infantry Division and the 18th Regiment of the 1st Infantry Division as they reached the beach.

The members of the U.S. Navy Combat Demolitions Team that led them into the maelstrom were the first Americans to touch down at Omaha. Among them was twenty-four-year-old Chief Petty Officer Jerry Markham from Jacksonville, Florida.

CHIEF PETTY OFFICER JERRY MARKHAM, USN
US Navy Combat Demolition Unit #46
Omaha Beach, Normandy, France
6 June 1944

A Navy lieutenant commander named Draper Kauffman convinced the Navy to form up our Combat Demolition Units. We nicknamed our team the "Tough Potatoes"—five men and an officer who were together because we wanted to be, not because we were ordered or assigned. At twenty-four, I was the "old man." We had great *esprit de corps* and knew each other and our jobs well. We had been well trained for combat reconnaissance and demolition work. When we finished our training in Virginia, all eleven Combat Demolition units shipped to England in December 1943.

We trained in Wales and in different parts of the Bristol Channel and English Channel in all kinds of terrain and different kinds of beaches and obstacles. Because we didn't know where we might end up, we trained for a little bit of everything.

About two months before D-Day, we were given the intelligence on the different landing sites and invasion beachheads for Normandy—though the maps and charts didn't have labels as to location.

The Omaha beachhead was a crescent-shaped curve about five miles long and 300 yards wide at mean low tide. It has a twenty-six-foot tide and the Germans had placed mines and obstacles at different tide levels—from low to high tide—to rip or blow the bottom out of landing craft or amphibious ships no matter when they came in.

Our job was to blow a fifty-yard path *through* those mined obstacles, all the way up to the high water mark, and mark it with buoys so that that the landing forces coming behind us could get ashore without hitting a mine. After the mines were cleared, we were to go in and remove booby traps on the beach. And after the beachhead was established, we were supposed to clear the ravines above the beach so that the troops could get off the beach quickly.

Our rubber boat hit the beach at mean low tide. Our explosives were made up of packs specially designed to detonate mines and flatten obstacles like the Belgian Gates that the Germans had built. We also had Bangalore torpedoes to blast through barbed wire and mine fields on the exits from the beach.

We were supposed to do all this during darkness but we were delayed getting to the beach and the Germans saw us coming. Even before we landed, their mortars knocked out some of our boats with direct hits. When we got ashore it was in a shower of machine-gun fire. They had every inch of that beach zeroed in for crossfire. The cliffs about a half-mile behind the beach were about 100 to 150 feet high and they had concrete gun emplacements inside the cliffs, firing down.

On our right and left they had their 88s—mounted in concrete pillboxes to fire down the beach. The velocity of an 88 mm projectile is so high that it would hit or go past before you heard the gun fire. As we got to shallow water we jumped out to haul our rubber boat up on the beach and a shell hit and killed my officer and two of our men. We never heard it coming.

Those of us who were left got about a third of the way up the beach, fighting strong crosscurrents. The demolition units on my right were pretty badly shot up and began to drift down to us. We took shelter as best we could behind the obstacles that the Germans had constructed in the water and did succeed in blowing a partial gap.

We had two units completely wiped out when direct mortar hits on their boats detonated their demolition charge and killed everybody. Within that first hour we had over 50 percent casualties.

When I finally reached the high water mark at the beach, the Germans lobbed a mortar in and hit the top of an embankment, and caved it in, covering three soldiers. Without thinking, I rushed over and dug their heads out with my hands and helped them get out, not realizing I was exposing myself to machine-gun fire. That's when I got wounded.

In order to help the soldiers get off the beach, two of our Navy destroyers came into the shallows, and fired their 5-inch guns point blank into the German gun emplacements on the cliff. They used their 40 mm guns to help clear the ravines and knock out the German machine guns and mortars.

I spent the night of D-Day in a foxhole I dug out on the beach. Lots of ration cans floated ashore with the tide, so we had plenty of food. I got off the beach the fourth day because I had started passing blood from a shell concussion. I had made the mistake of going down to a hospital ship for some medication to stop the internal bleeding. And they slapped a tag on me, threw me on a litter and took me back to England. About two days in the hospital there, I started badgering the nurses and trying to donate blood—because I heard they give you three ounces of Scotch if you donate blood. They said, "Get out of here! You don't have enough blood to spare, and you're driving the nurses crazy."

So I went back to our base. A few weeks later they put what was left of us on a transport ship and transferred us back to New York so we could get rested up to go to the Pacific theater.

As Jerry Markham's Navy Combat Demolition Unit struggled to clear the mines and obstacles on Omaha beach, the 2nd Ranger Battalion was struggling to scale the sheer 130-foot cliffs three miles to the west at Pointe du Hoc. Their task was one of the most difficult at Normandy: after attaining the heights, they had to cross the mined and obstacle-ridden crest under fire to destroy six 155 mm cannon mounted in reinforced concrete casements—all before the guns could bring fire to bear on the beaches below and the fleet offshore. Twenty-four-year-old New Jersey native Leonard Lomell was one of the handpicked volunteers chosen for the mission.

FIRST SERGEANT LEONARD LOMELL, US ARMY
Company D, 2nd Ranger Battalion
Normandy, France
6 June 1944

I was the first sergeant of D Company of the 2nd Ranger Battalion, formed in Fort Mead, Maryland, out of the 76th Infantry Division. We were always told that we were supposed to be the best of the best, but that we'd have the toughest missions. We went through 2,000 volunteers to make our team of 500.

We started preparing for in England in late April, for Pointe du Hoc. Lieutenant Colonel James Rudder, our battalion commander, pushed us hard—telling us that we were going up against the best-defended shoreline in the world. General Omar Bradley, commanding officer of the American ground forces, told us that this would be the most dangerous mission he ever assigned anybody. So, 225 specially chosen Rangers—and I was one of them—were picked to make that raid.

That day was terrible—stormy, cold, rainy, and windy. Our company had a three-pronged mission: First, climb the cliffs and destroy the six big guns on top so they wouldn't kill thousands of men on Omaha beach and Utah beach. Second, get to the coast road between Omaha beach and Utah beach and establish a roadblock so that the Germans couldn't reinforce their troops at the beaches. And third, destroy any German communications equipment we found so they couldn't communicate.

Though we didn't know it, several days before D-Day, the Germans relocated the guns inland to an alternate position. No aerial photos or intelligence showed that they were gone. The Germans had disguised the move by sticking telephone poles out of the casements to fool our reconnaissance.

On D-Day we had breakfast at about 0300, loaded British LCAs—about twenty-five men per boat—and we were lowered into the water at about 0400. We headed into the beach but our British guide boat led us to the wrong point—about three or four miles west of where we were supposed to be. When we got close to shore, our team leaders realized we were in the wrong place and told the coxswains—and then the LCAs had to run whole distance back to where we belonged—while about 200 yards off the coast—as the Germans fired mortars and small arms at us from atop the cliffs.

As we landed, we lost one of the LCAs—a lot of our officers and one-third of our company were gone in a few seconds. As our ramp went down and I jumped into the water, I was the first one shot—through the right side.

By the time we got to the cliffs we had lost the element of surprise and the Germans were waiting for us. We were very lightly armed and equipped because climbing hand-over-hand up a 100-foot rope is exhausting. All I carried was what I was wearing—a pair of trousers, shirt, and a light jacket—and a harness for grenades and ammunition, a first aid kit, my sub-machine gun, and a side arm.

The British LCAs that brought us in were equipped with six rocket launchers—three on each side—and the rockets were connected to grappling hooks and coils of climbing line. As soon as the ramps opened, the rockets fired—and soon the face of the cliff had all these ropes hanging down it—and Rangers climbing up—while the Germans fired down on us and dropped grenades on our heads.

The face of the cliff was clay—which is slippery when wet. Soon it was like the climbing line had been coated with grease. We finally got to the top of the cliff by sheer willpower—and with the help of a U.S. Navy destroyer that came in close to fire over our heads to pin down the Germans.

When we got to the top, we discovered that the big guns were gone so a dozen of us headed to the coast road. We let group of about 180 Germans pass by us while we hid behind a rock wall—and then followed them at a distance. That's how we found the guns at about 0830 in the morning.

Sergeant Jack Cume from Altoona, Pennsylvania, and I went down this road and came upon a group of about seventy-five Germans getting briefed by their officers. They were in various states of undress and putting themselves together.

Jack covered me while I took two Thermite grenades and put 'em into the gears of the big guns. Thermite is a magnesium—and it burns hot enough to melt metal. In an artillery piece it will weld a breech block closed or lock the elevating and traversing mechanism, rendering the gun inoperable. To me it was a chemical wonder. And it didn't make any noise—it didn't draw any attention from the Germans—so we got the job done.

To destroy the gun sights, I took my jacket off and wrapped it around my stock of my sub-machine gun so it wouldn't make any sound. Without that padding, it would sound like a hammer hitting it. And it worked out well.

These guns had a range of twelve miles, and that's where the invasion fleet was anchored. That's why it was imperative that these guns be destroyed. When we were done we ran like scared rabbits back to our roadblock.

We held the roadblock for three days and nights against all the German units that tried to get through to Omaha beach on that road. And though we took a lot of casualties, no German unit got past us. We started out with 295 men and by the time we were relieved we only had ninety men still standing that could fight on.

When the Rangers were finally relieved, Len Lomell's wounded side was severely infected and gangrenous. He was evacuated to England where he was operated on. After a two-month recuperation, he rejoined his fellow Rangers.

While 1st Sergeant Lomell and his Rangers were struggling to scale the cliffs at Pointe du Hoc, the soldiers of the 1st and 29th Infantry Divisions below them on Omaha beach were being cut to pieces. The German fire was so lethal that in some cases entire units disappeared before ever getting to the beach. Lt. Art Van Cook from the Bronx was an "old man" of twenty-six on D-Day. He trained as an artillery officer near his base at Plymouth, England, and landed on Omaha beach under a hail of small arms and mortar fire.

FIRST LIEUTENANT ARTHUR "ART" VAN COOK
111th Field Artillery Battalion, 116th Infantry,
29th Infantry Division
Omaha Beach, Normandy, France
6 June 1944

They sent me over to Europe in early 1943. I joined the 29th Infantry Division in England and I was assigned to the 111th Field Artillery Battalion—a 105 mm howitzer unit assigned to provide artillery support to the 116th Infantry Regiment.

When we put out to sea on the way to Normandy we could see thousands of ships of every kind, size, and shape. We were embarked on an LST—for Landing Ship Tank. Inside the well deck of the LST were our twelve 105 mm howitzers, loaded into DUKW amphibious trucks—we called them "Ducks."

Each one of the DUKWs also carried fourteen or fifteen men, and ammunition. The "Ducks" were supposed to "swim" ashore and then drive forward on their wheels to put our artillery tubes into position to support the 116th Regiment—the assault wave for the 29th Division.

We were meant to "splash" the DUKWs about a mile or so offshore. But instead, the LST dropped us off about nine miles out and the sea state was terrible. As we headed in just after dawn, the battleships, cruisers, and destroyers were blazing away but I was somewhat skeptical that we were going to make it into the beach.

My DUKW started to take on water faster than the pumps could handle it and we couldn't bail fast enough. Some of the DUKWs rolled down the LST ramp and went straight to the bottom. We had practiced this before—but never in heavy seas. As it turned out, we lost eleven of our twelve howitzers before we ever got to the beach.

I transferred over to what they call an LCVP—Landing Craft Vehicle Personnel. It didn't make it either. So I wound up on something called a Rhino Ferry—a flat barge powered by two diesel engines with a ramp. Once ashore the Rhino Ferries could be linked together as causeway sections. This one was loaded with trucks, half-tracks, a single howitzer, ammunition, supplies, and equipment and we slowly rumbled toward the beach.

About 100 yards off the beach one of the engines was knocked out by an exploding German shell. It seemed like it was raining lead and steel all around us—and we're all just standing on this flat barge!

As the Rhino Ferry beached, one of the soldiers was hit by machine-gun fire as he jumped off into the water. Several others were killed and wounded by machine-gun and small arms fire as they tried to get up the beach.

I was supposed to get to Omaha beach at 0700 but I didn't land until around 0845. And even then we were taken to the wrong place. We were 1,000 yards from where we were supposed to land—but with all the wreckage from the assault wave of the 116th, it was the only place we could get ashore.

There were medics working on the beach, but they couldn't cope with all the casualties. There were bodies, parts of bodies, and guys moaning and bleeding everywhere—it was a terrible sight and you felt so helpless that you couldn't do anything for these guys.

On D-Day I was supposed to be artillery liaison for the 116th Infantry. But we only had one howitzer that had made it to the beach. Since one gun can't do much, we turned it over to the 7th Field Artillery Battalion of the 1st Division and joined the infantry.

A Company, 1st of the 116th—the lead assault unit—was almost wiped out completely by direct hits from the German 88s firing from the flanks—part of the direct fire across Omaha beach. I went to check in with the battalion commander, Lt. Col. Mullins.

That morning he was everywhere—running up and down the beach, moving people along, trying to get things organized. He'd shout, "Get up and go—if you stay here you're gonna die! So you might as well get off this beach." It was that kind of leadership that gave us the incentive to keep moving. By D-Day afternoon he was dead—killed by a German machine gun.

When a captain was killed, a lieutenant took over. If a lieutenant was killed, the sergeant jumped in. We were well trained to get the job done, which was also another incentive to keep moving. Besides, if you didn't get off that beach, you'd be run over by your own stuff. Despite the German fire, wave after wave was still coming in—heavy artillery, tanks, and jeeps were coming ashore—the landing craft wending their way through the obstacles that were still in place.

Some very brave small unit leaders got the men up and the infantry and engineers blew pathways through the barbed wire entanglements,

American soldiers reach the shore after their landing craft are attacked.

mines, and obstacles. By mid-afternoon they were crawling—a foot at a time—up the draws and ravines that led up to the high ground where the German trench lines and fortifications were. By nightfall on D-Day we had pushed to the top of the cliff, probably half a mile from Omaha beach.

Though the 29th Infantry Division, landing on the right side of Omaha beach, had the toughest time and the highest casualties on D-Day, things were only marginally better on the left side, where the 1st Infantry Division landed. Staff Sergeant Walter Ehlers of Manhattan, Kansas, had to get his parents' permission to join the Army with his older brother Roland. They had both seen action with the 1st Infantry Division in North Africa and Sicily in the same rifle company. Roland had been wounded in Sicily, so on 6 June 1944 when they both landed at Normandy, they did so in different companies.

STAFF SERGEANT WALTER D. EHLERS, US ARMY
Company L, 3rd Battalion,
18th Infantry Regiment, 1st Infantry Division
Omaha Beach, Normandy, France
10 July 1944

Two days before D-Day my platoon was assigned a special mission. As soon as we landed in the second wave we were to punch through a ravine to the high ground about 500 yards off the beach. As it turned out we came in right after the *first* wave, about two hours ahead of the second wave. When we got to where we were supposed to punch through, the beach hadn't yet been cleared and everyone in front of us was pinned down.

It was something because all the way into the beach in our Higgins boat we had been watching all these waves of planes passing over us—and the firing of all those big naval guns from the battleships and cruisers—and then closer in, the rocket ships firing. But when we got to the beach, there were all these guys getting hit from these German emplacements. Some of the rockets struck the German pillboxes and hit them, but they didn't do anything to them because they were so fortified.

We hit a sand bar. And I asked the coxswain driving the Higgins boat, "Is this as far as we're going?" And he said, "We can't go any farther, we're on a sand bar." So he let the ramp down and we got out—and naturally, on the other side of the sand bar, we went down into the water almost over our heads. My second in command, a sergeant, was so short he was pulled under the water. But we all managed to get to the beach.

When we got to the high water mark there was this incredibly brave beach master—standing there under fire—and directing traffic! I ran up to him and asked, "What direction do you want us to go from here?" He said, "Go straight ahead, and follow that path—otherwise you'll be in a minefield." So we did, despite the many bodies on our right and left. They were the guys from the first wave who were killed trying to get through the mines.

We raced inland some distance, and came to a row of barbed wire and two men from an engineer unit were lying there. One of them said, "We're pinned down! As soon as we move, they fire on us."

I told him, "We'll cover you. We'll fire up into the trenches while you guys blow the barbed wire with your Bangalore torpedo." They did it— although one guy was killed in the process. We rushed into the German trenches and I was feeling pretty good because I had gotten my squad of twelve soldiers across the beach without being killed even though the first wave had 50 percent casualties, and the second wave suffered 30 percent casualties. Some of the companies and individual squads or platoons even lost *100 percent* to casualties.

None of these guys had ever been in combat before and some of 'em wanted to hold up and dig in. But I told them, "We can't stay here, you'll get killed." So I just kept them moving. As we ran up into the trenches, the Germans started running from us. We took a pillbox from behind and captured four Germans. I sent them back down to the CP with one man from the squad.

From the high ground where we were, we could look back and see the beach and the wave with K Company—my brother's company and the one we had served in together in North Africa and Sicily—as they landed. That night I heard that the K Company commander got killed on the beach. And so did a lot of other guys in the company—the guys I knew and some close friends. I asked if my brother had made it, but nobody knew.

On D plus two—the night of June 8—we had just dug in when a German patrol bumped into our lines. They opened fire right in front of us. Our company commander told me to take a patrol and go after the Germans, so I set out with four of my men to follow these guys. I was the only person in this squad that had seen action before, but after two days of pretty bad combat, they had learned quickly.

It was pitch dark and we couldn't see but we could *hear* the Germans—up ahead of us, and moving faster than we were. We were cautious but they must have felt threatened, and took off fast. Then we ran across a briefcase that one of them had dropped. I picked it up and brought it back to the CP. Our officers opened the briefcase; it had maps and documents inside, showing the enemy's second and third line of defenses.

The next day, the ninth of June, we were in the attack again and I was leading my squad from hedgerow to hedgerow across the fields when we were fired upon. I told the guys, "We don't want to get caught out here in this field, hurry to that next hedgerow."

When we got to the hedgerow where the firing was coming from we could hear voices and I warned my squad, "Here comes some Germans!"

They saw me and fired first but missed and I got all four of them. I crept further up the hedgerow and saw more Germans in a machine-gun nest. I told my guys to reload and fix bayonets, and we charged the machine gun. I shot the gunner and killed him, and the others ran away.

A little while later we practically bumped into another machine gun, right at the corner of the hedgerow. We knocked out that machine gun with rifle fire and grenades and then charged up the ridge on the other side of the hedgerow.

Just over the crest we came upon two big German mortar positions with about ten men in them. They were more surprised than we were and we killed them all and captured their mortar tubes. We captured one more machine gun before dark and some of the guys in the squad said that I had killed eighteen Germans that day.

On the morning of the tenth the Germans launched a counter-attack and we were told to pull back because we were about to be surrounded. We were told to cover the withdrawal of the rest of the company but before we could pull back we started taking fire from the hedgerows in front and both sides of us.

I saw some Germans setting up a machine-gun nest in the corner of the hedgerow so I shot them but I got hit in the side by a bullet that turned me around, and as I'm falling, I saw a German up in the hedgerow and I shot him, and he fell to the ground.

As I rolled over I saw my BAR automatic rifleman go down so I crawled over to him, put his arms around my neck, and dragged him back to the protection of our hedgerow. Then I ran back and got the BAR so it wouldn't fall into enemy hands.

By the time I got back to our lines with the BAR the medics were there, treating my wounded rifleman. As they started to load him into the ambulance I asked my company commander, "Captain, can you have the medics look at my back before they leave because I've been hit." He turned me around, and he said, "Oh my God, you should be dead! You've been shot clear through." When they raised my shirt they saw a bullet hit a rib, went in and out and into my pack where it hit a bar of soap, passed through my mother's picture and out the back of my pack.

I didn't want to leave my men so I had them dress the wound. It was okay as long as I didn't wear my pack because it rubbed up against the two holes where the bullet went in and out. So I carried a bandolier of ammunition across my shoulder instead, and it didn't bother my wound.

A month later, on the fourteenth of July, Captain Russell, the new K Company commander, came and told me that my brother Roland had been killed on D-Day.

Later on, in Belgium, I was promoted to second lieutenant and the company commander and first sergeant came to me and said, "Lieutenant Ehlers, we have to get you out of here." I asked, "What's the hurry?" I still had my battle fatigues on, and was planning to go back up to the line. But the CO said, "We've got to get you back to Paris to get your Medal of Honor before you get killed!"

I was put on a jeep and sent back to Paris, where General John C. H. Lee awarded me the Medal of Honor. It was first time I'd ever been in an officer's dress uniform. Afterwards I rejoined my outfit, and after we had crossed into Germany, I got wounded again.

On that occasion, the New Testament that my mother had given me must have fallen out of my pack. Years after the war, a German woman mailed it to my mother, because her address was in it. She was pleased to see that I had read from it a lot before it fell out of my pack. She told me that she prayed every day. Where would we be without mothers who pray for us?

Wounded Rangers are treated after they scaled the cliffs.

National Archives

The Germans that Walt Ehlers would fight all the way into their home-land were slow to realize what was happening at Normandy. It was mid-morning before Field Marshall Erwin Rommel was even informed of the attack. He abruptly ended his visit to his wife in Germany and hastened back to Normandy.

Hitler wasn't told about the invasion until even later—his military advisors and commanders were afraid to wake him. He didn't get up on D-Day until close to noon, and it was four in the afternoon before Hitler decided to release two Panzer divisions for a counter-attack. By then it was too late.

By nightfall on D-Day the Allies had landed over 150,000 troops on the five invasion beaches. There were more than 5,000 Allied casualties, but they had cracked Hitler's Atlantic Wall. Within days, a quarter of a million more men, thousands of tanks, trucks, and nearly a million tons of supplies would be pouring into Fortress Europe. And Dwight Eisenhower's unsent message accepting responsibility for a disaster at Normandy would wait four years before becoming public.

CHAPTER 12
FREEING FRANCE FROM HITLER
1944

itler's delayed reaction to Overlord cost the Wehrmacht dearly. By the morning after D-Day, the breach in his Atlantic Wall was all but irreparable. Despite horrific American casualties at Omaha on 6 June, the Führer's belated release of the 12th SS Panzer and Panzer Lehr Divisions meant that the German armor, now under repeated attack from the air, would be unable to prevent consolidation of the Normandy beachheads. By 10 June, Eisenhower landed sufficient forces to close the gaps and connect the separate British, Canadian, and American lodgments.

While German reinforcements struggled to get to the battle at the Normandy beachhead, Hitler turned to his "secret weapons." On 12 June he launched the first V-1 "Buzz Bomb"—a crude version of the modern cruise missile—against London. Though nearly half of the eighty V-1s per day that were launched against England misfired or went awry, the Führer believed that the weapons could save Germany—even after an errant missile hit his headquarters bunker on 17 June during his only visit to the Normandy front, hardly a good sign.

National Archives

U.S. soldiers celebrate after liberating Chambois.

Then on 19 June Hitler got some unexpected help—from the weather. A fierce, three-day-long Atlantic storm grounded Allied air power, allowing German armor reserves to move into position around Caen. High waves struck the Allies' artificial harbors—smashing Mulberry B at Omaha beach and damaging Mulberry A at Gold. The British effected quick repairs and were able to resume offloading troops and 11,000 tons of equipment and supplies daily, but the American Mulberry was destroyed—along with nearly 300 ships and landing craft. The storm did what the crippled Luftwaffe could not accomplish. For weeks thereafter, the Americans were forced to laboriously transfer personnel and materiel into small landing craft for deliveries ashore.

Despite these setbacks, less than three weeks after D-Day, the Allies had landed almost a million men—twenty-five divisions—at Normandy. And fifteen more divisions in England were ready to "come across" to back a breakout from the hedgerows of *bocage* country.

Despite years of Allied over-flights and intelligence collection in France, no U.S. or American commander had anticipated how difficult it would be to break through the nearly impregnable hedgerows that divided the Nor-

Bulldozer tank

mandy farmland into 100- to 200-yard-wide rectangles. Comprised of earth, tangled roots, and vegetation, the banks were often ten feet thick and equally high. Impervious to artillery, tank, and small-arms fire, the *bocage* were perfect defensive barriers, providing excellent cover and concealment for well-camouflaged German defenders—who turned the fields between them into death traps for the American, British, and Canadian attackers.

In the period 12 June–1 July, three British/Canadian offensives against the main German defenses at Caen foundered in the narrow roadways, canals, and hedgerows along the coastal plain. On the Cotentin Peninsula, the U.S. 29th, 4th, 9th, and 90th Divisions were all bloodied by battles in the *bocage*. When they finally broke through and captured Cherbourg on 26 June, the port Eisenhower had counted on utilizing immediately was rendered unusable. What the Allied bombing and artillery hadn't already destroyed, the 6,000-man German garrison demolished before they surrendered.

The night Cherbourg fell, General Friedrich Dollman, commander of the Wehrmacht 7th Army, committed suicide. On 3 July, after Hitler ordered courts martial for all involved in the loss of Cherbourg, von Rundstedt urged the Führer to sue for peace. The old Prussian general was fired immediately and replaced by Field Marshal Gunther von Kluge the next day. Little more than a month later von Kluge would also be dead at his own hand—on 18 August he committed suicide after being implicated in the plot to kill Hitler.

By 3 July, the Americans had secured the entire Cotentin Peninsula and began to push south. The new objective: St. Lô—a strategically important crossroads and railhead on the banks of the River Vire. Eisenhower, Montgomery, and Bradley believed that if St. Lô could be captured quickly, the long-sought breakout into open French countryside could alleviate the pressure on the British and Canadians at Caen.

Taking and holding St. Lô required that the Allies seize and secure Hill 192, the dominant terrain feature in the area. On 11 July, a company of the Wehrmacht's elite 3rd Parachute Division held this commanding terrain. The mission of capturing it fell to the 38th Infantry Regiment of the 2nd Division. One of the platoon commanders in that bloody fight was twenty-two-year-old Lieutenant Charles Curley from Virginia.

LIEUTENANT CHARLES CURLEY
Company E, 2nd Battalion, 38th Infantry,
2nd Infantry Division
Hill 192, Normandy, France
11 July 1944

Hill 192 really is not a big hill—it's only six hundred feet above sea level—but from the top of it you could see the English Channel and the rest of the countryside for miles around—including all the approaches to St. Lô. The Germans needed to hold it for their artillery forward observers—because they didn't have aerial observers flying over the battlefield like we did. A German parachute infantry company was holding this high ground and really meant to keep it.

We were ordered to take the hill, but to get to it we had to cross five hedgerows. These hedgerows were five to fifteen feet tall—six to ten feet wide at the base—and full of rocks, trees, and roots. We tried to dig into them to set up a base of fire but it was almost impossible. The army demolition engineers tried using TNT, put it on the ground, and blew that first hedge. There was a terrific explosion. Stuff went up into the air but when the smoke cleared, the hedgerow was still there. I told the engineers to stop because every German artillery forward observer for miles around could see these explosions and know right where to zero in on us.

The Germans usually stuck a machine gun right in a corner of the field opposite the hedgerow we were trying to get through, over, or around. The machine gun field of fire would cover the entire open field between them and us. And they knew we'd try to cross that field.

I developed a way of dealing with that. As we got ready to cross a field toward the next hedgerow, I'd call up a tank and have it stick its gun through the hedge and blast the corners of the hedgerow on the far side of the field. I would do that each time, regardless of whether we saw anything there or not. More often than not, the tank rounds would take out a machine gun that would have cut us down.

Eventually some bright soldier developed what we called the "Dozer-Tank"—it was a Sherman tank equipped with a bulldozer blade. With a couple of those we could punch holes right through the hedgerows for both the tanks and the infantrymen to go through.

When we got to the base of Hill 192, I deployed my platoon in a skirmish line and hunkered down while the forward observers called in fire. The barrage must have lasted an hour—with 105s, 155s and 8-inch guns blasting the hillside—over 20,000 rounds I'm told. But as soon as it stopped and we launched the attack, the German machine guns and mortars opened up on us. I had two killed, and two wounded. Some of the other units had ten or fifteen killed and a whole lot more wounded. We ended up taking Hill 192 by brute force.

Between Hill 192 and the center of St. Lô there was about eight kilometers of hedgerows and little villages. We had to take every hedgerow—and every house on the way into St. Lô—one at a time and the Germans fought back at every one of them. I lost one of my sergeants, a squad leader, when he got shot after climbing up on a hedgerow to shoot down on some Germans digging in on the other side.

As we got closer to St. Lô, the Germans were employing mines in the edges of the narrow roads to take out our tanks. The only way to deal with that problem is to have infantry out in front of the tanks to check for mines. As we approached one of these little villages outside of St. Lô I was walking point in front of a "buttoned up" Sherman—meaning all his hatches were closed—when I spotted a German Mark IV Panzer up ahead. I ran back to our lead tank to point out the German tank and was right in front of him when an enormous explosion went off just over my head. My helmet went flying and so did I. The gunner, who hadn't seen me—or the German tank I was trying to point out—had fired the main gun at a sniper up ahead. I can't believe it didn't blow out my eardrums. I couldn't hear for a while.

It took us eight days to take St. Lô—and by the time we got control of the city, it was in ruins. We all knew then that kicking the Germans out of France was going to be a very tough fight.

St. Lô was liberated on 18 July—the day after Rommel was severely wounded by an Allied air attack near Caen. Though Bradley wanted to press on, his 1st Army had suffered some 40,000 casualties in two weeks of combat. He had no choice but to pause the offensive while reinforcements, replacements, and fresh supplies were sent forward to the spent troops.

Some in Hitler's entourage claimed that the hiatus was proof that the Normandy landings could be contained and defeated. But others, including Colonel Claus von Stauffenberg, saw the Allied build-up at Normandy and the Red Army "Bagration" offensive on the Vistula east of Warsaw for what they were—the beginning of the end. He and a handful of senior officers decided it was time for a military coup—after which they would sue for peace.

On 20 July, von Stauffenberg planted a small bomb beneath the conference room table at Hitler's Rastenburg headquarters in East Prussia. The blast wounded but failed to kill the Führer—who launched an immediate

U.S. troops advance at St. Lô.

purge against any and all suspected of being part of the plot. Over the next nine months, some 5,000 Wehrmacht officers and civilians—most with no connection to the attempted coup—were rounded up by the Gestapo and summarily shot. Others—including the Desert Fox himself, Erwin Rommel—were forced to commit suicide.

Four days after the assassination attempt, with the British and Canadians still heavily engaged in the bloody fight for Caen, Bradley was ready to launch an American breakthrough from the Cotentin. Dubbed Operation Cobra, the attack was to commence immediately after 3,000 bombers and fighters from the 8th and 9th Air Forces "carpet bombed" German positions facing the four American infantry and two armored divisions west of St. Lô.

But Cobra had an inauspicious beginning. On the morning of 24 July the bombers dropped 4,000 tons of bombs through the heavy overcast— hitting the American lines with almost a third of the high explosives, killing thirty U.S. troops, wounding another 150, and causing Cobra to be postponed for twenty-four hours. The following morning, with Bradley and Lieutenant General Leslie J. McNair looking on, the waves of B-17s returned. This time they swept over the American lines—instead of parallel to them—and again they dropped 4,000 tons of bombs, hundreds of which hit the U.S. jumping off positions—*again*.

McNair and nearly all of his staff were killed outright. Another 400 GIs were killed and wounded. Bradley, watching from a café on a nearby hillside, barely escaped with his life. The 30th Infantry Division took the brunt of the casualties from the errant bombing, but still managed to get up out of their shallow fighting positions and launch the attack. Twenty-five-year-old Lt. Murray Pulver, a farm boy from upstate New York, a replacement in the 30th Division, was one of those who saw it happen—and still carried on. His resolve would be severely tested in the weeks ahead.

LIEUTENANT MURRAY PULVER, US ARMY
Company B, 120th Infantry,
30th Infantry Division
Near St. Lô, France
27 July 1944

We looked up and saw the B-17s coming from behind—instead of across our front. And then the bombs started to fall—and we all took cover. It seemed like they took forever to hit—and the explosions went on and on all around us. I guess I repeated the Lord's Prayer and the 23rd Psalm a half a dozen times. General McNair was just off to the left side of my platoon when he was hit.

After the bombs stopped going off, everybody was in shock—we were like a bunch of zombies. But even as the medics were treating the casualties, we were ordered to advance. I don't know how we did it, but everyone fell in and away we went.

I was new, having arrived on Omaha Beach on D + 6 as a replacement. A few days later I was assigned as a rifle platoon commander in B

Company, 120th Infantry Regiment, located near St. Lô. There was only one officer, besides the company commander, left in the company. After a few weeks of fighting through the hedgerows around St. Lô, there were probably only twenty-five to thirty men left in each of our three platoons.

The first time that I made contact with the Germans was when we made the first attack, along with A Company on our right. We had moved across two hedgerows, which was probably just 100 yards. And we were receiving heavy artillery and small arms fire. Then somebody hollered, "There's a tank coming down the road at us!"

I hollered for the bazooka man, and a young fellow by the name of Werner Yurtz—a German-American kid—came running up to me with the bazooka. I said, "Fire at that tank."

He looked at me and said, "I don't know how to fire it. I'm the ammunition carrier. The man that fires it was killed."

I'd had a dry run with a bazooka in England, during training—but I had never fired one before. But with Yurtz guiding my shot, I fired the bazooka, hit the tank, and it exploded. Within half an hour, I could hear someone from A Company calling for, "Bazooka, bazooka!" That time I got another tank behind a wall, about fifty yards in front of me. So now, *I'm* the bazooka man. In fact, I continued to be the bazooka man for the rest of the war.

During Cobra we were supposed to move rapidly through the hole that the bombers made in the German lines and attack St. Giles, just west of St. Lô. Once there, the 3rd Armor Division would pass through our lines and head south.

On the way, we ran into more German tanks and paratroopers. The bombing had hurt them, but they fought hard. The German paratroopers were among the best soldiers in the war.

A few days later, at the town of Tessy-sur-Vire, I took over Company B. The captain went back to become a battalion commander. That's how bad the casualties were. At that point, I had 140 men in my company and I was the only officer.

On August 6 we reached the town of Mortain and B Company relieved elements of the 1st Division on Hill 285. When we took over their position, they said they hadn't seen any Germans in days. There was just twenty-nine feet difference in elevation between Hill 285 and Hill 314. The 1st Division pulled out and left the 30th Division strung out across the two hillsides. By nightfall on the sixth it looked like we had the Germans on the run. But all that was about to change.

What changed was Adolf Hitler's belief that a surprise Panzer counterattack could somehow stop the American advance. With George Patton's newly formed 3rd Army dashing into Brittany and Courtney Hodges's 1st Army headed east, Hitler ordered Gunther von Kluge to send four Panzer Divisions—the 1st and 2nd SS, the 2nd, and the 116th—on a sweep south, then west to smash through the American lines and cut off Patton's rear at Avranches.

As the Führer conceived Operation Lüttich, the 300 tanks and 50,000 troops commanded by von Kluge would be reinforced in the battle by 1,000 more tanks from the 9th and 11th Panzer Divisions coming from the south of France and the 9th and 10th SS Panzer Divisions presently engaged at Caen. It would have been a brilliant strategy but for three factors: first, Allied bombing of the French rail and road networks made movement of armor on the scale envisioned impossible. Second, Ultra intercepts of German high command communications eliminated the element of surprise. And finally, for the German armor to get to Avranches, the Panzers would have to get through the 30th Infantry Division at Mortain—a quiet little village known for the Camembert cheese made on the dairy farms in the nearby rolling hillsides.

On 6 August 1944, as the German tanks started moving into position for the attack, Murray Pulver's Company B, 1st Battalion of the 120th Infantry Regiment occupied Hill 285, one of the two prominent terrain features in Mortain. Spread between 285 and the other commanding high ground, Hill 314, were Companies E, G, and H of 2nd Battalion, and K

Company of the 118th Infantry. Staff Sergeant Angel Garcia—the son of an alfalfa farmer from Los Angeles, California—led a machine gun squad in H Company and had his men deployed at the base of the hill. Second Lieutenant Robert Weiss, an artillery forward observer, was hoping for a quiet night when he climbed to the peak of 314 to establish an observation post late that afternoon.

Within hours, all three men would play key roles in the largest tank battle on the Western Front.

LIEUTENANT MURRAY PULVER, US ARMY
Company B, 120th Infantry,
30th Infantry Division
Hill 285, Mortain, France
7 August 1944

At 0430, just before dawn, a Sherman tank, guided by two French civilians—a man and a woman—approached the roadblock I had set up below my CP near the top of Hill 285. They spoke a little English, and they told my sergeant at the roadblock that the American tank had gotten lost and they were guiding it back into friendly territory.

But it was a trick. It was a captured British Sherman. The crew was German—and so were the soldiers behind it. In the firefight that followed, I lost most of my first platoon. From then on, it was solid fighting for two days.

I moved my CP behind some farm buildings so that I could be centrally located between my two remaining platoons. Later that morning, the Germans attacked with more tanks and motorized infantry and blasted holes in every farm building.

At about dawn, I informed HQ that we were under heavy armor attack and that they were breaking through my roadblocks. We only had two anti-tank guns and the Germans managed to get a tank past them and it came down the road to about thirty feet from us, just crawling along in the fog.

My first sergeant handed me a bazooka, and when I hit the tank, it stopped. But *where* it stopped, I could almost reach up and touch the muzzle of the 88 on that tank. That's how close they came to the stone wall we were hiding behind. Our radio was knocked out by heavy mortar fire, and the Germans either cut our telephone line, or it was knocked out by artillery fire so I lost communications with the second and third platoons. In fact we had no communications with anybody.

After we knocked off the tank, several Germans, came across the field yelling, "Americans! Kamerad! Kamerad!" They were surrendering!

The good Lord was helping us that day. Though most of us were wounded that day, not one man in my company headquarters was killed—but a whole lot of Germans were.

Fighting was sporadic during the night. The next day dawned clear and the Germans tried another tank-infantry attack across the open field. A British Typhoon fighter aircraft with a Canadian pilot saved us. He flew over and fired his rockets. They were so close that I could feel the heat from them—but it broke off the attack.

The Typhoons and the artillery saved us but we were out of food and running low on ammunition. So in the midst of all the firing, my communicator and I took my jeep and drove back to battalion HQ. On the way we were hit by mortar fire. He was seriously wounded but I just got my teeth shattered. When I saw the battalion commander, he looked at me and said, "Where did you come from?" And I said, "From Mortain."

"Well," he said, "they told me that all of B Company had been captured or killed."

I said, "No, we're still there. All I want is some food, water, and ammunition." I also got a few men from battalion headquarters and we went back with the munitions and food and water.

I was called back to battalion headquarters on the third day, and we went to see the regimental commander. He could see that I was about done in, but he said, "I want you to take two platoons of your company and fight your way onto Hill 314, and deliver batteries and ammunition to them." They had tried air-dropping supplies to the troops on 314 but it hadn't worked.

So my company pulled out in the dark the next morning and we went down into the valley, leapfrogging from one patch of woods to another. We ran into two German patrols, in strength, but we fought them off. At the crossroads we met our battalion's anti-tank company and a small contingent of infantry. The captain commanding the unit beamed all over when he saw us, and said, "Oh, thank God we got help."

I said, "I'm sorry…I'm not here to help you. We've been ordered to deliver supplies up that hill."

"You must be kidding!" he said, adding, "Come with me." We went up a little rise, where we could get a full view of Hill 314 and the road going up. There were hundreds of dead Germans soldiers and destroyed tanks and other vehicles. A lot of them had been knocked out by our air force and artillery. But in between, there were a lot of live Germans as well. When I called back to battalion HQ on the radio they cancelled our re-supply mission so in the dark we moved back to where we had started and resumed our old positions.

The fourth day was very quiet. But on day five of the battle we heard German officers giving orders from a tree line maybe fifty yards away as they got ready to attack us. I gave the signal for every man to fire at least two clips of ammunition, and toss hand grenades just when they started to advance in our direction. They must have thought we were a huge army, because the Germans pulled back and that finished 'em. Later that day we marched down the hill and into Mortain. The town was wrecked.

✪ ✪ ✪

STAFF SERGEANT ANGEL GARCIA, US ARMY
Company H, 120th Infantry,
30th Infantry Division
St. Lô, France
10 August 1944

Operation Cobra started out with our air force bombing the German positions in front of us. Unfortunately, they also bombed us—*twice.*

The bombers came right over top of us and I looked up and saw the bombs dropping and yelled, "Mother!"—I don't know why—and ran to the other side of the hedgerow and jumped into an old German trench that was already full of GIs. When the bombs hit, the ground and the trees flew up in the air and anyone who didn't get to the other side of the hedgerow was killed or wounded. We lost almost half our company.

The next day we were all ready to go again, and the bombers dropped bombs on us again. But this time they also got a lot of the Germans.

As we were attacking past St. Lô, a German shell hit in front of me as I was running with my rifle up in front of me. Shrapnel hit my rifle and broke the stock and rifle into two pieces. The fragment also got me but if I hadn't been holding my rifle up the fragment would have hit me full in the chest. But it hit the rifle first, so it was a minor wound. I didn't bother to report it.

On our way to Mortain, we were ambushed by a group of Germans from a cemetery beside the road outside this little town. The Germans were firing at us from behind the tombstones. I got mad—I got up—and ran towards the tombstones firing my rifle and the Germans ran.

As we headed into the village there was a German tank sitting in the middle of a "Y" intersection, with its barrel pointed at us when we came around a bend in the road. We couldn't get away because the houses are up close to the road on both sides. And so, instead of running back, we ran forward and got so close to the tank that it couldn't depress its barrel low enough to hit us. It turned out that the gunner in the tank was already dead—but we didn't know that at the time.

When we got to Mortain, I was ordered to set up my machine guns along a road that ran along the base of Hill 314. We moved into some shallow foxholes that had been dug by the 1st Division and waited. None of us were told that the Germans were expected to counter-attack—though I learned afterwards that we had intercepted their communications to that effect.

Early in the morning of August 7, well before first light, my machine gun position by the road started taking rifle fire, so they started firing back. I ran down to the gun and told them to wait until the Germans got closer so that we didn't give away our position.

There were about 700 of us on the hill—from E Company, two platoons from G Company, my machine guns from H Company, and K Company from the 118th Regiment. But that wasn't much to stand and fight against an entire Panzer Division.

After the first probe we could hear the German tanks moving toward us—and then our artillery started firing. But in between each salvo we could still hear their tanks coming up the road.

The artillery fire forced them to move in small groups of a couple of tanks supported by infantry. There was a lot of rifle fire from down below us in the town of Mortain and then we started taking heavy mortar fire. A round hit in the trees to my right and then another one to my left and I dove into a trench and the next round hit right next to my machine gun.

The concussion shoved me from one end of the trench to the other and broke the legs on the machine gun tripod. The ammunition in the ammo can was pushed halfway through the steel can and the ammo belt that was on the gun was wrapped around a branch above us. My section leader, gunner, ammo-man, and runner were all dead.

During the battle we found some water from a well, but no food. There was an attempt to drop food, medicine, ammo, and radio batteries by parachute, but it didn't work. The wind took them away from our lines and most of it ended up with the Germans. Since we had no aid station, we had to tend to our own wounded. When our radio batteries died, only the artillery forward observer on top of the hill had communications. After six days, the Germans must have realized that they couldn't take the hill and they began to retreat.

The artillery forward observer on top of the hill was twenty-one-year-old Lieutenant Robert Weiss. He had joined "Baker" Battery, 230th Field Artillery Battalion of the 30th Infantry Division, as a replacement. Like Garcia and Pulver, he had no idea that a German counter-attack through Mortain was in the offing on 6 August.

SECOND LIEUTENANT ROBERT WEISS
B Battery, 230th Field Artillery Battalion
120th Infantry Regiment, 30th Infantry Division
Mortain, France
22 July 1944

I was a forward observer, the official title was reconnaissance officer, and my job was to go wherever I was assigned—which could be with an infantry or armor unit. Sometimes we would set up an OP—an observation post—in a church steeple or on top of a building where we could observe the enemy. If I saw a target I'd tell my radio operator and he'd call the battalion with the target and its coordinates. I'd also tell the type of target it was—like infantry, tanks, assault weapons, and so on.

The area around Mortain was hilly country. The village was tiny—a little over 1,600 people—with a town hall dating back to the seventeenth century.

On the afternoon of 6 August 1944, I was told to get a forward observer party together. The four of us in my party set out in a jeep and met a liaison officer, Lieutenant Lee, in Mortain. I remember he had a big map and we looked at it. And there was the obvious place to be—Hill 314.

The number 314 on the map meant that that hill's elevation was 314 meters. The hill was significant because it had a commanding view to the east and south and, to the west, was the village of Mortain.

We were told that the enemy was retreating—and they had been. I expected we would just sit up there and if we saw any movement, we'd just call in fire.

Sunday August 6 was our first day on the hill. E Company arrived and got into position. Our communicators came up to check out the telephone lines. The infantry brought a hot meal in—in containers that they carried in jeeps. Late in the afternoon we had seen dust being kicked up in the distance and I called in fire on some German patrols.

But after dark, activity really picked up. We could hear the sound of German tank engines and the clanking of their treads on roads below us. And it didn't sound like they were retreating—like we'd been told. Shortly after midnight, all hell broke loose.

We weren't equipped to dig in and hold out. The terrain was rocky, and impossible to dig down more than eighteen inches or two feet. In addition, the infantry on the hill weren't equipped to do battle against armor.

They had a few mortars, almost no bazookas, virtually no medical supplies, no mines, and no anti-tank guns—just rifles and machine guns and a limited amount of ammunition. But we did have artillery, with the CP five miles away—and we had maps. They were Michelin *road maps*— but that was better than nothing.

Directing artillery requires a lot of precision—just as with rifles and pistols or even bows and arrows. There are people who are good shots and people who aren't. I just was one of the fortunate ones who could estimate distances accurately and as it turned out, I was one of the better shooters.

The Germans were to our east and north, and E Company took the brunt of the onslaught in the initial assault, but eventually all the infantry was heavily engaged. The Germans were from the 2nd SS Panzer Division, one of Hitler's favored and most seasoned units.

Early on the seventh, a German artillery officer in a jeep-like vehicle drove up to the base of the hill, reconnoitering a gun position and not really realizing what was going on. He was captured, along with his men. After that, every time a German unit approached the hill, they were blasted with my artillery.

H Company was on the south slope of the hill, right in the path of the German onslaught. They were totally overrun and most were either killed, wounded, or captured. And a few straggled up that slope to the E Company position and were absorbed by E Company—but there were only a few of them. We didn't really quite comprehend the immensity of the attacks until midday on the seventh. By then we realized we were surrounded, because now we were being fired upon from all directions.

Every night the Germans would try to get close in so that we wouldn't fire artillery for fear of hitting our own soldiers. And every time they tried this, they were pushed back. The infantrymen were holding on by sheer determination. It was essentially rifles against tanks as far as the infantry was concerned, plus of course, the artillery, which we were able to control and direct.

We were determined to hold on until we were triumphant or destroyed. Only that determination—to not yield ground—stopped the assault—for a while.

We never heard that reinforcements were on the way until the very end, and I think that's probably because no reinforcements were available. Our company still had working radio batteries, so all the guns of the battalion were at my beck and call. Plus we could call for fire from the other artillery battalions with 105s, 155 howitzers, Corps artillery, the Long Toms—a total of thirty-six guns. At one point, we were shooting over 2,000 rounds a day. That's a lot of artillery.

The Germans countered with a mobile anti-aircraft weapon—their 88 mm guns—with a diameter of about three and a half inches. This weapon was useful not only for shooting at aircraft, but could also be used against targets on the ground. They used the 88s as mobile, self-propelled guns and mounted them in tanks—clearly outgunning our Shermans.

On the second night of the fight, a German tank got almost into our position, very close to where we were, and fired a round over our heads that lit up the landscape. Then he called on us to surrender. The next day, the Germans sent an officer with a white flag to our lines and demanded that we surrender. Lt. Curly told him to go to hell.

We started out with about 700 men, and by the time the battle was over, 40 percent were dead, wounded, or missing. The Division G2, from five miles away at the CP, made the assessment on the fourth day of the battle that the Germans were essentially defeated. Well, he was correct in that assumption—as far as the overall picture was concerned—but what that G2 officer couldn't see was that they were still trying, fighting fiercely, to knock us off Hill 314.

Water and food ran out and an infantryman came by and gave me a slice of a rutabaga—which I'll never eat again. I had a single high-calorie chocolate bar, meant as one meal for a soldier. Five of us divided it, and that was our food for a day. And when that ran out, that was it.

The battle was over on 12 August, about noon as the Germans began withdrawing. The 320th Infantry Regiment of the 35th Division reached us later that day, and we were finally relieved. They had fought their way up, and got to us just as the battle was over. So we found our jeep, started it up, got in it, and drove back our battalion HQ.

All told, the 30th Division suffered some 1,800 casualties. Of the 700 men who walked up Hill 314, only 357—about half—were able to walk down. There was almost nothing left of the town of Mortain, except the church. The streets were littered with the bodies of fallen German and American soldiers. But even before the people of the ruined village returned to help bury the dead on the afternoon of 12 August, Bradley was already moving to exploit his victory.

The remnants of von Kluge's 50,000-man army, now under relentless air attack, struggled northeast to escape the oncoming Americans. Meanwhile the British and Canadians broke through at Caen. Bradley, convinced that this was a "once in a century opportunity" ordered Patton to make a "sweeping right hook"—a boxing term—in an effort to cut off the German retreat before they could cross the River Orne, south of Falaise.

U.S. troops walk through battered Mortain.

Patton's armor reached Argentan on 13 August—and held up as ordered—waiting for Montgomery's 21st British/Canadian army to close the noose on the beleaguered columns of German Army Group B. Montgomery delayed long enough to bring up more artillery and pound the retreating Wehrmacht with air strikes, while Patton fumed as 40,000 Germans managed to slip through a six-mile-wide gap between the American and British lines.

On 15 August 1944 the 7th Allied Army—three U.S. divisions, four Free French, along with U.S. Rangers and Canadian commandos—stormed ashore in southern France on Operation Anvil. That afternoon, a furious Hitler, calling this "the worst day of my life," fired von Kluge, replaced him with Walther Model, directed a retreat to the Seine—and ordered that Paris be held.

It was a flight of fancy. With more than 300,000 German soldiers trapped in the "Falaise Pocket," the Wehrmacht in France was facing total annihilation. The once mighty Panzer columns had been reduced to fewer than 150 tanks. Tens of thousands of German wounded were being transported on anything with wheels—much of it horse-drawn. And on 19 August, Patton reached the Seine, twenty-five miles northwest of Paris.

On 21 August, after three days of furious battle against the 12th SS-Hitler Youth Division, the 1st Polish Armored Division—one of the many expatriate units fighting under the British banner—managed to close the bottleneck at Falaise. The carnage was horrific. More than 50,000 German troops lay dead and another 200,000 were taken prisoner—most of them wounded or shell-shocked. While touring the battlefield on 23 August, Eisenhower remarked that, "It was literally possible to walk for hundreds of yards at a time, stepping on nothing but dead and decaying flesh."

All that remained now was the liberation of Paris. Though Hitler had ordered the city held, the French countryside was now up in arms. In Paris, resistance factions that rarely cooperated with one another began an uprising against the German occupiers on 19 August. Many of the French resistance units had been armed, trained, and equipped by British SOE and American OSS intelligence officers like French-born Rene Defourneaux. Rene's parents had emigrated to the U.S. in 1939 to escape the menace of Nazism. Shortly before America entered the war, twenty-two-year-old Rene enlisted in the U.S. Army. He was subsequently recruited by the OSS to help train Resistance fighters.

RENE DEFOURNEAUX
Provence, France
19 August 1944

I parachuted into France on the night of 8–9 August, 1944. My assignment was to link up with a French Resistance unit and carry out sabotage and "dirty tricks" against the Germans: blocking roads, blowing up bridges or destroying communication, knocking off railroads, and so on.

We did a lot of work in conjunction with the Air Force, because it's nice to have bombs going off to conceal the things we were blowing up. If you blow up a railroad switch or a telephone center and there is no other activity around—the Germans very quickly figure out who's doing it. So we liked to coordinate our effort with the Air Force.

We did pretty well. Our biggest mission was to prevent two German Panzer divisions west of us from going after Patton and his southern flank. To stop them, we had to knock off bridges, cut their communication, and sabotage their fuel. The resistance guys I was sent to help were pretty good. We made life miserable for the Germans.

I had started out in the Army as a POW interrogator in England. But one day, an officer came into my office, closed the door, and asked, "Defourneaux, how would you like to go back to France before anybody else?"

I said, "Yeah? How do you propose to send me there?" He told me that they'd drop me from an airplane, and he gave me two minutes to make up my mind. So I said, "Okay, I'm game. I'll go."

A few days later, I was in a castle, north of London. And there, they gave twenty-nine of us a series of tests—for two or three days. Afterward, they called us in and said, "The nine of you, over here—come this way. The rest of you, leave by the other way." So, they took nine out of twenty-nine of us.

All nine of us went to Scotland to learn guerilla warfare, dirty tricks, and all the "covert arts" for about two months. By the time we finished the Americans and British had just landed in Normandy. They told me, "We've got a job for you. You're going to join a Frenchman who has already been trained—his name is Leon. You will recognize him by a small scar on his lower lip. He's expecting you, so don't worry, everything's going to be fine."

We were then sent to Eisenhower's headquarters in London and we were sworn in as 2nd lieutenants. Nobody ever told us about the bad things that could happen, and never mentioned any casualties. They had made a set of civilian clothing for each of us. Two tailors made us suits typical of the part of the country we were going to so that we could blend in.

After we finished our training, they informed us that, "since most of you will be dropped, you'd better learn to jump out of an airplane." Well, I thought, jumping out of an airplane is something anybody can do. It's the landing that's tricky—so most of the training was how to land properly.

Then of course we complained about why we had only one para-chute. We had heard that in America, you jump with a reserve chute. Their reply was, "We drop you so low, a reserve chute won't have time to open anyway, so one chance is all you're getting."

The night of 8 August, I got aboard a B-24 and when we got over the part of France where I was supposed to jump, the "dispatcher"—the guy who knows the mission—tells me to jump out of the hole where the belly turret was when the green light came on. So I did.

A few seconds later I was safely on the ground and a little while after I landed, two men from the resistance unit I was being sent to help met me with the proper recognition signal and took me to the local head of the Resistance. He had been with the Vichy secret police and he defected. He went from France to Spain to England, and was trained like I was, and sent back into France.

I started with this twelve-man unit, teaching them the basic funda-mentals of guerilla warfare, making bombs, and how to help get downed airmen safely out of France. Within days I had fifty men with me. And within two months, I had a hundred. We were on our way.

The OSS didn't win the war—but we helped. As the Allies broke out of Normandy, we helped the French resistance go after the Germans—demoralizing them—and helping them to decide that they really didn't want to stay in France after the fall of Paris. Our work undoubtedly helped save the lives of a lot of American soldiers.

The uprisings in Paris and throughout the French countryside did indeed help the Germans decide that the French capital wasn't worth dying for. On 22 August, Hitler reiterated his order to hold the city—or failing that—to destroy it. But the broken army that straggled back into Paris from the disaster in Normandy had lost the will to fight. As Allied forces closed in on the French capital—German soldiers were taking "French leave"—and heading home by whatever means possible. Nearly 100,000—many of them wounded—deserted the Wehrmacht in those last days of August, only to be rounded up when they arrived at the German frontier.

National Archives

Members of the French resistance celebrate.

Late on the evening of 23 August, the lead elements of the 2nd French Armored Division, commanded by General Phillippe Leclerc, entered Paris. The next day the remainder of the division fought their way, with the help of several resistance units, through the last German defenders. On August 25—eighty days after the landings at Normandy—Charles de Gaulle, who had made his own way to France without the help of the British or Americans, made a triumphal entry atop a Sherman tank carrying the French tri-color. Hitler's worst days were still to come.

CHAPTER 13
THE BATTLE OF THE BULGE
1944

B *erlin by Thanksgiving—Home by Christmas.* They were words none of Allied generals encouraged—but after the liberation of Paris on 25 August, more than a few GIs expressed words like these. The once mighty Wehrmacht was on the run. Many American soldiers—and even some of the war-weary British in Montgomery's 21st Army Group—thought the war might actually be over before the end of 1944. They had reason for such hope.

The Red Army was closing in from the East. Germany's cities and means of production were being bombed around the clock—by the American 8th Air Force during the day and British Bomber Command at night in Operation Pointblank. By 4 September, the British and Canadians had liberated Brussels and Antwerp, Belgium. On 15 September, the U.S./Free French 6th Army Group—having marched more than 350 miles from their Anvil-Dragoon landing beaches in southern France—linked up with the right flank of Patton's 3rd Army at Epinal. With all of Belgium and Luxembourg liberated, the Allies had a continuous front from the English Channel to the Swiss border.

Between Normandy and Belgium, Hitler had lost 400,000 irreplaceable soldiers killed and captured, over 1,300 tanks, more than 2,000 artillery

National Archives

German soldiers mounting their last offensive in the Battle of the Bulge.

pieces and assault guns, and 3,500 aircraft. But he wasn't about to give up. And the Allies had a major problem of their own making: supply.

Though Antwerp—Europe's largest port—was in Allied hands, the harbor and the forty-five-mile-long Schelde River estuary opening on the English Channel were heavily mined and the low-lying Dutch offshore islands guarding the approach were all still in German control. Until the mines and German troops were cleared—no Allied ships could enter the anchorage—requiring all ammunition, fuel, food, and other supplies to be trucked 400 miles from Normandy.

Montgomery believed that a quick breakthrough to the Ruhr River valley—Germany's industrial heartland—might hasten the end of the war and negate the need for a bloody fight through the marshlands west of Antwerp. Eisenhower approved a two-part plan Monty dubbed Operation Market Garden. It called for the British 1st Airborne—along with the U.S. 82nd and 101st Airborne Divisions designated as the 1st Allied Airborne

Army—to launch a surprise airborne assault to seize key bridges over which the British Guards Armored Division would charge across the Rhine and into the west German plain. It was a disaster.

On 17 September, the 82nd and the 101st Airborne landed and quickly seized most of their objectives—the bridges over the River Meuse at Nijmegen and the Wilhelmina and Zuid Willems Canals near Eindhoven—both in Holland. The British 1st Parachute Division, however, was dropped a full six miles from the Rhine crossings at Arnhem—and was quickly surrounded by the veteran 9th and 10th SS Panzer Divisions. The advancing Sherman tanks of the Guards Armored Division—restricted to a single narrow road for their approach—never made it to Arnhem. On 24 September, the 9,000 valiant, lightly armed paratroopers, outnumbered, outgunned, and fighting house-to-house, were finally overwhelmed. Only 2,000 of them made it back across the river. All the rest were killed or captured by the Germans.

Hitler was emboldened by the bloody "victory" at Arnhem and the overall Allied offensive slow-down precipitated by lengthy supply lines. Despite the looming advances by the Red Army in the east, Hitler ordered his generals to "harden" their defenses and prepare for a counter-attack. The effect of his order was almost immediate. By early October, Wehrmacht "personnel officers" had culled through every command and rear-echelon unit to find any able-bodied man able to fight.

On the river approaches to Antwerp, 65,000 troops under General Gustav von Zangen fought desperately to hold off Montgomery's Canadians from 6 October until 8 November as the Brits fought in terrible weather to open the port. Fortifications on the Siegfried Line—the "west wall" along the Saar River—were improved by the Germans and manned against the U.S. 1st and 9th Armies. In the Hürtgen Forest—a fifty-square-mile swath of densely wooded steep terrain along the Belgian-German border—Hitler Youth, Home Guardsmen, and *Volksgrenadiers* inflicted more than 25,000 casualties on the Americans, fighting them to a bloody standstill, in their futile effort to capture the Ruhr River dams.

As autumn turned cold, even Patton, strapped for lack of adequate fuel for his tanks, found it difficult to maneuver in Lorraine against the remnants of German Army Group G that had escaped the Allied landings in southern France. At the fortress city of Metz, the U.S. 95th Infantry Division, in which my father served, was decimated in a month-long battle that started on 18 November. Meanwhile, in the deep draws of the Eifel Mountains, on the German side of the Ardennes forest frontier with Belgium, Hitler was gathering eight Panzer Divisions, two Parachute Divisions, and a Panzergrenadier Division in preparation for a counter-attack called Autumn Mist.

It was the gamble of a desperate man. Hitler ordered his reconstituted Panzers and SS troops—under the overall command of von Rundstedt and led by his devoted follower, Waffen-SS General Sepp Deitrich, at the head of the 6th SS Panzer Army—to capture Brussels and then break through to Antwerp. The Führer's fantasy was that his SS units could somehow push 100 miles from the Ardennes to the Channel coast, divide the Americans from the British, and permanently deny the Allies a new logistics base. His hope was that an armor attack out of the Ardennes in weather too foul for Allied airpower to fly would come as a complete surprise—and that they could capture enough American and British fuel to keep his tanks in the fight all the way to the Channel. His first hope would be realized. His second would not.

At 0535 on the morning of 16 December, a barrage of German artillery, rocket and mortar rounds came crashing down on the U.S. 4th, 28th, and 106th Infantry Divisions as the 9th Armored Division deployed along an eighty-five-mile swath of the Belgian frontier. It was damp, foggy, and bitterly cold and the American units were totally unprepared. Few of the U.S. soldiers were equipped with winter-weather gear for what turned out to be the coldest Western European winter in fifty years.

Both the 4th and 28th Divisions had already been badly battered in the Hürtgen Forest and their cantonments on the edge of the Ardennes were supposed to be "rest and recovery" camps. Because the Germans had strictly enforced radio silence, Ultra intercept operators had no inkling that von Rundstedt had massed hundreds of thousands of troops, hundreds of tanks, and more than 1,000 artillery pieces less than five miles away in the thick forest to their east.

Nearly all of the 28th Division was overrun almost immediately, and to their north, the inexperienced 106th Division was surrounded in a matter of hours. Farther south, the 4th Infantry Division, supported by the 9th Armored Division, managed to hold up the advancing SS columns for much of the day, but when ammunition supplies dwindled, they were forced to retreat—leaving other supplies, vehicles, and many of their wounded behind.

Bradley's 12th Army Group—whose area of operations included the Ardennes—was slow to react. Lacking Ultra intercepts or any aerial reconnaissance because of the low-hanging clouds, Bradley believed the German assault was merely a localized attack. Eisenhower, summoned from an aide's wedding in Paris, thought otherwise—and ordered the 7th Armored Division to cut into the German thrust from the north and Patton's 10th Armored Division to move north in an effort to interdict the "tail" of the attack.

The following morning the 7th Armored Division ran headlong into the 1st SS Panzer Division at St. Vith—a key road junction on the way to Antwerp—and the American fuel stores. By then it was clear that a major offensive was under way and Bradley finally moved to contain it. He issued a warning order to the 101st Airborne Division to move as fast as possible from their rest-training camp at Reims to the town of Bastogne—a crucial crossroads on the way to Antwerp.

The 101st raced the 100-mile distance by truck and arrived during the night of 18–19 December and started digging into the frozen ground. At dawn the following morning the Panzer Lehr Division with 100 tanks arrived on the outskirts of Bastogne—only to find their way blocked by the lightly armed but determined paratroopers. Michigan native Sergeant Donald Burgett was one of them.

SERGEANT DONALD BURGETT
Company A, 1st Battalion,
506th Infantry Regiment, 101st Airborne
Ardennes Forest, Belgium
19 December 1944

We normally parachuted into combat, but for the "Battle of the Bulge" we were trucked overland—more than a hundred miles in open trucks. I was a sergeant and squad leader of the 2nd Squad, 2nd Platoon, Company A, and at nineteen, was one of the "old men" because of my combat experience. The paratroopers got hit pretty hard, so every time we went in, I rose in seniority.

I had been wounded twice during a bayonet attack in Normandy, so I spent some time in the 216th General Hospital in Coventry, England, and rejoined the division on 13 July. We parachuted into Holland on September 17. When the Germans attacked through the Ardennes we were in a "rest area"—getting replacements, putting our gear back together, and repairing our machine guns, mortars, and other crew-served weapons.

We had about three hours notice to mount up and move out to defend Bastogne. There were seven roads and one railroad that went through the city—like the spokes of a wagon wheel. The Germans had to have Bastogne to move their tanks, fuel, men, equipment, artillery, and supplies forward and to bring their wounded back into Germany.

The Panzer units that attacked us the morning after we arrived had Mark IVs, a small Tiger tank, and some of the "Royal" Tigers—their biggest—and of course all sorts of assault guns, half-tracks, and wheeled vehicles. We already knew to let the tanks go by and then pop up and shoot off the infantry. We had four TDs—Tank Destroyers—that were mounted with 90s, from the 705th Tank Battalion. They could knock out a Tiger with that 90 mm gun at close range.

I jumped into a hole at one point and a German tank ran over the top of me. He was probably there three seconds, but when you're underneath sixty tons of enemy steel, that seems like a long time. If they knew you were beneath them, they would lock the track and and spin the tank around and grind you into hamburger. I saw them do it to one of my men.

You know, if you're fighting a war in a ditch, the whole war is in that ditch. You don't know what's going on in Africa and don't care. When you're in a hole, pinned down by mortars and machine guns have you in a crossfire, it's impossible to get a sense of the overall picture. That's how it was for us at Bastogne—where we were encircled, with no communication in or out.

We were shot up so bad that my company—which started the fight in Bastogne with 170—within a couple of days we had just fifty-eight men left. We ran patrols outside our perimeter day and night—just like we had for the seventy-two straight days and nights we had been in combat during Market Garden.

That also meant we went seventy-two days we didn't shower, we shaved with cold water out of a steel helmet, and washed one foot at a time; in case Germans hit again, or you got the call to attack. We had a very rough time with our equipment—after seventy-two days of constant combat, our machine guns and mortars were all beat up. We had lice, scabies, and I had trench mouth so bad I could move my teeth around with my tongue. Pus oozed out of my gums.

At Bastogne we were in constant enemy contact—a lot of it small arms fire at distances from three or four feet to maybe a hundred yards at the most. When I got shot one night, the bullet went into my hip and I could see part of the bullet under my flesh so I used my trench knife to dig the bullet out myself, because the Germans had overrun our hospital on the first night. They took all of our surgeons, medics, and medical equipment with them.

The real turning point was when the weather cleared enough for the C-47s to parachute supplies to us. We also got support from P-47s—strafing and shooting up German tanks and troops.

Finally the 4th Armored Division broke through to us but we couldn't leave because tanks are very vulnerable without infantry around them. They brought a few replacements—my squad received one man. Best of all, they brought us ammunition, overcoats, and overshoes. They took care of our wounded but some of the men with severe frostbite needed amputations.

Then, after the 4th Armored came in, the 11th Armored Division arrived. The 11th Armored was green—they had never been in combat but they had the newest tanks, with 76 mm guns and muzzle breaks. As they arrived near Bastogne, our patrols were telling us that the Germans were preparing to mount another attack on the northwest end of Bastogne.

Patton said, "We have to attack now—before they do. Let's go." He took the new 11th Armored and they did a good job. They went forward, hit the Germans head on, and pushed them back.

I liked being a paratrooper. When you go out the door with a parachute, you don't know if your chute's going to open, but if it doesn't you've only got nine seconds to worry about it.

Brigadier General Anthony McAullife was acting commander of the 101st Airborne when they were ordered to Bastogne. For three days after arriving at the small Belgian city, the paratroopers and a handful of tanks fended off the German Panzers. Then, on 22 December, four Germans carrying a white flag approached the American positions at the edge of the besieged city.

The leader of the group, a Panzer officer, told the U.S. soldiers who stopped the group of envoys that he had a message for the commanding officer of the U.S. unit. The Germans were blindfolded and taken to the 101st Division HQ, where they delivered their message to the Division G-3, a tall Texan and West Point graduate, Colonel Harry Kinnard.

COLONEL HARRY KINNARD
G-3, 101st Airborne Division
Bastogne, Belgium
22 December 1945

I parachuted into Normandy with the 101st as a twenty-eight-year-old lieutenant colonel. Before I was twenty-nine, I was a colonel—which was quite unusual in the Army. In our case, it was just a matter of survival. Eleven of my classmates started out in the 101st, and I was the only one in the end that hadn't been at least wounded, and many of them had been killed.

A typical U.S. Army division has three regiments but the 101st had four. In addition to the three parachute infantry regiments, the 501st, 502nd, and 506th, we also had a glider regiment, the 327th.

On September 17 we had parachuted into Holland for the Market Garden operation. I had the planes drop my battalion from 400 feet— which was very low—because I wanted to get a very tight drop between a canal and the river, so that the Germans couldn't cut us off before we got to the bridges we'd been sent to capture.

I told my guys, "Don't even try to assemble. Just get up and go for the bridges."

We secured our objectives, killed a lot of Germans, and captured 417. After that, General Maxwell Taylor made me the G-3—the operations and plans officer of the division.

When we jumped into Holland we were told that we'd be fighting for about seventy-two hours and be pulled out. Well, we were there seventy-two *days*—fighting every day. When we finally pulled out and went back to Reims, France, we were told, "You guys have done a great job—you can take a much needed rest." So General Taylor went back to the United States, and General Higgins, the assistant division commander for Infantry, went to England.

I got a call from Brigadier General McAuliffe, our division artillery commander, about 2100 on the seventeenth. General McAuliffe was the only general officer present when we got the alert, so he was the acting division commander. He said, "Harry, come over here. We've got something going on. There's been a German breakthrough, and we're moving out in the morning."

It was well after dark on the night of the 18–19 by the time we got the whole division into Bastogne, a small city of maybe 30,000. It was bitter cold and there had been a light snowfall in the area. Eisenhower had already sent in Combat Command B, of the 10th Armored Division. They had about fifty tanks that were working—and had taken up positions on the roads coming into Bastogne.

When our 501st Parachute Infantry Regiment arrived, we sent them out immediately to reinforce the 10th Armored—and they had just gotten in position when the first fight erupted on the morning of the nineteenth. It was that close. A handful of tanks and 3,000 paratroopers engaged the German tanks just three miles out of town.

The next unit we put out was the 506th. And then the 502nd and every time the Germans started breaking through someplace, we got there just ahead of them, forming what turned out to be a perimeter. But by 20 December, the Germans had us completely surrounded and outnumbered five to one.

We put our field hospital in what would have been a safe area. But when you're surrounded there's no longer *any* safe area. The Germans captured our entire hospital, which was really bad news, because we had a lot of casualties throughout this battle. Without the hospital we treated our wounded as best we could, but it was very bad. Altogether we suffered 4,100 casualties—wounded, killed, and missing in action.

On 22 December a party of four Germans—two officers and two enlisted men—under a white flag made from a bed sheet, approached a platoon of our 327th Glider Regiment. The platoon didn't fire on them, and went out to meet them. One of the Germans said, "We want to see your commander."

So, my guys blindfold everybody and left the two enlisted men to where they came in to the platoon headquarters, taking the officers, blindfolded, to the company headquarters. The company commander brought the message to our G-2, the intelligence officer, and to me, the G-3. And we took it to the chief of staff. The message says, basically, "We have you surrounded. And the humanitarianism of Americans is well known. We know you wouldn't want us to have annihilate you and your men along with innocent civilians, so you'd better surrender or we *will* annihilate you."

The chief of staff decided we needed to take this message to Tony McAullife.

The general said, "Let me guess. They want us to surrender?"

I said, "No, sir. These Germans are *demanding* our surrender."

McAullife said, "They *demand* that we surrender? Nuts!"—which is just the way he talks. There was a long discussion about whether the message should be answered. "Oh yes, it should be answered," McAullife said, "and it should be in writing. They wrote to us; we'd better write back to them. But I don't know what to tell them."

I said, "What you said first would be hard to beat."

He said, "What do you mean?"

I answered, "You said, 'Nuts!'"

So General McAullife writes, "To: German Commander. Reply: Nuts. From: American Commander." He gave his reply to the chief of staff and says, "See that this gets delivered."

The reply was given to the blindfolded Germans and they were escorted back to their vehicle. Our platoon commander watched them read McAullife's response. They clearly couldn't figure it out. But they went on their way. That was it.

The German commanders *were* perplexed about the meaning of the strange American reply, but it became one of the most famous military communications of all time—and when it was reported to the press by Bradley's headquarters, it cheered the American people back home. But the battle was far from over and the SS would wreak more deadly havoc on both soldiers and civilians.

The next morning, 23 December, the weather cleared—allowing U.S. C-47 transport planes to drop supplies to the beleaguered American garrison in Bastogne. On Christmas Eve the vanguard of Patton's armor arrived on the outskirts of the city and the following morning, his U.S. 4th Armored began a limited counter-offensive—despite air attacks by the Luftwaffe against targets in and around Bastogne.

On 26 December, British Lancaster bombers attacked the Germans at St. Vith and that afternoon, the skies were still clear and calm enough to permit twenty-five Waco CG-4A gliders to land near Bastogne with essential supplies of ammunition, food, and medicine for the pinned-down GIs.

Over the next four days the British 30th Corps in the north and Patton's 7th Armored Corps from the south started pinching off the "bulge" that the Germans had made in the Allied lines. Though it was not yet evident to Hitler, the threat to Antwerp was over. On New Year's Day he launched the last massed attack made by the Luftwaffe in the war—sending more than 600 aircraft against Allied airfields and installations in Belgium. Although nearly 200 U.S. and British aircraft were destroyed—most of them on the ground and many of them shot down by German anti-aircraft batteries as the planes returned from their raids—it cost the Luftwaffe dearly, as they lost twice as many planes—nearly 400 aircraft.

By 8 January the Panzers were practically out of fuel and von Rundstedt appealed to Hitler to withdraw the remaining Panzers back to the frontier while they still had fuel and ammunition enough to make it. The Führer refused—but then, a few hours later, granted an identical request made by Sepp Dietrich. By 16 January, Patton and Montgomery had linked up at Houffalize and began "mopping up" German units scattered behind the new Allied front line. It was only then that senior U.S. commanders became aware of the atrocities perpetrated by the SS troops during the battle.

Early in the Ardennes offensive some German troops had donned American uniforms in order to penetrate American positions. Though this act was regarded to be "unlawful" it paled by comparison to the wholesale murders of U.S. prisoners of war who were captured by Dietrich's storm troopers in the initial stages of the battle. At Malmedy, St. Vith, and at several smaller engagements, more than 350 Americans and nearly 100 Belgian civilians were machine-gunned to death in cold blood by their German captors—many of them on the order of SS *Standartenführer* Jochaom Peiper, one of Dietrich's most fanatical SS commanders. Staff Sergeant Bill Merriken of Bedford, Virginia, was wounded and then captured near Malmedy. He was one of the few survivors of an SS killing spree near the little village of Geromont.

STAFF SERGEANT WILLIAM "BILL" MERRIKEN
Battery B
285th Field Artillery Observation Battalion
Geromont-Noville, Belgium
17 December 1944

I was an artillery forward observer. My team conducted surveys for artillery batteries, laid-in wire to the Fire Direction Center from other forward observers, plotted the locations of enemy targets, called for fire—we did it all.

On 16 December when the Germans came through the Ardennes, we had been in the same area of Belgium for about two weeks. Most of the time, my team had been responding to incoming artillery fire from the Germans—and called in "counter-battery fire."

This was a very active area. Occasionally a German aircraft would fly in low and strafe our artillery battery. The day after the Ardennes battle started, our battery commander got orders to move west because German armor had broken through our lines to the east.

We were moving in a convoy of about thirty vehicles on the morning of 17 December—with perhaps 120 men in the trucks. We stopped one time for chow—just off the road. A short while later we were stopped again because German paratroopers had landed in the wooded area near the road. But as we started up again, the convoy was taken under fire by German artillery and we were forced to stop, dismount, and take cover.

Most of us jumped in the ditch beside the road for some sort of protection. A short while later we heard the rumbling of tanks approaching. When the lead German tank came around a bend in the road, it opened fire on us—taking out our vehicles and shooting at us in the ditches.

A German officer was standing in the turret of the tank and he was firing the machine gun on the turret. When he got to where we were, the tank stopped and he shouted to us—in English—"Get up! Get up! Up!"

When we got out of the ditch, he motioned us to the rear of his tank where another German officer told us, "If you don't all surrender, you will be killed." We were outnumbered and there wasn't anything we could do against the tanks so we did. We were told to follow at the back of the column of German tanks.

After walking for a few miles we arrived at a field that we thought was going to be a holding area for POWs. The Germans had their tanks and half-tracks lined up on the road, with the barrels of their weapons pointed in our direction. A small group of German troops searched each prisoner—taking any watches, rings, or weapons that they found. They then motioned for us to gather in the center of the field. My group was among the last to get to the cluster of American POWs, so we were out front of the whole group,

While we were standing there, a German officer standing in the back of a half-track took out his pistol and shot one of our guys. I guess that was the signal, as all the machine guns started firing. The one closest to me swung around and started chattering and I turned around and fell flat on my stomach. As I fell, two machine gun bullets hit me in the back. As I lay there I could hear the bullets hitting the ground, hitting the bodies around me. There was terrible screaming from those who were wounded.

Then, the firing stopped and a squad of Germans came out into the field checking on those who were still alive. If anyone moaned or moved they shot them immediately. And then to make sure, they would kick the bodies or hit them with rifle butts. I could hear one of them say, over and over, in English, "Are you all right—are you all right?" And if one of our boys said anything, the German would shoot him with his pistol. That went on for quite a while, because it takes a good bit of time to murder more than a hundred men, even with machine guns.

I could hear all this going on, but I couldn't see it because a dead American soldier had fallen on top of me. I could hear the sound of the Germans talking and their boots crunching through the ice in that field. At one point they stood directly over the two of us, speaking in German and then, one of them fired his pistol. The bullet went through the guy on top of me, and hit me in the right knee. It hurt terribly, but I didn't move or make a sound. My face was being pressed into the ground so they couldn't see the vapor from my breath in the cold air.

I guessed that the Germans left—and after awhile I heard other guys in the pile of bodies whispering to each other. Somebody said, "Let's make a break." I thought, this might be the only opportunity I have. I either have to do it now or I won't make it. So I struggled to get up and stand but because I had lost a lot of blood and the injury to my right knee, I knew I couldn't go very far. That's when I saw a shed, not far from the edge of the field.

As I started to drag myself toward the shed, most of the other survivors of the massacre took off in the opposite direction, toward the woods. The Germans began firing at them again, swinging their machine guns around to shoot at the group. They didn't see me. I got across the open field to a fence, climbed over, and got into the wooden shed where I passed out.

Just before dawn I came to and looked out. In the light from a burning building down this little lane, I saw a GI that I knew, crawling along on the opposite side of the road. His name was Chuck Redding—and his unit had been overrun the previous afternoon and he was trying to get back to American lines. He was the first person to save my life.

Chuck and I made our way over another field to some high ground where we spent the rest of the day in a thicket. I was too weak from loss of blood to go any further and he stayed with me. The next morning we couldn't see any Germans around so we started on our way again. As we were passing a house, a Belgian man, milking his cow, looked up, saw us, and motioned for us to come inside. He and Chuck got me into the house, and put me on a bench behind the kitchen door.

The man left to talk to his wife, and then she went around and closed the shutters and doors. I suppose he went back to milking his cow. The woman came over with a pan of water and wanted to know where I was hurt.

She wanted to take my shirt off. I said, "No, no, no!" And that was a good thing, because if she had pulled it off, she couldn't have helped me. All the blood had clotted to my shirt and if she had taken it off, I probably would have bled to death from the wounds in my back. She gave me a few sips of potato soup and I passed out again.

Somehow the farmer and Chuck got me upstairs to their bedroom. When I came to I was in a huge bed, and when the woman came into the room I said, "I'm sorry. I bled all over the sheets, everywhere."

Chuck was at the window, watching for Germans. He came over and said, "Sergeant, I've been downstairs in the kitchen, trying to tell her that we need to get you some medical help but I couldn't make myself understood so I wrote a note for her to take to the American lines to get a medic or some aid to come and help you." He also told me that one time during the night the Germans came and banged on the door and questioned the old lady. And evidently she gave the right answers, because they left.

Chuck said he had watched out the window as the woman put the note in her brassiere and start down the road. He assumed she took the note to the American line at the town. Or so we thought at the time.

Some time later an ambulance came. I heard the vehicle coming up the road, but I didn't know what it was. Chuck wasn't in the room then— he was downstairs. Then I heard this guy in heavy boots running up the steps. He pushed open the door, picked up everything that was attached to me, including their bedding, and carried me down the steps, and outside. He and the other Americans waiting outside put me on a litter.

The lady of the house came over, bent over and kissed me on the cheek, and she was crying. And before you know it, we took off down the hill in the ambulance. In a few minutes we were at the warehouse they were using as an aid station. After looking at my wounds, they put me in another ambulance and took me to the school they were using as a hospital, then took me into the surgery and removed the bullets.

The next day I went on a hospital train to Paris. From there they put me on another hospital train all the way to Le Havre, close to the docks, where they loaded me on the hospital ship and we crossed the channel on 27 December, and I was admitted to a hospital in Melbourne, England.

It would take fifty years for Bill Merriken to find out what really happened to that note. Madame Blaise, wife of the farmer, was much too frightened to go through the American and German lines. Instead, she went to the house next door that belonged to the family of sixteen-year-old newspaper delivery boy Emile Jamar.

EMILE JAMAR
Noville, Belgium
21 December 1944

Madame Blaise was very worried about the fighting and was afraid of the Germans. So were my parents. She was very fearful of going into town to find the Americans. When the Germans returned, most people stayed inside because of all the shooting—and because you never knew what the Germans might do to you if they caught you. But I had seen the Americans and I liked them—even though we were all very concerned that the Germans had come back into our country.

I had been into the town the day before and had seen the Americans at the School for Girls in the town. I told Madame Blaise that I would deliver the note for her. My parents didn't want me to go, but I told them, "Someone must deliver this message—otherwise this soldier is going to die. So I am going to take this message to the Americans. The Germans will not stop me—I am just a boy, after all."

I went on the road part way to Norville until I saw German soldiers ahead setting up a gun and putting in mines along the road. So after watching them for a while, I went through a field and then through some woods—looking very carefully for mines.

When I got to Norville—it was a very small town in those days—a soldier took me to an American officer and I gave him the note. I could speak a little English so I understood what he wanted when he asked me to show them the way.

The American soldiers put together a group of trucks—some of them had large guns on them—and we went back down the road to where I lived. On the way I showed them where the Germans were placing the mines and where they had been setting up a gun. But by the time we got there, the Germans were gone.

We went to the Blaise home and the American soldiers went inside. My parents called to me then and I went to tell them that all was well. As I returned, they were carrying the wounded soldier out of the house and put him into a truck with a red cross on it. As they carried him out, I saw Madame Blaise bend over and give him a kiss, but I did not get to talk to the wounded man. They left immediately and went back toward Norville.

But Bill Merriken and Emile Jamar did finally meet—in 1999 at the site of the Malmedy Massacre. Merriken had written Belgian friends that he would visit them during a trip he was taking to Europe to commemorate his WWII experiences. Emile, now in his sixties, wanted to meet the wounded man who rode away that day in an ambulance that he had made possible, and thereby saving Bill's life.

As the two men came together, Bill began to weep and laugh at the same time. He said, "I'm so thankful."

Emile said of the meeting, "To know him not five minutes and see the tears streaming down his face . . . there was a bond that formed between us in that moment."

✪ ✪ ✪

This "Battle of the Bulge" was Hitler's last futile attempt at any kind of offensive operation. Though it cost the Allies nearly 20,000 killed and

15,000 POWs, it had destroyed two Panzer armies—nearly 100,000 killed, wounded, and captured. None of those troops, their 800 tanks, 3,000 vehicles or 400 aircraft lost in Autumn Mist would be there when Hitler needed them to stop the Red Army as it closed in on Berlin.

During the Battle of the Bulge, the sheer courage of the American fighting man prevented a disaster and eventually won a bloody victory. This epic triumph wasn't achieved by the brilliance of military strategists. It was won by hundreds of thousands of ordinary GIs in their foxholes... exhausted, low on ammunition, hungry, freezing—who simply refused to give up— men who witnessed their friends blown to pieces, but who mustered the courage to fight on day after day, denying Hitler the success he so desperately needed.

CHAPTER 14

THE LAST DAYS OF HITLER AND THE THIRD REICH
1945

T he Battle of the Bulge, Hitler's Autumn Mist December 1944 offensive in the Ardennes, had proven to be an unmitigated disaster for the Third Reich. By New Year's Day 1945, American, British, and Red Army offensives were closing in on Germany's industrial heartland and Berlin from the east, south, and west. At the Argonaut Conference in Yalta—4–11 February—Churchill, Stalin, and an ailing Roosevelt met to map out final strategy for how the Führer would be finished off—and the shape of postwar Europe.

Churchill left Yalta disappointed. Roosevelt, clearly ill and in failing health, was unable or unwilling to stand up to Stalin's demands for hegemony over Eastern Europe. To his chagrin, the "United Nations"—as the Allies had taken to describing themselves in press releases—announced "unanimous" withdrawal of recognition for the Polish government in exile that had been resident in London since 1940. Even before Hitler's final defeat, the fissures that would dominate European politics for more than four decades were beginning to show.

Roosevelt departed from the Crimea convinced that a plan had been put in place for the "cooperative administration" of postwar Germany—divided into four "occupation zones"—U.S., British, Russian, and French. He had also won acquiescence from the Soviet and British leaders to publicly try the leaders of the Reich as "war criminals" before an international tribunal. But he also left the Black Sea port a dying man.

Stalin returned to Moscow determined to become the arbiter of continental Europe and with an understanding that Berlin would fall to the Red Army. While the "Big Three" posed for photographs at the conference, Soviet Field Marshall Georgi Zhukov's Red Army columns were barely fifty miles from Berlin.

None of the three leaders foresaw that Hitler—or the German people—would invite Armageddon by continuing to resist the Allied onslaught. Once again, the leaders of the "Grand Alliance" had underestimated their adversary.

On both the eastern and western fronts, the Wehrmacht was being battered incessantly. And in the east, millions of terrified German civilians were fleeing the approaching Russians. The brutal savagery of the vengeful Red Army was well beyond anything that even Paul Goebbels' propaganda could envision. Rape, torture, and murder of German civilians became so prevalent that many fathers killed their wives and daughters rather than subject them to the "tender mercies" of the Russian enemy. The atrocities made the Wehrmacht fight even harder.

By the time the Allied heads of state gathered at Yalta, all of Germany was being subjected to round-the-clock air bombardment, reducing whole cities to gutted, smoking ruins. There was little food, fuel, heat, or electricity available in much of the country. Yet the Germans resisted.

The day before the Yalta Conference began, Staff Sergeant Joe Regan, an Iowa farm boy turned B-17 ball-turret gunner, was part of a 2,400-plane raid over the German capital. He learned firsthand how hard a desperate enemy could still fight.

STAFF SERGEANT JOE REGAN, USAAF
92nd Bomb Group
03 February 1945

My dream was to be a pilot, and it was a possibility, until they washed out 10,000 cadets in early '44, because they weren't losing pilots as fast as they had been. It was a big disappointment that I wasn't going to get my pilot's wings. But I did get gunnery wings, and assigned to a B-17 crew.

We trained in England and Scotland and were assigned to the 92nd Bomb Group. I started flying missions about the same time we were bombing targets around the Bastogne and towns along the western part of the Bulge.

On 3 February 1945, my fifteenth mission, we took off and headed for Berlin. There were over 1,000 B-17s, 424 B-24s, and 900-plus fighters. Now, they never gave us any parachute training, because they didn't want gunners bailing out. They just told us, if you ever need it, put your parachute harness on and tighten it up. I used to put my parachute on the floor up above the ball turret.

We had just dropped our bombs, and I looked out and saw that number four engine was on fire. The pilot knew it too, and he dived to blow the fire out, as I sat there bouncing around in the ball turret. We were going straight down, and I didn't know what was happening. But he put that fire out and then pulled the plane out level at about 20,000 feet. In that maneuver we got three more hits.

We were still heading east. The pilot thought we could make it to the Russian lines, less than sixty-five miles from Berlin. But, we'd taken too many hits from the flak—some of them really bad—and the pilot rang the "bail out now" buzzer.

The ball turret is hard to get out of—you have to have your guns pointing straight down in order to get out. There's a trap door behind you that you have to open up first. So, I stood on the seat, looking for my parachute and I retrieved it. Well, there was a door just in front of the horizontal stabilizer, where you had to pull the hinge pins out. I did that and kicked the door until it fell out, and I followed it out.

Other crew members were going out from the hatch in the nose, but the pilot stayed with the plane until he was sure everybody was out. The pilot and co-pilot went out through the bomb bay. This was my first parachute jump, and I figured I'd better get it right the first time. When the crew jumped it was like throwing leaves out—we were scattered all over. And because we opened our parachutes at different altitudes, none of us saw each other as we landed.

The B-17 apparently came down about twenty miles northeast of Berlin. When I jumped I saw the ground coming up pretty fast. And so I pulled the ripcord and after a couple minutes I crashed through some trees, and my knees came up under my chin when I hit the ground.

A few minutes later, a German truck drove up with seven or eight German soldiers sitting in it, obviously looking for where I came down. Not finding me, they went back up the road. As soon as they left I headed east. I walked for five days before I got captured.

I almost made it to where the Russians were shelling a village off to my right. And I figured I was in Russian territory, but I wasn't—a German soldier took me prisoner. I was taken to a headquarters of some kind and they asked me a lot of questions, checked my dog tags, and then took my Parker 51 pen set, my wristwatch that I'd won in a poker game, and put me in a room with a bunch of German enlisted men. I was given a blanket and went to sleep. When I woke up the next morning a German soldier was looking down at me.

He turned me over to a civilian—I suspect he was Gestapo. Of course I couldn't understand what he was saying in German. But, I think they were trying to locate the rest of my crew—who must have been picked up—because he kept asking me if I knew Lieutenant Morrow, Lieutenant Early, and he went right through the list of my crew members.

By that time the Germans had a pretty good contingent of prisoners, mostly Americans. They put us on a train, and took us north to a place called *Stalag Luft,* a temporary prison camp for airmen. That's where I caught up to my crew members—they were in line for some food. When I walked up, they didn't know who I was, because I'd lost fifteen pounds and they had shaved my head. We were there for a while before they moved us down to Nuremberg.

In the weeks that followed we got news from new guys coming into camp. They'd tell us how where Patton was, so we expected liberation any day. But then they decided to move us again. They moved 9,000 of us on a march that took about two weeks, covering ten kilometers a day.

The new prison camp was a hell-hole—filthy and overcrowded. I heard one time there had been 135,000 prisoners of war in that camp. Not all were Americans, some were Allies. Hitler ordered all prisoners moved when our troops got close. He had visions of holding us hostage. There were no barracks left, so we were sleeping in big circus tents. We were just like sardines in there.

One day an American P-51 Mustang flew over, and did barrel rolls over the camp. That was signal that Americans were coming. I think the guards fled when they saw our planes come over.

On 29 April, American tanks came crashing through the barbed wire—and General George Patton was in one of the tanks. He walked through the main street of the compound, and some GI standing next to me says, "You can slap me now, General Patton." And the general laughed like hell. He was a pretty happy guy. And by then, so were we.

After Patton's 3rd Army tanks smashed through the gates of Joe Regan's POW camp, the captured airmen had to wait several more days to be taken out. Food and transport trucks finally arrived and the former POWs were taken to Reims to be deloused, given first aid, then convoyed to St. Valerie, France, where Joe was hospitalized for a couple of weeks before shipping home.

On 8 February the Canadian 1st Army launched Operation Veritable, an effort to secure the remaining ground west of the Rhine. They met stiff resistance from the German 25th Army and remnants of the 1st Parachute Division. The U.S. 9th Army, bogged down in the flooded Ruhr River valley, were unable to link up with the Canadians until 23 February—delaying a late-winter offensive east by Montgomery's British armor.

But by the first weeks of March, with the Red Army closing in on Berlin from the east, German defenses in the west began to collapse. On 23–24 March 8,000 U.S. soldiers of the 9th Armored Division forced across the Rhine River just south of Wesel—and the Rhine was the last natural barrier into the German heartland. The U.S. 1st Army, in Operation Lumberjack, captured Cologne on 5 March and two days later, Hodges's 1st Army seized the Ludendorff Bridge at Remagen. The span was taken intact—German demolition teams had failed to blow it as they retreated. Further to the south, Patton's 3rd Army cleared the Moselle River basin, pushed the Wehrmacht out of the Saar Valley, and on 11 March he crossed the Rhine—pausing only long enough to make a statement by urinating in it.

In a last-ditch effort to stem the Allied advance in the west, on 10 March, Hitler had replaced the aristocratic von Rundstedt with Field Marshal Albert Kesselring—the man who had so effectively delayed American-British advances in Italy. But it was too late—even the master of defense could not stem the Allied tide.

The German ranks were now filled with old men and boys. Kesselring was plagued by inadequate equipment, insufficient fuel, and deficits in ammunition, weapons—even food. Patton, Hodges, and the other Allied commanders rolled right over his western army in every engagement. On 22 March Patch's 7th Army joined with Patton in the Saar and Palatinate regions, and captured a bridgehead on the Rhine at Oppenheim.

By the end of the month, the American 1st, 3rd, and 9th Armies had encircled Germany's nearly ruined industrial heartland. There, Joachim Fest, a seventeen-year-old German conscript, came face-to-face with the Americans.

JOACHIM FEST
Freiburg Gun Battery
Breisgau, Germany
27 March 1945

At age fifteen I was drafted into the military, but in May 1944 at age seventeen I transferred into the Luftwaffe. But none of us had any idea of flying anymore. By then, it was much too late for that.

Goering had organized the Luftwaffe into so-called air force infantry divisions, and I was assigned to one of those—not knowing if I would be sent to either the Eastern Front or the Western Front. In the east there was the danger of being taken as a Russian prisoner of war. No one wanted that—but there was still great danger in the west, due to the Allied air superiority.

I saw action at the famous bridgehead of Remagen. I thought about what would happen if the Americans captured me—how would I be treated? During the battle we went six days with nothing to eat. So I ate my "last resort" rations, as they were called—I ate them up.

Off to the left side of my position, about 100 meters away, there was a farm. I was sent there to see if there was any food but as I approached the main building through a narrow passageway for the harvest wagons and mowers, I ran into an American soldier, and he immediately yelled, "Hands up!"

I also said "Hands up!" to him. But then other American soldiers showed and I was taken captive. They led me into a room in this farm and imprisoned there. The next day I was brought to the Rhine River and during the night was brought over Remagen Bridge to the other side of the Rhine. There, several dozen of us were locked inside a school building.

After that we were driven in trucks to a prisoner of war camp near Paris—where almost half-million German soldiers had been detained. We were all together in primitive tents and conditions. My family was in Berlin and for weeks before I was captured I had heard nothing from them. There hadn't been any mail—and of course it had been impossible to phone during the last weeks of the war. So I was very worried about my parents and my sisters.

When the war was finally over I learned that my father had been taken as a Russian prisoner of war, and my mother and my two sisters were displaced from the area of Berlin where they lived. Within the space of two hours they had to vacate their apartment to accommodate Russian soldiers. They were only permitted to take what one person could carry in one suitcase. They tossed in whatever they could, but then they were suddenly on the street.

In January 1947 I was released from the American prisoner of war camp. My father was one of the lucky few who made it back from being a Russian prisoner of war. He had lost about half his weight. We slowly nursed him back to health and he lived another fifteen years, in spite of his terrible captivity.

When I came back to Germany, I first had to finish my schooling since I had been drafted before finishing school. Half a year later I graduated with the so-called German *Abitur* certificate. And then from that moment on, I was allowed to read anything, say anything, think anything, and publish anything. And suddenly I realized that there is indeed a new freedom that is worth something.

In 1948, the Americans organized the "Berlin Airlift" to feed the people of the city while the Russians blockaded the trains and roads into Berlin from the west. The airlift has always engendered a feeling of deep thankfulness in me and in my entire generation. We will not forget—and I know many of my friends feel the same way—what America has done for our freedom.

On 19 March a tormented Adolf Hitler sought refuge in his Berlin underground bunker—caught in an undeniable downward spiral, measured only by the continuing injections that his doctor administered regularly. One of Hitler's own staff members described him as, "a dreadful sight . . . saliva frequently dripped from the corners of his mouth." Yet, the Führer continued to issue orders—including a directive drafted by Albert Speer, calling for war production to continue until the last possible moment, then—if factories or facilities were unable to function—they should be crippled or destroyed.

By the evening of 23 March, the 21st Army Group and the U.S. 17th and British 6th Airborne Divisions had followed Patton across the Rhine and the next day, the rest of the U.S. 9th and British 2nd Army had also entered Germany's heartland. The U.S. 7th Army crossed the Rhine further south, at Worms on 26 March, along with the French 1st Army.

But then, on 28 March, Eisenhower, at Marshall's direction, sent word to Stalin that the western Allies would not advance on Berlin. Instead, the British and Americans would proceed along the Efurt-Leipzig-Dresden corridor to split German defenses and then link up with the Red Army. When General Omar Bradley called Patton and told him that Eisenhower did not want him to venture any farther into Germany, it is said that "Old Blood

National Archives

Hitler shortly before the end of the war.

and Guts" had tears in his eyes. By 1 April 1945, the final Red Army drive to Berlin was on.

A disheartened General George Patton turned his army east toward Czechoslovakia, and on 7 April, his troops literally struck gold, uncovering a hoard of Nazi treasure—$250 million in gold bars—hidden deep inside a salt mine in the town of Merkers. After receiving a tip from local residents, Patton's engineers blasted their way into the salt caverns outside the town and found millions more in priceless works of art—paintings, jewels, and 8,000 gold bars—along with more than fifty boxes of gold bullion, gold and silver coins, and *hundreds of bales* of currency from various nations worth hundreds of millions of dollars. It appeared that most of the gold reserves of the German Central Bank had been stored there.

Excitement about the discovery was tempered with a grisly realization— Hitler's SS had also used the mine to hide gold and jewels stolen from Nazi death camp inmates—including dental fillings, wedding rings, and other jewelry and personal effects.

Although the Merkers mine was located in an area designated as a Soviet-controlled zone, Patton ordered the booty to be removed before the Red Army arrived.

The death of Franklin Delano Roosevelt on 12 April did nothing to slow the momentum. The following day, Soviets troops occupied Vienna, Austria, and subdued the last German defenders in Hungary. Though American and British troops paused briefly out of respect to the American president, Russian troops continued their offensive and by 13 April, 2.5 million Red Army soldiers of the 1st and 2nd Belorussian Front and the 1st Ukrainian Front effectively encircled the capital in a ring of massed artillery and mortar fire. Two days later, American and British soldiers overran the Ruhr Valley, capturing 320,000 German troops. The Third Reich was in its death throes.

Hitler marked his fifty-sixth birthday on 19 April 1945 by decorating several Hitler Youth defenders of Berlin for their valor. The next day, the 3rd Infantry Division entered Nuremberg, the seat of Nazi power. American troops lined up in Adolf Hitlerplatz and ceremoniously raised the Stars and Stripes over a huge Nazi swastika.

With the end near, Hitler was spending nearly every moment in his bunker beneath the Reich Chancellery with his closest Nazi Party officials. Nonetheless, Heinrich Himmler, one of his most steadfast followers, still managed to slip away long enough to meet in secret with Swedish diplomats in an effort to see if he could negotiate some kind of conditional surrender on the Western Front.

Now, only a select few remained loyal to Hitler. One of them was Eva Braun and another, a Hitler Youth soldier, sixteen-year-old Armin Lehmann, on courier duty, was dodging Russian bullets to deliver messages to and from Hitler's bunker.

CORPORAL ARMIN LEHMANN
Hitler Youth—*Jungsturm Adolf Hitler*
Berlin, Germany
19 April 1945

When the war started, I volunteered for the mountain *Jungsturm* unit. These were AA units to shoot down enemy bombers. I was fifteen at the time. At Christmas '44 I had the papers at home to report to the pre-military training for mountain soldiers.

I reported to my Jungsturm unit of the Hitler Youth, and our commanding officer was an army first lieutenant, who had been wounded and only had one lung left. He said, "I need a courier," and picked me for the job. That was good news for me, because to a certain extent as a runner you're on your own. You are given a destination; you deliver your dispatch, and get back to the unit. You are mostly responsible to yourself.

I was never afraid of death. But I was afraid of the Russian soldiers. We were told that they slaughter to *sterben Sie einen langsamen Tod*, which means they let you die a painful, slow death.

Twice I was given the Iron Cross for bravery, after being wounded, and for getting some of my wounded comrades out of the line of fire. We had encountered a Russian tank. A German *panzerfaust*—like an American bazooka—was the only weapon available to me at the time so I knocked out one of the Russian tanks, and completed the mission without any more casualties.

After attending to my wounds they put me on a hospital train, and then later I was sent back to our unit. But my orders changed—I was to go and defend Berlin. The unit was comprised of the students of a Jugensturm, and some others from a pre-military training facility—altogether about 150 young people.

I was there getting ready when a German-type jeep drove up and a man jumped out right in front of me, and pointed to the medal I had been awarded, and said, "Where did you get the Iron Cross?"

I explained it to him. And then he went to my commander and pointed to me and said, "Are there two more like him? I need three decorated boys to present to the Führer on his birthday." The celebration was on the nineteenth, but the reception for us was postponed to the twentieth, at five o'clock in the afternoon. We were driven right into the garden of the Chancellery. Hitler was shaking so badly he couldn't even really shake our hand. He had to hold on to his jacket.

When I first saw Hitler seven years earlier, in 1938, he was strong, healthy looking, wearing his Nazi uniform, and his medals from the First World War. He had radiated energy, and people went wild. But when I saw him on April 20, he looked older than my grandfather who was in his seventies. Hitler's birthday was that day—he was fifty-six. He also looked smaller, which might have to do with age.

As Hitler prepared for the end, American and British troops were discovering the deepest horrors of the Reich—the Führer's death camps—and evidence of the Holocaust that had been his "Final Solution." In late April, 1945, Lt. Alvin Ungerleider from Carbondale, Pennsylvania, received a call with new orders from his battalion commander.

LIEUTENANT ALVIN UNGERLEIDER
Company I, 115th Infantry Regiment,
29th Infantry Division
Nordhausen, Germany
27 April 1945

My battalion commander said, "Take I Company and two tank destroyers and move down to the vicinity of Nordhausen. See if you can find an area large enough to contain the whole regiment."

Well, I did as ordered. It was about 110 kilometers away—and though there was some minor enemy opposition, we arrived in the vicinity of Hanover, a central city that lies between the Bergen-Belsen concentration camp and a place called Nordhausen.

As we got near Nordhausen, I saw these two towers—maybe twelve or fifteen feet high. Suddenly, we started getting some machine gun fire from them. I brought the tank destroyers up and said, "See if you can knock out those two towers and go forward. When you get there, swing in and see what they're protecting."

The tank destroyers had 105 mm guns on 'em to destroy German tanks and they promptly knocked out the towers. We then broke through the barbed wire surrounding this place and the sight I then witnessed was so appalling i still have nightmares about it. People were walking around in prison garb—ragged, torn, and dirty—emaciated as you could imagine. They cheered when I came inside the compound and then some of them started falling over, they were so weak.

I got my whole company in there and said, "Go around and see what you find." After checking it out they captured forty-four SS troopers, some pretty tough guys. But they all surrendered. Billy Millhander, one of my soldiers, and I entered a large building in the center of the camp and discovered ten huge ovens—crematoriums—but I didn't know that at the time.

The ovens were cold and the doors were closed. I looked at Millhander and said, "Billy, have your M-1 rifle ready. I'm going to open each door of these things and see if anyone's hiding inside." Well, the first four doors I opened, I saw only ashes. But when I got to the fifth oven, I pulled that door open and threw it back. All of a sudden, *bang, bang, bang*—Billy fired eight rounds as fast as he could.

There had been a German SS guard hiding in there with a Luger pistol. He just toppled forward, dead, and Billy got himself a nice Luger pistol out of the deal. Then, we checked the other five ovens. But it turned out that he was the only one hiding inside.

When we went back outside into the yard, more people had come out of the barracks. We told them who we were and that we were there to free them. When they heard that they cheered and clapped. Then they saw the body of the guy Billy had shot, and they got even more excited because the dead German was apparently the meanest SOB in the whole camp. He had been beating, kicking, and abusing everybody.

I started talking in a mixture of Yiddish, French, a little German, English, and I asked them, "What are you doing here? What is this place? And how many are here?"

A prisoner spoke up and said, "Somewhere between 250 and 300 of us are left."

I asked, "How many did you start out with when they opened up this camp?"

The prisoner replied, "At least a thousand. This is one camp among twenty-three that are just outside of Nordhausen. The camps house slave laborers for the factories."

As he talked I realized there's something bad going on here, and I asked, "What were you making in this factory?"

He said, "V-2 missiles—the missiles they're firing against England."

And that's when the enormity of the evil that the Germans were doing to these people hit me. And this was a slave labor camp, not a death camp. They were making a product for the war effort. The first thought that came into my mind is how the Germans could take 1,000 people— but it was really *many thousands* when multiplied by the twenty-three different slave labor camps—and put them to work. How could they not feed them, take care of their medical needs, not clothe them?

I got on the tank destroyer radio and called my battalion commander. After I told him what I had found there, he said, "I'll send a military government team in there. They're trained on how to take care of seriously sick people, feeding them, clothing them, the whole works. So wait there until they come. Then rejoin us back north of Hanover." And he gave me the coordinates of where to meet him.

It took us two days to get back to the rest of the unit. On 25 April we got to the Elbe and met the Russians. They were on the other side of the river. Ironically, the Germans were streaming across the river as fast as they could—*toward us.* They surrendered to us, rather than be taken by the Russians.

Richard Marowitz was a talented trumpet player. Rich had set aside his horn and joined the Army to fulfill his draft obligation. He was a green soldier at the Battle of the Bulge at the end of 1944, but after a few months of intense combat he was an experienced part of an intelligence and reconnaissance platoon in the 42nd Infantry "Rainbow" Division. During a routine mission on 29 April he thought that he had just walked through the gates of hell.

PRIVATE RICHARD MAROWITZ
222nd Infantry, 42nd Infantry Division HQ
Dachau, Germany
29 April 1945

When we crossed into Germany—that was when we started to feel like we were really winning the war. But I remember the biggest thing was constantly being on the road. I had transferred to the intelligence and reconnaissance platoon and the trouble is, you're on combat duty all the time.

When we got into Würzburg, the city had been so effectively bombed that there was hardly a roof on any house. Despite that, the people seemed glad we were there. Nobody liked Hitler. And the civilians were scared when we came, because they assumed that they were going to raped or killed. You could tell that they were relieved and surprised, because we weren't doing what the Russians did.

Schweinfurt was one of the big German industrial cities we took. As we rode into town, there were dead guys hanging from lampposts. We wondered why they were hanging Germans. Somebody thought maybe the SS decided that these guys were going to surrender and they put them up there to teach the others a lesson.

We didn't spend much time in Schweinfurt. But then, we didn't spend a heck of a lot of time anywhere. We were given maps, and told to go to Dachau, then Munich. We took Dachau on 29 April, and Munich on the thirtieth. It was a mission I'll never forget.

On the way we went right straight through the middle of a German army convoy crossing the road we were on. We crossed in a hurry, firing as we went. And they just went off the road into the woods. They clearly didn't expect any Americans to be where we were at the time.

Going through one village, a German Panzer crossed behind us and fired. The round went over our heads but the concussion blew us out of the jeep. No one got seriously hurt, but getting back to the jeep, I felt something sticking through my trousers and into my leg and I pulled out a piece of shrapnel. It wasn't enough to slow us down.

As we were coming around the bend out of the woods, there was a village directly in front of us and somebody fired on us. So we piled out of the jeep for cover. But as we got out, I remembered we had a lot of stuff kicking around at the bottom of the jeep that we had liberated—like grease guns, bazookas, and 60 mm mortars—lots of little things to make a noise with. So we dragged some of the stuff up on the hill and we made a lot of noise. The people in that village must've thought they were being hit by a whole division.

Lieutenant Short sent three men from our platoon of twenty-eight to assault the town. The three guys were Pvt. Heard and myself, with

Howie Hughes the BAR man—the three of us went in and cleared the first few houses and waved the rest of the guys in.

We quickly accumulated over 150 prisoners. We lined them up, broke up their weapons and told them to put their hands on their hands and walk up the road. But then we wondered—what're we gonna do with them? While they were marching off with their hands on their heads we got back in the jeep and took off the other way toward Dachau.

Before our platoon got to Dachau, we started to get this awful smell—like cows, farm animals, horses—that've been killed and left to rot in the fields. It was a terrible stench.

We finally got to Dachau. But there was an SS camp attached to the concentration camp. A tank came out of Dachau and the gun aimed down on us. We were pinned down. Fortunately, a U.S. tank destroyer came up behind us and took the tank apart.

A lieutenant colonel was riding on top of the tank destroyer and it escorted us as we went into Dachau. Our INR platoon didn't know that a concentration camp was there. We went inside and there's *thousands and thousands of bodies.* There were 30,000 in the camp. And on a railway siding alongside the camp, there were *forty boxcars of bodies.* All were dead except—going through the boxcars they found one man still alive. He couldn't stand up—he was such a skeleton. Our medics took him out and put him in the jeep and brought him to the aid station to try and save him. I don't know if he survived or not.

So many in the camp were already dead—and many others were dying. Large numbers had recently been shot in the head, others had simply died of starvation or some disease. It was an impossible scene. Human skeletons walking down the street dropped dead in front of you. And there were piles of bodies—just piles and piles of bodies.

The prisoners pointed out SS troops who had taken off their uniforms and put on prison garb to hide among the condemned. But the prisoners knew who they were and pointed out the guards to the Americans.

Before we could stop it, two extremely brutal SS guards were grabbed by prisoners, taken to the ovens, and shoved in. Then a hand grenade was tossed in and the door slammed shut.

That camp was a grisly scene that nobody should ever have to see and it changed the attitude that our troops had toward the Germans we were fighting. Our view of them definitely got worse. These were not human beings, because human beings don't do what they did. These were maniacs. I mean, can you think of a bigger crime?

On 26 April (1300 hours Eastern War Time in Washington) President Harry Truman advised the American Legation in Stockholm, Sweden, to reply to Himmler's conditional surrender overture of 20 April. Truman's response was blunt: a German surrender would only be accepted if it were *unconditional.*

President Roosevelt's death had catapulted Hitler's psychosis to new heights of fantasy. He discussed with Speer, Himmler, Goering, and some of his aides the possibility that Truman might be more amenable than Roosevelt had been to forming a pact between Germany and the United States for attacking the Soviet Union. Yet when Hitler learned about Himmler's secret talks with the Swiss on 28 April, he dismissed his longtime Nazi collaborator from his post as the number two Nazi in the Third Reich, head of the SS and Gestapo. And several times each day the Führer issued new orders and instructions to an army in its death throes. In those last few days, many of those directives were carried by sixteen-year-old Hitler Youth courier Armin Lehmann.

CORPORAL ARMIN LEHMANN
Hitler Youth—*Jungsturm Adolf Hitler*
Berlin, Germany
29 April 1945

As a courier, I was sent all over Berlin delivering dispatches—often while being fired upon by Soviet artillery, mortars, tanks, and foot patrols. Once, three of us were being sent with dispatches across Berlinstrasse. The other two were Catholics, and they stopped to cross themselves just before they went. But I went by instinct. Somehow I could tell by the air pressure, even before the detonation, that a mortar or artillery round was coming in and could time it for when to run across the street. I was the only one who made it—my two buddies were blown apart.

Arthur Axman used me, and a couple of others, as couriers for Hitler. Initially, I had my own car and driver and it was very exciting, being a sixteen-year-old courier without rank or anything, carrying orders from the chief. Axman issued us all the appropriate papers. Otherwise we could have been executed for desertion.

When it got too difficult for a car to get through, Axman asked me if I knew how to ride a motorbike. I told him that I could—and that I was a very good driver.

Arthur Axman, the head of the Hitler Youth from 1940 to 1945, was a veteran who had lost an arm. It seemed to some that he was making every effort to save the Hitler Youth. But I thought he was determined to please Hitler and to prove that the Hitler Youth would be loyal enough to die for the Führer—and because of that, he didn't spare anyone.

In the last days, Axman had at least twenty Hitler Youth units surrounding the bunker in Berlin, defending Hitler. He sacrificed the youth instead of saving them, just to please the Führer who was moved by their self-sacrifice. Axman would tell them, "Keep fighting to the end—the Führer is with us."

I had the feeling that Axman would make it, and that if I were close to Axman, that I would somehow be spared. I tried not to think of my lieutenant friend who led my unit. He was at the front line with 150 boys and some other units. Those were their orders—stop the Russians.

In those last days of April 1945, my actions were dictated more or less by Axman's responsibilities, which were first, to get Hitler out of the bunker to safety. We were supposed to move Hitler with by covering him on every side with our bodies, and take him to the subway to get him out of Berlin, and to safety.

Hitler apparently never considered that. Instead, he and Eva Braun were married in a German civil ceremony performed by an official from the Berlin city government that Goebbels arranged to have come to the bunker.

The bunker became a very strange place. Hitler was there, of course—as was Eva Braun. Herr and Frau Goebbels were there with their six children. Eva Braun looked like a movie star. The last time I saw her, she was with Frau Goebbels and a third woman—that I think was one of Hitler's secretaries.

It was very sad that Goebbels' six children were there. Two of the little girls looked just like two of my sisters. I think the oldest was fifteen and the youngest was six. One was a boy, the others were girls. The night of 30 April–1 May, Axman offered to have one of his special units get the Goebbels' children out of Berlin and west to the American lines but Goebbels said no. The day after Hitler killed himself, the Goebbels killed their own children and then themselves. This is after Hitler was dead.

Axman made plans to break through the Red Army lines from several positions. When we left, we got as far as the river. And then a tank exploded and hell broke loose. Axman ordered me to tell all the members of our group to assemble at a certain bridge. I made it to three units, but when a Red Army artillery shell exploded very close by, I was wounded and must have collapsed.

My next memory is being on a stretcher, in front of a Russian army doctor who told me I had shrapnel in my back at my spine and was paralyzed from there down. They decided they couldn't treat me there, and they gave me whatever additional papers to clear Russian checkpoints, and I was transported in Russian trucks to the farm of my uncle.

It took me many weeks to recover but the paralysis was temporary. When the contusion on my spine healed, the sensation and movement returned to my legs.

By 29 April 1945 Marshall Georgi Zhukov had closed the noose on Berlin, ringing the city with 40,000 mortars and artillery pieces. As his Red Army troops poured into the city through the Brandenburg Gate, squads of NKVD secret police followed immediately behind. Their mission: find Hitler and the Reich leadership—dead or alive.

The first news they had of Hitler was on 29 April, when Zhukov's troops captured a ventilation engineer, who'd been summoned to a bunker beneath the Reichchancellory bunker to deal with a damaged air conditioning duct. The German revealed that it was the Führer's refuge and that the day before, Hitler had married his mistress Eva Braun in a civil ceremony.

Just after noon that same day, the U.S. 42nd and 45th Divisions captured the infamous Dachau concentration camp in Germany, liberating 32,000 survivors. The following day, Allied forces reached Moosburg, freeing a POW camp of 110,000 British and American troops.

Late on the afternoon of the twenty-ninth Hitler appointed Admiral Karl Dönitz as Reich president, Joseph Goebbels as chancellor, and Martin Bormann as Nazi Party minister. The small group assembled in the bunker and toasted the Führer and Eva with champagne, and Hitler then went to his office and dictated his two last testaments to his secretary, Traudl Junge. He then instructed that after his and Eva Braun's deaths, their bodies were to be burned. At 1530, Hitler and Eva retired to their private quarters in the bunker, where both took cyanide capsules. According to Martin Bormann, Hitler then shot himself in the head.

As their bodies burned, Nazi propaganda minister Joseph Goebbels and his wife, Magda, poisoned their six children, and then killed themselves. An hour later, American 7th Army took control of Munich, and at 1835 hours local, Admiral Karl Dönitz received a radio message from Martin Bormann claiming that he, Bormann, had been designated as Hitler's successor. Dönitz rejected Bormann's claim, pointing out that the German *Reichchancellery* had already confirmed Dönitz as *Reichspräisident* and Supreme Commander of the Armed Forces.

On 1 May, Karl Dönitz began trying to make contact with Eisenhower in an effort to seek some kind of conditional surrender of the German armed forces. At 1518—almost twenty-four hours after the Führer's suicide—Dönitz learned from Russian radio broadcasts that Hitler was dead. From that point on the Reich's collapse cascaded.

That afternoon German military resistance in Berlin ceased as 70,000 surviving German troops capitulated to the 1st White Russian and the 1st Ukrainian Armies. In the twelve days of defending their city, 343,000 Germans had been killed.

On 2 May, more than a million German troops in Italy surrendered unconditionally and Dönitz moved his headquarters to Flensburg, on the Baltic coast off Denmark, after ordering all U-boat commanders to cease hostilities and return to their home bases.

On 5 May the German High Command agreed to Eisenhower's demand for the unconditional surrender of the remaining German forces still fighting. Later that day, 9th Army units in Westphalia discovered another Nazi treasure trove in a dank copper mine. The haul included paintings by Rembrandt, Van Gogh, and Rubens; a gold sarcophagus of Emperor Charlemagne; jewelry; and an original manuscript of Beethoven's Sixth Symphony. On 8 May a total cease-fire of all German forces took effect, ending the war in Europe, and by 5 June, less than a month after the end of hostilities, Germany was officially partitioned into American, Russian, British, and French occupation zones.

The pursuit of final justice for the architects of the Third Reich continued for months after the fighting was over, but the manhunt wasn't always successful.

Though Heinrich Himmler disguised himself as a Wehrmacht private, a British soldier captured him. Unfortunately, he escaped a war crimes trial by committing suicide with a cyanide capsule.

On 20 November a war crimes tribunal convened at Nuremberg, with twenty-one defendants. Nearly a year later, on 1 October 1946, the tribunal's findings were published. Eleven high-level Nazis were convicted and each sentenced to death:

- Hans Frank, the so-called "Butcher of Krakow"
- German interior minister Wilhelm Frick

- Luftwaffe commander Hermann Goering
- Alfred Godl, chief of operations for the German High Command
- Ernst Kaltenbrunner, head of the Gestapo and SD police
- Wilhelm Keitel, chief of staff of the German High Command
- Foreign Minister Joachim von Rippentrop
- Reichminister Alfred Rosenberg
- Chief of Slave Labor Fritz Sauckel
- Austrian chancellor Arthur Seyss-Inquart
- *Der Sturmer* editor Julius Streicher

The executions were carried out on 16 October—but Goering cheated the hangman by swallowing cyanide the day before.

Three defendants—Erich Raeder, commander in chief of the German navy; Deputy Führer Rudolf Hess, and Economics Minister Walther Funk—were given life sentences.

Albert Speer and Hitler Youth leader from 1931 to 1940 Balder van Schirach were each sentenced to twenty years in prison. Konstantin von

Judgment at Nuremberg.

Neurath, Reich protector, and Admiral Karl Dönitz were given fifteen-year and ten-year sentences, respectively.

Reichbank president Hjalmar Schacht and Franz von Papen were acquitted, but Schacht was later found guilty by a German court and sentenced to eight years in prison.

In the end, the defeat of Adolf Hitler's Third Reich exacted a staggering cost. According to Russian statistics, in 1,418 days of military operations, nearly *twenty million* Soviets were killed, and *another forty million* were wounded. The Russians also reported that on the German-Russian front, ten million Germans were killed or wounded.

Allied estimates of Soviet and German losses were generally about the same—with nearly nine million Soviet soldiers and seventeen million civilians killed in the USSR—along with 3.5 million German soldiers and nearly three million German civilians killed. More than 200,000 Americans made the ultimate sacrifice to liberate a captive people from the grip of the merciless dictator.

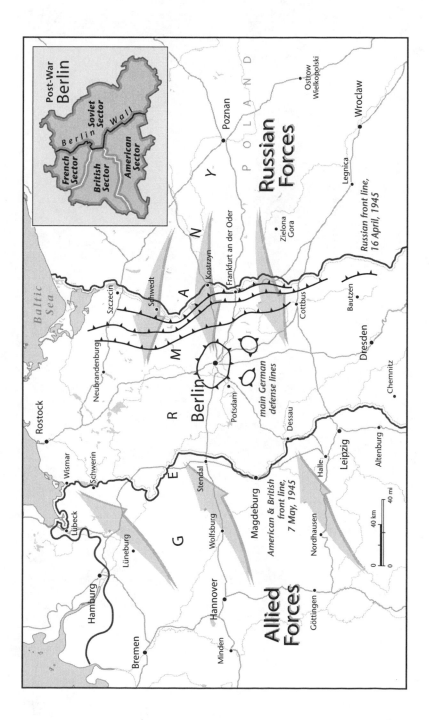

EPILOGUE

 **JOHN ALISON**, after the war, became the youngest-ever assistant secretary of commerce for aeronautics. He returned to military service during the Korean War and eventually retired as a major general in the Air Force Reserve. He was national president, then chairman of the board, of the Air Force Association and retired from Northrop Aviation as a senior vice president.

 **JOSEPH BOITNOTT** decided to stay in the Army Air Force after the war and made the transition to the U.S. Air Force in 1947. He served in four different services: National Guard, Army, Army Air Force, and USAF— and was on active duty during the Korean War.

 **DUANE STONE** spent three long years in a POW camp and was liberated at the end of the war. He returned to his hometown of Council Bluffs, Iowa, on 15 June 1945, married, and raised five children, including three boys—all of whom served in the U.S. Armed Forces.

ANGELO MONTEMARA was awarded a medal for valor by the French government for his courage during the invasion of Normandy. He and four brothers all survived the war and returned to a celebratory family reunion in New York. He married, raised five children, and has ten grandchildren.

CHRISTINE "CHRISSY" QUINN survived the Blitz and the long-distance correspondence with her fiancé, a British soldier. When he finally returned to England in 1946, the two were married.

RON DICK was so influenced by the bravery and resolve of his countrymen during World War II that he joined the Royal Air Force in 1950. He served as a squadron officer, flight instructor, USAF exchange officer, and eventually as the commander of a Royal Air Force squadron in Cyprus. Today he is a writer-lecturer and European-tour leader for the Smithsonian Institution.

CHARLES LEAH served throughout the war for the Air Raid Precautions organization, rescuing his fellow Britons. He subsequently joined the British army as a Royal Engineer, where his duties included defusing bombs—as he had done during World War II.

GUNTHER RAAL, the Luftwaffe ace, returned to the German air force after WWII, rising to the rank of general and chief of air staff. He also served as the German military representative in Brussels on the Military Committee of NATO.

 **BILLY DRAKE** was awarded a Distinguished Service Order and Distinguished Flying Cross for heroic service in WWII. He earned a bar for the DFC from the United States, and spent a career in the Royal Air Force, with service as group captain commanding RAF Chivenor, Devon, until his retirement in 1963. He then lived for more than twenty years in Portugal.

PETER BROTHERS, a RAF fighter ace with sixteen kills, flew during the Battle for France and the Battle of Britain with No. 242 Squadron and later No. 457 Squadron. His decorations include the CB Distinguished Service Order and Distinguished Flying Cross with bar.

 **BETTY SHEA BOYD** married a fellow ferry pilot whom she had met at 10,000 feet above Madison, Wisconsin. He stayed in the Air Force and served two tours in Korea. The couple has remained close to their many friends from both wars.

 **MARIA FASTOVA** volunteered when the Red Army asked for thirty girls from her town to become communicators. She was trained to defend herself with a rifle and served in the 199th Division of the 38th Field Army. Wounded in the Battle of Stalingrad, she recovered in time to celebrate the Russian victory.

 **KEN CROSBY** left the FBI after the war and joined the financial firm Merrill Lynch, where he worked for twenty-five years. Today he works with the Center for Counterintelligence and Security Studies, running courses for government agencies and private groups on terrorism, counter-terrorism, espionage, and counter-espionage.

CHARLES CALHOUN served in the South Pacific against the Japanese after his experiences in the Atlantic and the European theater. He retired as a captain in the U.S. Navy in 1967. Since then he has written three books on his wartime experiences.

CHARLES HANGSTERFER was with the 3rd Battalion, 16th Infantry, 1st Infantry Division, when they breached the Siegfried Line—among the first U.S. troops into Germany. In the Hürtgen Forest a reoccurrence of malaria hospitalized him in England. After the war he returned to the U.S., where he married Geneva, a fellow veteran, on 31 October 1945.

PEARL MCKEOUGH met and married her husband Michael ("Mickey") while he was the orderly for General Eisenhower. They continued to serve Ike throughout the war and remained close to Eisenhower after he became president.

ROBERT GREEN taught at Fort Benning, Georgia, went to medical school on the GI Bill, and was commissioned in the Medical Corps. A practicing U.S. Army physician, he eventually served as a deputy in the surgeon general's office.

JEFFERSON WHITE participated in three invasions, seven major battles, and earned the Silver Star for valor. He was wounded in action at the Battle of the Bulge and spent more than seven months recuperating in a Florida hospital.

GEORGE PERRINE was wounded three times during WWII. Treated in four U.S. military hospitals, his last wounds required hospitalization until 1947.

A. H. "ED" SPEAIRS came back to Oklahoma City, wrote a book about his World War II experiences, and stayed in touch with his friend Bill Mauldin, whose famous Stars and Stripes cartoons helped GIs keep their sense of humor during WWII.

EDWIN "ED" SAYRE recovered from his serious wounds, stayed in the Army, and retired as a colonel in 1968, after serving in Viet Nam. He described his most satisfying moment as the day he and a fellow officer convinced 3,000 Axis soldiers defending a small Italian town to surrender—thereby precluding the need for an attack.

TIMOTHY "TIM" DYAS, liberated from a German POW camp on 27 April 1945, made it across the Elbe River to American lines. He used the GI Bill to attend and graduate from Harvard.

EDWARD "ED" STAFFORD, after serving in the European theater, was posted to the South Pacific to join the fight against the Japanese at Leyte Gulf and Okinawa. After the war he wrote a book based on his experiences in WWII.

FELIX SPARKS settled in Colorado after the war. During the 1961 Cuban Missile Crisis, he was recalled to active duty and eventually rose to the rank of brigadier general. He became a lawyer, judge, and state supreme court justice and in 1968 he was named ground commander for the Colorado National Guard.

RAY SADOSKI stayed in the Army until 1947 and played football at the Army War College. He married Eleanor (now deceased) in '46, and they had four children. Ray worked for Prudential Insurance and was a health inspector for the city of Hartford, CT.

VAN T. BARFOOT was awarded the Medal of Honor for single-handedly destroying two enemy machine-gun nests and capturing the crew of a third—taking a total of seventeen enemy prisoners. He also disabled an enemy tank, killed its occupants, and carried two seriously wounded men of his platoon to safety through enemy fire.

ROBERT "BOB" DOLE was hospitalized for thirty-nine months recovering from the wounds he received in Italy. He earned a law degree on the GI Bill and entered politics in 1952. He subsequently served in the U.S. House of Representatives, in the U.S. Senate as majority leader, and in 1996 was the Republican nominee for president of the United States. In 1997 he was awarded the Presidential Medal of Freedom.

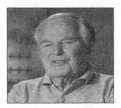

WALKER "BUD" MAHURIN downed twenty-one enemy planes in Europe and one more in the Pacific theater. During the Korean War his F-86 was shot down over North Korea. Bud was a POW until the end of the Korean War.

CHARLES "CHUCK" YEAGER stayed in the USAF after the war and became a test pilot. On 14 October 1947, while flying the X-1, he became the first man to break the sound barrier. He flew his last combat missions in Viet Nam, where he logged 127 missions.

ROBIN OLDS returned to the U.S. after World War II and continued to fly fighters. During the 1960s, while flying missions over North Vietnam, he shot down four Russian MiGs. He retired from the USAF as a brigadier general and went on to be Director of Aerospace Safety in the Air Force Inspection and Safety Center, a separate operating agency and an organization of the Office of the Inspector General, Headquarters, U.S. Air Force.

RICHARD BUTLER and his copilot both returned to the U.S. in March 1944 after sustaining serious injuries when an engine of their B-24 exploded and they crash-landed on Katania, Sicily. Rich remained on active duty after recovering and retired in 1971 as a USAF colonel.

LEE ARCHER flew more than fifty missions as a "Tuskegee Airman" during World War II and stayed in the service to make the transition from Army Air Corps to the U.S. Air Force. His commitment and courage were rewarded in 1947 when President Harry Truman officially ordered the de-segregation of the U.S. Armed Forces.

GEORGE DUFFY, captured by the Germans but turned over to the Japanese, was brutally treated as a slave laborer until liberated in September 1945. Though not eligible for veterans' benefits under the GI Bill, he put himself through college and returned to the sea as a Merchant Mariner.

PETER PETERSEN was released from a British POW camp after Germany surrendered but was placed in an internment facility for several months until he was discharged to work on a farm in his now-divided county. He later immigrated to the U.S. and then became an American citizen.

DAVID BATE, after serving aboard two destroyers in the Atlantic waters, went to the Pacific theater in April 1944 where he served aboard the USS *Dewey* until the end of the war. After his discharge from the service in October 1945, he went to law school and became an attorney.

DOROTHY DEMPSEY, one of the original U.S. Coast Guard SPARs, was discharged at the end of the war, married, and had two children. The SPARs were disbanded in 1948. During the Korean War she was asked to return to service as a full-fledged member of the U.S. Coast Guard, but as a young mother, she declined the request.

EDGAR "ED" NASH made it back from the war in time to enroll at Yale for the spring term of '46 and graduated with a degree in industrial administration. A successful heavy equipment salesman in Pittsburgh, he designed heavy hydraulic machinery and eventually moved to Visalia, California, where he made a career in real estate.

PHYLLIS MCKEY left her job as a welder at the end of the war so that she and her husband could raise five children. She subsequently became a bookkeeper, then an interior decorator, and has since traveled by RV throughout North America.

 **JOHN CULLEN** received the Legion of Merit for discovering and reporting the first landing of German saboteurs on the U.S. coast on 13 June 1942. After the war he worked for Macy's and United Parcel Service and later for National Dairy, on Long Island.

 **LOURELEI PRIOR** and her husband, Herb, started a small business and raised two daughters. She has four grandchildren, five great-grandchildren, and has served as a Disabled American Veterans volunteer at an Indiana VA hospital, and was auxiliary chaplain at American Legion Post 296 for more than twenty years.

 **DR. BERNARD J. RYAN**, wounded at Normandy, Operation Market Garden and the Battle of the Bulge, is the recipient of two Silver Stars and two Purple Hearts. After the war he returned to New York to practice medicine.

 **WALTER D. EHLERS** is a Medal of Honor and Purple Heart recipient who was wounded four times. In 1946, after a tour of duty with the U.S. occupation forces in Germany, he left the service and returned to California, where he worked for the Veteran's Administration, married, and raised three daughters.

 **LEONARD LOMELL** was awarded the Distinguished Service Cross, our nation's second highest decoration for valor, for his courage in France. He participated in the fortieth and fiftieth D-Day anniversaries in France.

ARTHUR "ART" VAN COOK came home in September 1945, rejoined the National Guard as a captain, and was recalled to active duty in 1948. He served in Korea and retired as a lieutenant colonel in 1964 to become a civilian administrator in the office of the secretary of defense. He retired a second time in 1984, started a consulting firm and retired "for good" in 1988.

JERRY MARKHAM, awarded the Navy Cross for valor at Normandy, went to Harvard on the GI Bill and became a labor relations negotiator. He worked for Continental Can Company and led its subsidiary, Hazel Atlas Glass Co., with fourteen plants and 9,000 employees. After heading several other corporations, he returned to Omaha beach in 1984 to mark the fortieth anniversary of D-Day.

CHARLES CURLEY stayed in the Army for a year after the war and met his future wife in 1947. They married, raised five children, and now have six grandchildren. In 2004, sixty years after the invasion of Normandy, Charles was awarded the French Legion of Honor in ceremonies in France.

ROBERT WEISS was awarded the Silver Star, Purple Heart, Presidential Unit Citation, Croix de Guerre with Bronze Star (France), Fourragere (Belgium), and European Theater ribbon for his participation in four major battles. After the war he became an attorney, married, raised two children, and wrote a book about his experiences at Hill 314, *Fire Mission! The Siege at Mortain.*

ANGEL GARCIA was awarded the Silver Star, the Bronze Star, and two Purple Hearts for his courage and wounds. After leaving the service in 1945, he married, raised his family in California, and wrote about his experiences. He has been honored in France for his service and has participated in 30th Infantry Division reunions in Normandy, France.

MURRAY PULVER received the Distinguished Service Cross and Silver Star for his service in the 30th Infantry Division. After the war he managed a cold storage business, returned to farming, and later became the owner-manager of a service station. His book, *The Longest Year*, chronicles his experiences in World War II.

RENE DEFOURNEAUX served with the OSS in Indo-China after V-E day and is a recipient of the Silver Star. He left the OSS in 1946, but continued to serve in military intelligence and counter-intelligence assignments until he retired in 1965.

DONALD BURGETT returned to the U.S. and was discharged in 1946. He is the recipient of the Bronze Star for valor, three Purple Hearts, and numerous other decorations. He married Twyla in 1953 and they have five children and nine grandchildren.

WILLIAM "BILL" MERRIKEN went back to college after the war, earned a degree in business administration, and became the head of a successful small business. After selling his business he worked for the Commonwealth of Virginia and in 1999, he returned to the site of the Malmedy Massacre in Belgium, where he nearly lost his life in 1944.

HARRY KINNARD made a career of the Army, served in the Korean War, did two tours in Viet Nam and retired as a lieutenant general. He is professor emeritus at the University of Vermont and author of several books on military history and strategy.

EMILE JAMAR, the paperboy who helped save Bill Merriken's life, graduated from college, became a successful businessman, and later served as the mayor of his town where the Germans and Americans fought during the "Battle of the Bulge." He and Bill Merriken met for the first time when Bill returned in 1999 for a visit.

JOE REGAN returned to his job as a ship fitter after World War II ended and married his sweetheart, Kay. After working for Centennial Flour Mills, he was employed by Boeing Aircraft for thirty-six years.

JOACHIM FEST became a successful and prolific author and lecturer. His six books on the Third Reich emphasize the gratitude he feels toward the United States for rebuilding Germany and establishing a democratic framework for the modern German state.

ARMIN LEHMANN recovered from his wounds and after helping his family rebuild their lives, he emigrated to the United States, where he worked thirty-five years in the travel industry. He is the author of *In Hitler's Bunker*, and uses his experiences to warn young people about fanaticism.

ALVIN UNGERLEIDER received two Purple Hearts during his service in World War II and stayed in the Army. He subsequently served in Korea and Viet Nam and retired as a brigadier general. He is a much sought after speaker at civic and historical events.

RICHARD MAROWITZ was training in Austria for the invasion of Japan when World War II finally ended. After returning to the U.S. in June of '46 he successfully auditioned for a job as a trumpet player for a band in Spanish Harlem. He subsequently became a successful magician and entertainer in his native New York City.

GLOSSARY

AA—Anti-aircraft

AAA—Anti-aircraft Artillery

Abwehr—German military intelligence service

ALT—Altitude.

AO—Variously used for Area of Operations and Aerial Observer

APC—Armored Personnel Carrier

API—Armor Piercing Incendiary

ARP—Air Raid Precautions (Great Britain)

ASW—Anti-submarine Warfare

AT—Anti-tank

ATA—Actual time of arrival

AWOL—Absent without leave

Axis—The 22 May 1939 "Pact of Steel," formal alliance between Germany and Italy with which Japan became aligned in 1941

Bandit—Hostile or enemy aircraft; also sometimes referred to as a Bogey

BAR—Browning Automatic Rifle

BB—Battleship

Blitzkreig—German slang for "Lightning War;" the term first appeared in the British and American press in 1939, describing the German air-armor assault on Poland

CAG—Carrier Air Group

CAP—Combat Air Patrol

CC—Combat Command

CinC—Commander in Chief

CNO—Chief of Naval Operations

CO—Commanding Officer

ComNavNAW—Commander, Naval Forces, North African Waters

CP—Command Post

CPT—Variously used to abbreviate Captain (Army and Air Force) or Civilian Pilot Training

DD—Destroyer

DE—Destroyer Escort

D-Day—The day on which a military operation commences

DIV or Div—Division

DUKW—A multi-purpose, diesel-powered amphibious truck equipped with propellers for moving through water and wheels for use on land

DZ—Drop zone

E-Boat—A German motor torpedo boat, similar to the U.S. PT-Boat

ETA—Estimated time of arrival

ETO—European Theater of Operations

FO—Forward Observer

Führer—German for Leader, the title assumed by Adolf Hitler in 1936

Gestapo—Geheime Staatspolize, the internal security organization of the Third Reich, Hitler's secret police

Herbstnebel—German for Autumn Mist, the code name for Hitler's Ardennes offensive in December 1944 that the Allies called the "Battle of the Bulge"

H-Hour—The time at which a military operation commences

Higgins boat—The smallest of the U.S. amphibious landing craft, originally designed and built by Higgins Boat Works, New Orleans, LA. The plywood-hulled, diesel-powered, bow-ramp equipped craft could carry thirty-six troops or a jeep and trailer. Also see LCVP

HMS—His (or Her) Majesty's Ship, an abbreviated prefix for British naval vessels

Il Duce—Italian for "The Leader," the title assumed by Italian dictator Benito Mussolini

INF or Inf—Infantry

JCS—Joint Chiefs of Staff

JTF—Joint Task Force

KIA—Killed in Action

Knot—A nautical mile, equal to 1.15 land miles, or to 1.85 kilometers

LCA—Landing Craft, Assault

LCI—Landing Craft, Infantry

LCVP—Landing Craft, Vehicle & Personnel, also "Higgins boat"

LMG—Light Machine Gun

LST—Landing Ship, Tank

Luftwaffe—The German air force

MIA—Missing in Action

NCO—A non-commissioned officer; sometimes called non-com

MTB—Motor Torpedo Boat; also E-Boat

MOS—Military Occupational Specialty, for armed forces job descriptions

NKVD—Narodny Komissriat Vnutrennykh Del, the Soviet internal security organ and intelligence service, predecessor to the KGB

NM—Nautical mile, equal to 1.1508 statute miles, and 1/60th of a degree

OKW—Oberkommando des Wehrmacht, Supreme High Command of the German Armed Forces, created by Hitler in 1938 to coordinate the High Commands of the Army (OKH), Navy (OKK), and Air Force (OKL). The OKW was directly responsible to the Führer as commander in chief

OP—Observation Post

OSS—Office of Strategic Services, U.S. military intelligence service created in WWII, the forerunner of the Central Intelligence Agency (CIA)

Pluto—Abbreviation for Pipeline Under the Ocean, the cross-Channel fuel line installed between England and the continent after Normandy

PM—Prime Minister

POW—Prisoner of War

RAF—Royal Air Force (Great Britain)

RAAF—Royal Australian Air Force

RCAF—Royal Canadian Air Force

RCT—Regimental Combat Team, a task force formed around an infantry regiment that usually included armor, artillery, and transportation units

ROTC—Reserve Officer Training Corps, an officer training program at civilian colleges and universities

SHAEF—Supreme Headquarters Allied Expeditionary Force, Eisenhower's headquarters for the Allied invasion of Europe

SOE—Special Operations Executive. British military intelligence organization created to support partisan activities and espionage in occupied territories

SOP—Standard Operating Procedure

Sortie—In military air and naval operations, pertains to an operational flight by an aircraft or the dispatch of a vessel or vessels from a port

SS—Schutzstaffel, elite Nazi Party military personnel and units operating within the German army and organized as Waffen SS battalions, regiments and divisions

Stavka—Staff of the Soviet Supreme High Command. Under Stalin the Stavka coordinated all military and political activities in the USSR during WWII

TD—Tank Destroyer; a mobile armored vehicle mounting a heavy caliber gun

TF—Task Force

Ultra—Code name for the decryption of German radio communications by MI-6, the British secret intelligence service

USAAF—United States Army Air Force

USS—United States Ship, the prefix to identify a U.S. naval vessel

WASP—Women's Airforce Service Pilot

Wehrmacht—The German Armed Forces from 1935 to 1945

WPA—Works Projects Administration, a "New Deal" program created by President Roosevelt to alleviate unemployment by creating public works projects during the Great Depression of the 1930s

XO—Executive Officer

ACKNOWLEDGMENTS

This book and accompanying DVD, a collaborative effort of FOX News Channel and Regnery Publishing, is a tribute to heroes—those who fought and won the war against Hitler. Thanks to the vision of Roger Ailes at FOX News and Marji Ross at Regnery, this multimedia chronicle of courage serves as a reminder to future generations of the sacrifices necessary to preserve this nation as the land of the free and home of the brave.

Like the two FOX-Regnery books that preceded this one, we again draw heavily on the accounts of eyewitness-participants—those who make *War Stories* an award-winning television series. Though I am blessed to host these documentaries, the real "stars" are the men and women who serve—and have served—on battlefields all over the world. The words of the soldiers, sailors, airmen, Guardsmen, Marines, merchant seamen, and civilians who fought World War II in Europe are the heart and soul of this book. Their self-effacing, matter-of-fact descriptions of battles, wounds, injuries, and privation reflect the brutal reality of war—and inspired all of us who worked on the television series and this book. Our liberty is their legacy.

Writing this book about the heroes who won World War II in Europe has been, in various ways, similar to preparing for a combat operation. To be done well, military planning requires the work of many to assimilate vast amounts of information to determine what is accurate and relevant. Time is rarely sufficient to easily carry out the task. Unforeseen events often disrupt the original plan. And as in warfare, there is always the enemy—in this case a deadline! Even the word—"deadline"—sounds ominous.

In completing this work, all of these factors applied. The volume of information about World War II in Europe is extraordinary and challenges authors far more gifted than I. Complicating an already ambitious schedule for this book about the heroes who beat Hitler were my protracted absences to document a new generation of warriors in Iraq and Afghanistan for FOX News. Thankfully, there were others—just like in the military operations we chronicle in our *War Stories* television series—willing to step into the breach to help accomplish the mission.

Much of the burden fell on the shoulders of Joe Musser, my friend, collaborator, and research partner of many years. With the help of Freedom Alliance Fellow Tom Crowe and *War Stories* executive producer Pamela Browne at FOX News, Joe pored through mountains of transcripts, tapes, and interviews from our now extensive *War Stories* archives to prepare a workable draft manuscript.

David Deis, the gifted cartographer who lent his considerable talent to the first of our World War II books—*Heroism in the Pacific*—has done so again for the European theater. His maps—and the remarkable photos selected by Andrew Stenner—illuminate the events described in these pages.

Thanks to the active engagement of Roger Ailes, Bill Shine, and Dianne Brandi, the preservation of eyewitness accounts and an accurate, documentary record of battles past and present has become a passion for the *War Stories* unit at FOX News Channel. Executive producer Pamela Browne, who has headed the unit since its inception, personally supervised the production of the DVD included in this book and exercises oversight over every episode. Producers Martin Hinton, Greg Johnson, Steve Tierney, Cyd

Upson, and Ayse Wieting spend countless hours with every hero who appears on the air and in this work. Associate producers Kelly Guernica, Jason Kopp, Michael Weiss, and Bevin Mahoney and production assistants Christina Diaz and Andrew Stenner have devoted themselves to finding material worthy of being preserved for posterity.

Peter Bregmen provided invaluable assistance with the archives at FOX Movietone News. Rich O'Brien's graphics department helps us every day—and none of this would have been possible without the help of business manager Rey Erney.

Because of my protracted absences, Ben Domenech, my patient editor at Regnery, was compelled to edit this book a chapter at a time—sent to him electronically—often from thousands of miles away. Art director Amanda Larsen, managing editor Paula Decker, and publicity director Angela Phelps all had to wait for a belatedly delivered manuscript—and still ensure that this book would make it into the hands of readers. Without their diligence—and perseverance—this book would not have been completed.

My friends Bob Barnett and Deneen Howell at Williams & Connolly helped put this great collaboration between FOX News Channel and Regnery Publishing together so that these War Stories could be told in book and DVD format. Marsha Fishbaugh, my executive assistant, and Damon Goude, my faithful travel companion, have borne the brunt of my frenetic schedule.

Betsy, my wife of thirty-seven years and best friend, gave the most to see this work finished—tolerating my lengthy travels to faraway battlefields and frequent trips to interview those who fought there. Without her support and encouragement—and that of our children and their spouses: daughters Tait and husband Tom; Sarah and husband Martin; our son Stuart and his wife, Ellen; and daughter Dornin—this book would have been impossible.

Also deserving of special recognition and praise are the authors, historians, curators, and museum directors who have participated in our European *War Stories* documentaries. The breadth and depth of their knowledge and experience has made this a better book:

- Rick Atkinson, historian and author of *Army at Dawn*
- Walter Boyne, author of over thirty books on the history of aviation
- Dr. Robert Browning, Jr., chief historian, U.S. Coast Guard
- Burl Burlingame, historian and author of *Advance Force Pearl Harbor*
- Prof. Thomas Childers, World War II expert and author of *Wings of Morning*
- Chad Daniels, director, Armed Forces Museum, Camp Shelby, Mississippi
- Carlo D'Este, author, historian, and expert on the Normandy invasion
- Dr. Eckhart Dietzfelbinger, Nazi Party Documentation Centre, Nüremburg, Germany
- Susan Eisenhower, author and granddaughter of Dwight D. Eisenhower
- Joachim Fest, authority on the Third Reich and author of *Inside Hitler's Bunker*
- John Hanson, senior vice president, United Service Organizations (U.S.O.)
- Sir Max Hastings, historian and author of *Armageddon: The Battle for Germany*
- Don Holt, director, Eisenhower Presidential Library
- Keith Gill, curator, U-505 exhibit, Museum of Science and Industry, Chicago
- Col. David Glantz, author of numerous books on the European Eastern Front
- Kristian Marks, U.S. Army historian, U.S. Military Academy, West Point, New York
- Marvin Miller, expert on U.S.-German history and author of *Wunderlich's Salute*
- Terry Miller, executive director, Tin Can Sailors, Natl. Assn. of Destroyer Veterans
- Patrick O'Donnell, author and military historian
- Robert Patton, author and grandson of General George S. Patton
- Richard Powers, professor, City University, New York City, author of *Secrecy and Power*

- Lt. Col. Mark J. Reardon, senior military historian, U.S. Army
- Thomas Reilly & Lynn Homan, co-authors, *Black Knights: The Tuskegee Airmen*
- Gary Robinson, historian and author of *By Order of the President*
- Henri Rogister, authority on the "Malmedy Massacre" of WWII
- Ed Ruggero, military expert and author of *Combat Jump*
- Dr. Helmut Trotnow, director of Allied Museum in Berlin
- Ernest Volkman, authority on the OSS and author of *Spies and Espionage*
- Dr. John Votaw, executive director, Cantigny 1st Division Foundation
- Flint Whitlock, president, Colorado Military History Museum, author of *Soldiers on Skis*
- Hans Wijers, Dutch historian and author

BIBLIOGRAPHY

John Keegan, ed., *Atlas of the Second World War* (New York: HarperCollins, 2003)

Dwight D. Eisenhower,*Crusade in Europe* (New York: Doubleday & Co., 1948)

E. B. Potter, ed., *Sea Power: A Naval History* (Annapolis, MD: Naval Institute Press, 1984)

James Dunnigan & Albert Nori, *Victory at Sea* (New York: Quill/William Morrow & Co., 1995)

Ken Polsson, *Chronology of World War II* (Island Net.com, 2005)

INDEX